1934 Bobby and Alfonso Errico, Alice Patterson, Harriet, Ernie and Bill Errico sit in front of Miramar cabin. Courtesy: Errico Family.

For orders, please contact Bill Errico Jr.
at MIRAMARIIGAMBIERIsland@gmail.com

Most Trafford titles are also available at major online book retailers.

Content Coordinator: Dana Ramstedt

Back cover: The old Sea Wolf leaving Grace Harbour, 1950. Courtesy: Ted Smyth.
Front cover: 1934, Errico family. Courtesy: Errico family.

Printed in the United States of America.

ISBN: 978-1-4269-0463-9 (sc)

Trafford rev. 12/20/2011

 www.trafford.com

North America & International
toll-free: 1 888 232 4444 (USA & Canada)
phone: 250 383 6864 ♦ fax: 812 355 4082

"You have a responsibility to tell history because people forget history."

—Leslie Brody: *Red Star Sister - Tell it Slant: Writing and shaping Non-Fiction:* Leslie Brody and Suzanne Paola.

From the inside looking out of the Douglas Bay prospecting site. Courtesy: Steve Errico.

Dedication

Miramar II: Gambier Island's History is dedicated to all those who visited, worked, lived, and loved on Gambier Island.

Special thanks to Leiani Anthony for her tireless efforts at tracking down pictures and stories. Her interviews give us a chance to experience the lives of those early Gambier Island residents.

I would like to thank everyone associated with the production of this book. Especially Dana Ramstedt, who, without the hours spent coordinating the material, her constant phone calls and questions, this project would not have made it to publication.

Thank you to everyone who contributed their stories, photographs and sketches to this book: *Miramar II: Gambier Island's History*.

Many thanks,
Bill Errico Jr.

Above: Photo taken from Houston family veranda at Grace Harbour. Courtesy: Houston family.
Below: 1956 The Gambier Clan. Courtesy: Houston family.

Table of Contents

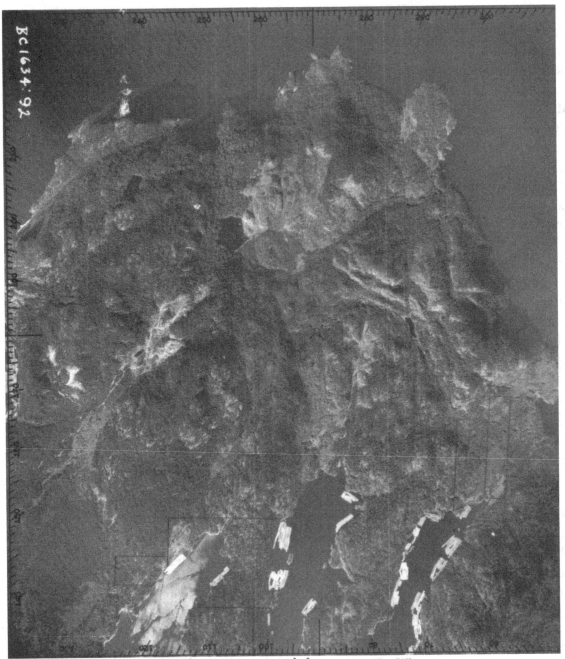

Gambier Island October 14, 1952.   Aerial photo courtesy: Pat Winram.

Table of Contents

Harriet and Alfonso Errico. Courtesy: Errico Family.

Table of Contents

1920 Grace Harbour. Courtesy: Houston Family.

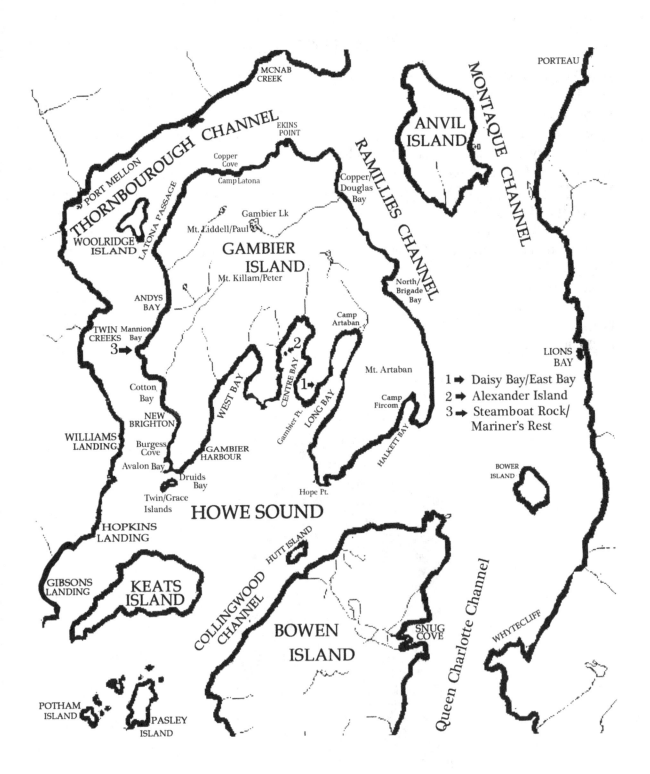

PORTEAU

MONTAQUE CHANNEL

ANVIL ISLAND

MCNAB CREEK

THORNBOROUGH CHANNEL

EKINS POINT

Copper Cove

Camp Latona

RAMILLIES CHANNEL

Copper/ Douglas Bay

PORT MELLON

LATONA PASSAGE

Gambier Lk

Mt. Liddell/Paul

WOOLRIDGE ISLAND

GAMBIER ISLAND

Mt. Killam/Peter

North/ Brigade Bay

ANDYS BAY

Camp Artaban

LIONS BAY

TWIN CREEKS

Mannion Bay

3

2

Mt. Artaban

1 ➡ Daisy Bay/East Bay

Cotton Bay

WEST BAY

CENTRE BAY

1

Camp Fircom

2 ➡ Alexander Island

NEW BRIGHTON

Gambier Pt.

LONG BAY

3 ➡ Steamboat Rock/ Mariner's Rest

WILLIAMS LANDING

Burgess Cove

GAMBIER HARBOUR

HALKETT BAY

BOWER ISLAND

Avalon Bay

Druids Bay

Twin/Grace Islands

HOWE SOUND

Hope Pt.

HOPKINS LANDING

HUTT ISLAND

GIBSONS LANDING

KEATS ISLAND

COLLINGWOOD CHANNEL

BOWEN ISLAND

SNUG COVE

WHYTECLIFF

Queen Charlotte Channel

POTHAM ISLAND

PASLEY ISLAND

Miramar II: Gambier Island's History

Mid 1920s Bowen Island Wharf, Hutt Island in center with Keats to right. Courtesy: Jackson Family.

The Islands of Howe Sound

Home of the Squamish—a sudden northerly wind, Howe sound lies 10 miles northwest of Vancouver. Snowy mountains over 5,000 ft. high overlook an indented coastline and islands with both sandy coves and rock or pebble beaches. Salmon fishing is good here, and commercial and sports fishermen in all types of craft are out in most weathers. Freighters and ferries pass the patient tugs, and on blustery days, the sailors turn out.

The first European to sail into the sound was Narvaez, the Spanish explorer. In 1791, the year before Captain Vancouver arrived; Narvaez came as Captain of the *Santa Saturnina*. He called Bowen Island "Isle de Apodaca" probably after a small village in Spain.

Gambier, the largest of the fourteen main islands, with an area of 25 square miles, has had its share of shipwrecks.

Although Bowen and Gambier Island had been logged from time to time and there was once a small sawmill on Keats, the islands are now mainly a summer haven for city dwellers. Paisley, Ragged, Worlcombe and Bowyer Islands are all privately owned. Waterfront on the other islands is fast disappearing, which is hardly surprising. What other large Canadian City has such a lovely recreational area at its front door?

Excerpt from Leslie Wright and Rolfe Limited. Monthly Letter January 1970. Courtesy: J.R. Thomson.

Gambier Island

Tucked into a division along the Southern West coast of BC, Gambier Island rests at the mouth of Howe Sound directly North of Bowen Island. From the air, the island appears as an open, welcoming hand with long, outstretched fingers protecting sheltered bays. Its three mountains, Mount Killam, Mount Liddell and Mount Artaban are splendid in their cloaks of glistening forest and trimmed with a sometimes mist. Gambier provides its visitors and long-term residents with a life style rarely found anywhere else in the world.

Gambier Island, New Brighton, Mount Liddell on right. Courtesy: Errico Family.

"Gambier Island was named in 1860 by Capt. G.H. Richards for H.M. surveying vessel, Plumper, after Admiral of the Fleet, James, Lord Gambier (1756-1833), who as captain of H.M.S. Defence distinguished himself in the battle of the "Glorious First of June," won by Lord Howe against the French."

This quote is from the BC Archives that recommend we see: J.T. Walbran, British Columbia Coast Names, Ottawa, 1909.

The name Gambier Island does not appear in the directories until 1910.

Judge Harper's house on left, New Brighton wharf in center with Harper store on shore. Courtesy: Errico Family.

1939 New Brighton with Harper's Big House and store at the head of the wharf. Courtesy: Errico Family.

Lady Cynthia *leaving Gambier Harbour. Courtesy: Harper family.*

The 1920 photo that started it all.

The Inneses owned this property. They fixed up the cabin in the center and moved in in the mid 20s. The Holmes family purchased this land in the 40s. They rented the cabin to the Thrashers and the Dawsons in 1944. Alfonso, Bill Jr's Grandfather told him the cabin was likely built by Japanese loggers in the 1890s when logging was in its early stages. Tommy Austin's land is to the right of this photo. Courtesy: Bill Errico Jr.

1930s Lady Cecilia *on the rocks, waiting for the tide. Courtesy: Betty Forbes.*

1930s Grace Harbour. Left-Arthur Lett's home, right-Hazlitt's place, Mrs. Drage's mother and sister.
Courtesy: Betty Forbes.

Preface

My family settled on Gambier Island in 1912 in the New Brighton area. For me, spending my life on Gambier Island is like living in paradise, but of course, as time goes on one has to allow things to change. I have watched the island and its people as ideas and projects were implemented; some failed, some succeeded.

This island was being logged in the 1870s, prospectors came looking for gold in 1897 and the first settlers broke ground at the turn of the century. Still, when people first come to Gambier they act as though it is a community still in its childhood. They want to have a post office, a busy store, and much of what they have on the mainland. While there are others who want to raise the drawbridge and keep our way of life just the way it is. We have had all of those conveniences over the years and now this is how we choose life on the island to be.

I have always had an interest in history, particularly the history of Gambier Island. Then about thirty years ago, I walked into an abandoned house, here on Gambier, and came across an old photo company envelope. In it

1952 Carolynne, Yvonne and Billy Errico Jr. Courtesy: Errico family.

were photos of the people and the house they had lived in on that same property in the 1920s. The fifteen pictures were spectacular and so well preserved I knew I had to protect them. It clicked in my head; here was someone's history! I held their images in my hands with no one to tell me their story.

I decided the island's history was too precious to lose, and I knew there were families and older people still surviving that would know Gambier's history and who would hopefully have some photos. That was when my first book, *Miramar*, got its start.

For the next twenty-five years, I worked at collecting as much as I could on the history of the island. *Miramar*, which in Italian means, "by the sea" was painted on a sign over the deck of my grandfather's first cabin. It was my inspiration for the title of that book.

Miramar, published in 2005, took a lot of time and patience to complete. I would like to thank all the contributors for the photos and information. I would especially like to thank Daphne Dawson and Elaine Davies for helping put my first book together.

After the first edition was printed, I discovered a batch of photos from the 1930s but

1928 Left - Don Crocker, top center - Andree Harper, Muriel Clarke, Sid Clarke,
Art Harper, Right of Art - Vernon Clarke and Bill Burchill,
Centre bottom – unknown. Courtesy: Lynn Bell.

since many people from that era have passed away, there is no one to put names to those faces. As a result, I am thankful that we published that first book preserving that material.

I continued to receive letters, phone calls, material and photos from many folks from the second and third generation of Gambier Island dwellers. Some of these people are now in their seventies, give or take a decade. With this new material, I have put together *Miramar II*. It will bring us into the mid-sixties with the prospect of *Miramar III* to be written by my children, the fifth generation of Gambier residents.

Tommy Austin with Shirley Innes' mother and friend at his old shack on his back land in the 20s.
Courtesy: Shirley Innes.

Gambier Island. Lot numbers taken from map 2B, 1914.

Lot #	1883	[Frankion]		
477.	23.4.83	Joseph Harion	purch. 142 ac.	A c.g. 23 May, 1884
1653	10.1.87	Arthur R. Davies	pre-emp. 180	c.g. 13.6.04.
1588	3.6.87	John Funke	pre-emp. 175	c.g. 10.1.95
847	9.5.88	Robert Leatherdale, Joseph H. Gill & Wm. McGirr	" 551	c.g. 20.2.91
3161	24.10.88	Malcolm McDonald	" 129	c.g. 13.11. 1912.
1259	25.10.88	J. Simpson	"	c.g. 28.12.91.
1258	25.10.88 / 7.7.04	H.W. Myers / T.D. Cyes	"	c.g. 18.7.04
1297	11.7.89	F.A. Bochlotsky	" 207	c.g. 9.2.92
836	18.9.89	J.C. Keith	purch. 216	c.g. 27.4.91
1257	31.12.80 / 7.10.91 / 19.3.04 / 14.1.07	Angus Popplewell / William J. Bell / E.J. Peck / Geo. Pearson	pre-emp.	c.g. 1.11.12.
1639	29.7.90 / 13.10.04	H.E. Huxham / William A. Bishop	pre-e,p 164	xx c.g. 18.12.08
1299	2.5.90 / 20.11.05	G.A. Aldous / Frederick P. Murray	" 83 / purch.	c.g. 26.3.08.
1256	29.9.90	M. Costello	pre-emp. 123	c.g. 4.6.92.
1300	26.6.91	Carl Kosche	purch. 157.5	c. 19.3.92.
1780	22.4.91	F. & T. Keeling & J. Sisson	pre-emp. 432	c.g. 31.10, 02.
xxxxxxxxxxxxxxxxxxxx			"	xxxxxxxxx
1566	5.5.91 / 6.2.07	Thomas D. Cyre / Hugo Hjorthoy	purch.	c.g. 4.6.08.
1298	18.12.91	W.L. Johnson	pre-emp. 91	c.g. 10.7.99
1564	8.3.92 / 10.8.10	James Leithead / T.W. Davey	purch. 120 / purch.	c.g. 20.1.93 / c.g. 30.9.10
1576	1.5.92	T. Campbell Hope	purch. 66	c.g. 30.12.92.
1533	25.2.92	Lewis Hind	purch. 37	c.g. 23.12.92.
1654	26.8.95	Hugo Hjorthoy	pre-emp. 161	c.g. 5.7.03.

2705	20.9.04 / 9.4.10	Hugo Hjorthoy / Christian Hjorthoy	pre-emp. 75 / purch.	c.g. 31.1.11
2706	22.8.05	Christian Hjorthoy	pre-emp. 80	c.g. 22.2.15
2586	22.8.05	Thomas Austen	" 84.66	c.g. 5.1.11
3765	19.9.05	Wm.Hy. Hitchcock	" 83.5	c.g. 13.1.16
2704	14.12.06	F.W. Wright	" 80	c.g. 13.8.10
2259	17.2.06	J.H. Meusse	purch. 88	c.g. 20.5.07
2810	7.6.08	Frederick Chaffey	pre-emp. 65.2	c.g. 29.5.11
2979	11.5.08	Otto Joseph Ffitzonmaier		c.g. 8.3.11
2845	25.8.08	James Skelley	pre-emp. 119	c.g. 13.3.11
2809	4.4.08	George Austin	" 72.6	c.g. 23.3.11
2768	12.8.09	Joseph A. Fisher	purch. 29.25	c.g. 7.3.10
3107	22.12.09	Chester S. Rollston		c.g. 26.1.12
23201	18.3.10	Robt. F. McLennan	purch. 53.45	c.g. 5.10.21
3164	29.10.10	Henry Ramsey		c.g. 27.2.12
3184	31.10.11	Thos. Wickham Davey	pre-emp. 88	13.c.g. 13.10.
3110	14.2.11	William Townshend		c.g. 4.4.12
2519	13.4.11	John Gibson Whitworth	pre-emp. 88	c.g. 21.8.15.

Timber Licences. Lease.

				Date gaz. as surv
807	22.8.90	Henry R. Morse	881 ac.	1890
2209	22.10.04	A.R. Davis	2411 ac.	15.12.04
2457	MxM.	H.H. Taber & F.P. Cameron	369 ac	1.11.07
2445		Joseph Chew Lumber & Shingle Mfg. Co.	387	20.8.08
24438		"	639	30.5.09
2079		J. Chevy (Chew?)	616	4.11.09

"Responsibility for keeping records of the land now passed to a Land Title office. If the new owner defaulted on taxes, the land reverted to the Crown."

2086		Alexander Barnet	624.1	11.11.09
2588		"	355.3	11.11.09
2590		"	200	11.11.09
2458		McFaden Bros. & Browne	428	28.1.09
2460		"	630	23.9.09
2587		Anglo-American Lumber Co.	533.5	11.11.09
2588 89		Alexander Barnet	346.9	21.4.10
3027		"	610	3.10.12
3111		A.R. Bettes	556	19.1.12

Crown Grant records for Gambier Island 1883 to 1922 from BC Archives. Courtesy: Leiani Anthony.

British Columbia Pre-emption Claims

Claiming land for settlement and agricultural purposes was possible if one followed the pre-emption process of the Land Act. From as early as 1859 up to 1970, individuals, companies and partnerships who were willing to settle, work and "improve" the land were able to apply for a Crown Grant. A Crown Grant had to be registered with a Land Title office, and the pre-emptor had to make specific improvements to the land as well as meet citizenship requirements to complete the process to pre-empt land in British Columbia.

According to the British Columbia Archives Research Guide details of the pre-emption process varied over the years and generally consisted of the following steps:

- *A block of vacant, non-reserved, unsurveyed Crown land was selected by the pre-emptor.*
- *The land was staked and a written application submitted.*
- *A Certificate of Pre-emption was issued in triplicate (copies to the pre-emptor, the local office, and the department in Victoria.)*
- *After improvements, residency qualification, and land surveying, a Certificate of Improvement was issued and the land purchased at a discount rate or at no further charge.*
- *A Crown Grant was issued and ownership of the land passed into private hands (alienation). The Crown Grant had to be registered at the Land Title office and a Certificate of Indefeasible Title (land title deed) issued for the process to be fully completed.*
- *Responsibility for keeping records of the land now passed to a Land Title office. If the new owner defaulted on taxes, the land reverted to the Crown.*

Killam Wharf by Ruthie Massey.

Above left: 1932 Johny Hoosen. Art Harper is driving. Courtesy: Lynn Bell.

Above right:Ellen Harper, Art Harper's mother. Johnson's orchard. Courtesy: Lynn Bell.

Left: Robert and Helen Jeffery, Bill Errico Jr's Aunt Peg's parents. Courtesy: Errico family.

Mining on Gambier Island

Miner on hillside. Sketch by Eliza Killam.

Mining on Gambier Island: the Early Days

Mines and claims were in full operation on Gambier Island in the late 1800's. Of all these once active mines, all that remains are the shafts and tunnels that were blasted or dug out of the living rock of Gambier Island.

Carmelo Point mine shaft. Courtesy: Ron Pratt.

The book: *Mining in Southern British Columbia,* edited by L.K. Hodges is an extract from: *Mining in the Pacific Northwest; A Complete Review of the Mineral Resources of Washington and British Columbia*, edited by L. K. Hodges, published in Seattle, Washington in 1897 and reprinted in 1967. The title page states: Entered according to Act of Congress, in the year 1897 by James D. Hodge Jr. and L.K. Hodges, in the office of the Librarian of Congress at Washington.

Mining in the Pacific Northwest: A Complete Review of the Mineral Resources of Washington and British Columbia contains a collection of articles which are the accounts of writers sent on a tour of the mining districts of the Pacific Northwest by *The Post-Intelligencer* in 1895. It contains articles and mining advertisements of the day with real facts, in real time. They were written over 100 years ago.

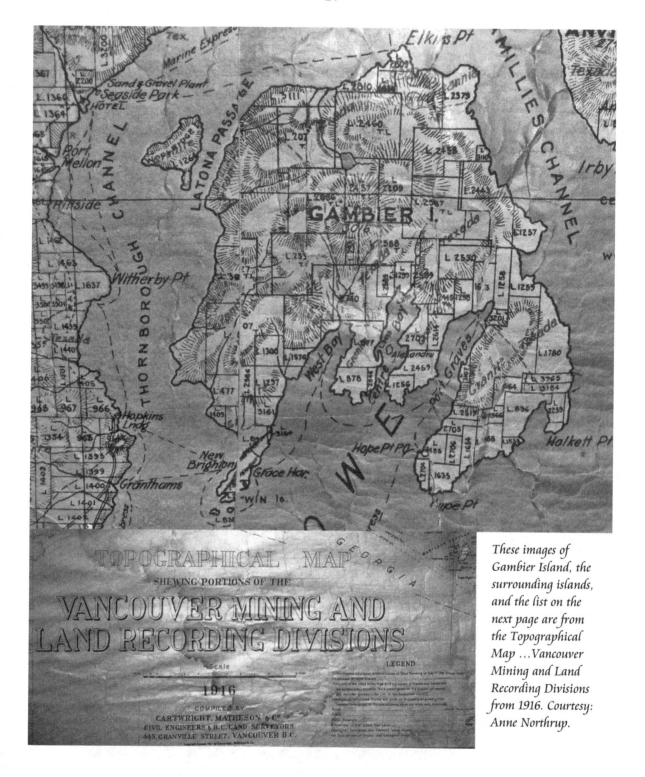

These images of Gambier Island, the surrounding islands, and the list on the next page are from the Topographical Map …Vancouver Mining and Land Recording Divisions from 1916. Courtesy: Anne Northrup.

LEGEND from the 1916 map

"Crown Granted & Surveyed Mineral Claims in Good standing at Feby 1st 1916
Shewn thus . . . . .16 in a square, Unsurveyed . . . . 16 in a circle.
The lists at sides of Map give the names of Claims and Owners and are divided
into Localities. The Numbers given on the Claims correspond with the Index
Numbers in the List of the Respective Locality. [SIC]
Locations of Unsurveyed claims are given as accurately as possible from Locators
Descriptions on Records of Claims which are often indefinite."

"West side Howe
Sound including
Gambier Island" is
one of the lists
referred to in the
above legend.

Map courtesy: Anne
Northrup.

West side Howe Sound including Gambier I.

50°

INDEX No	LOT No	NAME OF CLAIM		GRANTEE OWNER OR LOCATOR
1		Louisa D		George G. West
2		Canadian		Robert D. Buchanan
3	1792	Alp No 2	C.G	James Douglas
4	1786	Alp	C.G	B.C Standard Mining Co. Ld
5		Silver Drop	*	J.L. McTaggart
6		Lucky Mack	*	H.W. Archibald
7		Fraser	*	P.H. Fraser
		Neptune	*	A.A. Davidson
		Lucky Jim	*	do.
10		Molybenite	*	Percy H. Fraser
		Copper King	*	J.L. McTaggart
		Dixie No 1		J.P. Miller
		Bell		Percy H. Fraser
14		Dixie		Edmund Guy Deneen
15		Dixie No 2		Robert Olliver
16		Silver		H.W. Archibald
17		Cold		Jas. W. Archibald
18	1793	Condor	C.G	James Ironside
19	1794	Vulture	C.G	W. J. Keerfoot
20		Blue Jay		Nelson Perrault
21		Red Jay		Charles Mandel
22		Lucky Todd		A. Chapman
23		We Lead		A.B Bettes
24		Squirrel		A. McNair
25		Ida May		S G. Cunningham
26		Sunday		G.C. Bailey
27		Lydia		William Wood
28		Joey		H. Chaffey
29		Rosa		J.A. Russel
30		Wren		S.E. Austin
31		New Moon		George Powell
32		Lucky Baldwin Fr.		Albin Chapman
33		Wanda		Walter J. Barton
34		Lucille		Isaac Gowler
35		Clayton		George A. Jacobs
36		Argile		J.W. Grey
37		Lucky Prince		F. H. Haskell
38		Russeline		L. Russel
39		Cliff		Robert Walker
40		Black Diamond		George Black
41		Lucky Todd		Donald Todd
42		Sandy		A. McNair
43		Squirrel	*	George D. Martin
44		Sunset	*	Job Greasley
45		Sunrise	*	George Hartley
46		Shamrock	*	Edmund Murphy
47		Thistle	*	Jas. A. Thomlinson

The following text is from an article in *Mining in Southern British Columbia*. In which John R. Wolcott of Seattle reports in reference to the Coastal District of Southern B.C.:

> *"The first development work in the [coastal] district was during 1896, and as a whole, has proven so satisfactory that the attention of capital is being strongly directed to the district: this region presents the unusual feature of English capital taking hold of undeveloped properties in a district in which but a comparatively small amount of development work has been done. A number of English mining engineers, most of them with South African and Australian mining experience, have inspected the district during the past year with the result that five or more English companies have acquired holdings and are arranging for development during 1897: some already being at work.*
>
> *The indications for paying properties and prosperous camps at a number of points are excellent. Several properties are already sufficiently advanced to warrant the belief that they will become dividend paying mines. The large bodies of ore, much of it capable of being concentrated and situated for economical handling, combined with the certainty of low freight rates, all tend to make this a most inviting field of capital. Freight rates on ore to Everett or Tacoma are $1.25 per ton in 50-ton lots: freight on camp supplies is moderate…"*

This account by Mr. J.R. Wolcott continues including this paraphrased section as it refers to the mines on Gambier and Bowen Island:

As the area is practically unprospected, the coastal district of British Columbia would be of great interest to the practical prospector.

Twelve miles from Vancouver, Howe Sound projects into the mainland in a northerly direction for twenty-five miles. At the entrance to the Sound are Bowen, Gambier and Anvil Island. On Bowen Island, there are thirteen claims that are the property of the syndicate represented by: Cowen and Shaw, of Vancouver. The property is developed, with a forty-foot shaft and sundry open cuts to explore several veins. The principal vein is eight or nine feet wide and carries gold and silver, making this a considerably valuable property. A Tacoma company also owns a group of claims on the island.

On Gambier Island, the Gold Standard, owned by Stokes and Hartley, has a four-foot vein between slate and granite walls. The ore from this claim assays from fifty dollars to eighty dollars per ton of gold. The following persons own mines as extensions of the Gold Standard claim: G. S. Logan of Seattle, owns the Nulla Secunda, and Dr. S. F. Martin and John R. Foster, of Seattle, owns the Wall Street. Close to this claim, Messrs. Stokes, Hartley, Martin and Foster own the Vancouver, Thorley, Ecclefechan and Westminster claim on a well-defined vein of rose quartz, eight to ten feet wide, assaying from eight dollars to fifteen dollars gold. Dr. Marten of Toronto, owns the Croesus, a fine property with surface assays being five dollars to eight dollars in gold.

Thankfully, timber is abundant on Gambier—an essential element for shoring up walls and ceilings in the mines, and for constructing shelters and outbuildings.

Complete set of assay tools found by Bill Errico Jr. in New Brighton area. Photo by Steve Errico.

Prospecting site at Camp Latona/Copper Cove. Notice the sedimentary rock layers; they were clues to possible riches for those early prospectors. Photo by Steve Errico.

In 1905, claims were being staked on Gambier Island; at the same time exploration and development began at Britannia mine (1905 –74).

A huge copper-molybdenum porphyry, estimated to contain over 200 million T of ore runs from the head of Howe Sound under Gambier Island and out to the Pacific Ocean.

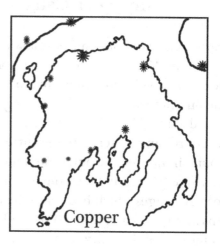

Copper

Right: This map shows copper deposits on and around Gambier Island. Note: The concentration of the findings on all "deposit" maps are represented by the size of the symbols.

Below: Douglas Bay prospecting site. In 1905, due to the copper findings, this area was called Copper Cove. Bill Errico Jr. found this site with the help of Joe Mitchell's son, Gordie Mitchell. Photo: Steve Errico.

Mining on Gambier Island: What Lies Below the Trees?

The west coast of British Columbia was formed by the intense action and reaction between the Pacific and North America tectonic plates. Over 10 million years of tectonic upheavals formed the chain of volcanoes that run along western North America. The buildup from those volcanic segments (or *terranes*) extended the edge of the continent westward and brought rocks, ores and minerals to the surface resulting in two mountain ranges; the outer mountains of the Queen Charlotte Islands and Vancouver Island, *and* the inner Coastal Ranges which back onto the City of Vancouver and runs along the coast to the Alaskan Panhandle. The Coastal Trough, from the Georgia Strait up to Hecate Strait, separates these two ranges. These actions also brought to the surface, the necessary clues for the prospectors in the late 1800s.

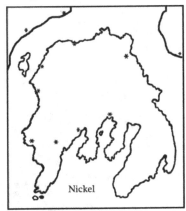

Nickel

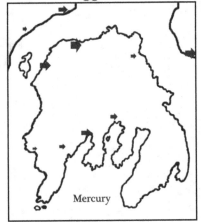

Silver

Gambier Island is one of the many islands referred to as part of the Lower Cretaceous Gambier Group. Its rocky shores held the promise of gold, silver, iron, copper and molybdenum, manganese, mercury, nickel, lead and uranium.

For the miners to identify the possibility of ores or minerals below the trees and grass they needed to be able to recognize the rocks of the cliffs, and the rugged shoreline. The three basic types of rocks are Igneous, Sedimentary and Metamorphic.

<u>Intrusive Igneous Rocks</u> are from deep inside the earth (plutonic rocks) and are formed from molten matter. These types of rocks never reach the surface but are squeezed into cracks, called dikes or sills later to be exposed by weathering or upheavals in the land they occupy.

Granite, being coarse-grained, is representative of an intrusive rock. A perfect example of grandodiorite is the Stawamus Chief, of Squamish at the head of Howe Sound; it covers approx. three-square kilometres. A distinct black two meter wide dike of hornblende diorite runs up the right hand wall of the rock's west face.

Mercury

<u>Extrusive or Volcanic Igneous Rocks</u> are brought to the surface by magma. This molten rock cools quickly to form a lava flow. The results are fine grained rocks. When the magma is high in iron and magnesium silicate minerals, they will be dark in colour and are called mafic rocks. Other intrusives such as *pegmatites,* frequently house the best gemstones and *peridotite* an ultramafic, often contains important commercial materials.

<u>Sedimentary Rocks</u> are of two categories:

Clastic sedimentary rocks are produced when fragments of eroded rock are brought together by the action of wind, ice and water and are usually found in flat areas like river beds. As time passes, many layers are created. This process known as "bedding" is easily recognizable in the "layered-look" of the Rocky Mountains.

Fossilized clam shells. Photo: Steve Errico.

Chemical sedimentary rocks are formed when dissolved materials settle out of the solution they are in. Limestone, (fine-grained calcium and magnesium carbonates) is composed of the compacted shells of sea creatures. The White Cliffs of Dover in Great

Britain are a fine example of this process.

<u>Metamorphic Rocks</u> are igneous or sedimentary rocks that have been dramatically changed due to extreme thermal, chemical, or physical forces acted upon them. The metamorphosis of these rocks can be so severe that their original identity is obscured. Slate

was once a sedimentary rock called shale. Marble is another metamorphic rock formed from recrystallized limestone.

Metamorphic sedimentary rock. Photo: Steve Errico

Gambier Island is mostly underlain by mafic volcanic strata, or a sedimentary layer that generally runs northwest with steep northeast dips. Granitic rocks of the Jurassic to Cretaceous period underlie the southern part of the island. Isolated post-mineral dacite porphyry (igneous rocks in which large crystals are set in a fine-grained ground mass) dikes and dioritic rocks (intrusive igneous rock composed chiefly of sodic plagioclase, hornblende, biotite, or pyroxenen) are part of the Coast complex. The rocks of the Gambier Group are a northwest trending series of volcanic rocks and rocks metamorphosed by hydrothermally pressures. The zone at the south end of this group has been converted to a granoblastic assemblage of quartz, biotite, epidote, sericite and chlorite as a result of multistage metamorphosis of phyllic, propylitic and potassic mineral assemblages. These dioritic rocks show only small amounts of pyrite.

Phenocrysts up to two cm are enclosed by altered feldspar phenocrysts anhedral aggregates of chlorite, sericite and quartz.

The granitic rocks are of an unrelated assemblage of quartz, breccias and subporphyritic in a Northwest trending oval-shaped stock up to 500 meters in diameter.

A broad area of mineralized rocks runs with the south and west contact of the quartz porphyry stock. It encloses a low-grade core rich in quartz veinlets. Most veinlets trend

The rock layers are shale and white quartz that contains golden flecks of iron pyrite (Fool's gold). Photo: Dana Ramstedt.

north-west and form a south-closing porphyry mass accompanied by altered and mineralized volcanic rocks. Small amounts of pyrite, molybdenite and chalcopyrite can be found in the selvage-free veinlets. These barren to low-grade pyritic rocks can contain sphalerite, galena and chalcopyrite.

In a narrow extension of the deposit north of Gambier Creek fracture coatings, veinlets and finely disseminated aggregates of pyrite, chalcopyrite, and molybdenite occur in altered volcanic rocks close to the south contact. Locally present on fracture surfaces, small rosettes formed of molybdenite can be found in quartz stringers.

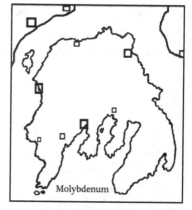

Major fault zones are believed to exist along Gambier Creek Valley, South Fork Creek and East Fork Creek. Over the millennium, these have created a spider's web of sheer zones, cataclastic zones and mineralized zones that pass parallel through, separate the mafic volcanic strata, and are associated with the sedimentary layer under the Cretaceous Gambier Group.

All of the above were great motivators for the early prospectors to sink test shafts into the rock of Gambier Island.

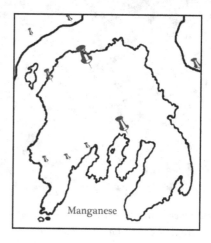

Top of the shaft at the Copper Cove/Camp Latona prospecting site. Photo: Steve Errico.

Copper Cove/Latona Beach/Camp Georgia/Camp Latona

In 1860, Captain Richards named the channel between Woolridge Island and Gambier, Latona Passage after the warship—*HMS Latona*, a thirty-eight gun frigate.

In 1905, prospectors were busily staking mining claims on Gambier Island. This area, west of Ekins Point, due to the copper found here, was called Copper Cove.

Later, in 1914, Edward Linfoot settled here and the area became known as Latona Beach.

In the 1940's, this property was purchased for a naval training center. The Federal

government provided the original construction of the site naming it Camp Georgia and later, renamed it Camp Latona. This site on Latona Beach was used for a Navy Sea Cadet Camp.

In 1958, Latona Beach was purchased by the Archdiocese of Vancouver for $25,000 and Camp Latona was developed on the 118 acres of DL 2809. Camp Latona opened its doors in the summer of 1959. This summer camp featured a Western-style mess hall, mezzanine and seven lodges with capacity for close to one hundred and fifty people. Over the next forty years, the Latona Catholic Camp welcomed thousands of children from all walks of life. They arrived by boat for a week of: hiking, swimming, and cookouts. The campers could catch-up with old friends, and meet new ones. Together, they would ward of the mosquitoes and the occasional bouts of homesickness. All took away with them memories and lessons to keep with them for a lifetime.

Lost and lonely, this mussel-encrusted lifeboat rests on the beach in front of Camp Latona. Photo: Bill Errico Jr.

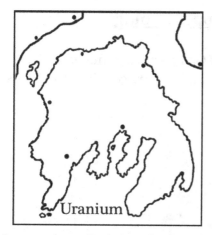

Below: The opening into the shaft at the Copper Cove/Camp Latona prospecting site. Photo: Steve Errico.

Above: Entrance to Copper Cove/Camp Latona prospecting site. Photo: Steve Errico.

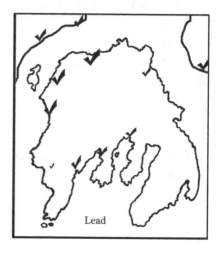

Copper/Douglas Bay Copper Mining

Douglas Bay, once Copper Bay, on the northeast side of Gambier is another area where they were doing some prospecting. In my younger days, Grandfather Errico told me that bits of gold were found in all the creeks on Gambier.

Looking into the tunnel at the Copper/Douglas Bay prospecting site. Notice the natural smoky look to the walls. Photo: Steve Errico.

The other place for copper prospecting, was at Massey's Point in the 1920s when the Massey's owned property from the point of the Centre Bay peninsula into the head of Centre Bay.

Many mine shafts were abandoned because the required concentration of ore was missing, usually, there was only one mine out of 100 that showed any promise. On Gambier, all the mineshafts were abandoned.

A closer look at the prospecting site at Carmelo Point, west of Massey Point. Photo: Ron Pratt.

Rock Quarry

There is another site on Gambier Island that is very hard to locate unless you have a good eye and know what you are looking for. The remains of a rock quarry are located on the left of Centre Bay after you pass Alexander Island. Layers of broken rock are visible on the steep bank at high tide point. You would swear there is nothing there as trees and moss camouflage the tumble of rocks.

This quarry is from the turn of the twentieth century and covers about one half acre. Pieces of exposed pipe are proof that the quarry was man-made but only one or two people I have talked to even know about it.

The granite from this Centre Bay quarry was of such great quality it was barged to Vancouver and used in the construction of many buildings.

The supply was limited and once these rocks were removed, the mine was shutdown.

In center back of photo, Bill Errico Jr. studies pipes from the quarry operation. In left back is Centre Bay. At right back is a tumble of quarry waste. Photo: Steve Errico.

Centre Bay quarry site is behind the top of the trees. Notice the discarded granite waste on the bank. Mark Jewitt provided the directions to this site. Photo: Steve Errico.

Breakaway rocks tumble down side of bluff at Centre Bay quarry site. To the left of image is Centre Bay. Photo: Steve Errico.

The back of the quarry site of the above bluff. Centre Bay is beyond the trees on the right side of image. Photo: Steve Errico.

Frozen in Time

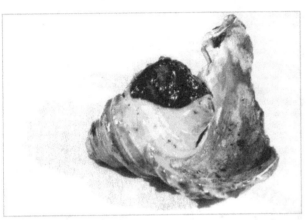

Remnants from the last glaciers,
roughly 10,000 years old.

Top right: An ancestor of the horse neck clam.
Above: Fossilized snail.
Right: Fossilized snail shell. Photos: Steve Errico.

Clay Deposits on Gambier Island

Rocks and minerals were not the only substances prospected for on Gambier Island; clay was

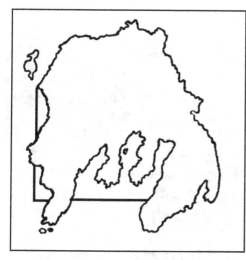

At low tide, blue clay is visible along the west and south shores of Gambier Island.

also a product of interest. There are areas along the west and southern shores where blue clay is visible at the low-tide point while red clay is mostly found on Anvil Island.

In those early days, the clay was mostly used for pottery. Still, while this clay was a valuable item for Artisans, I have not heard of it being extracted for that purpose in times that are more recent.

In bulletin No. 30 of the British Columbia Department of Mines, *Clay and Shale Deposits of British Columbia*, printed 1952, the following general references are made to the clay in the Lower Mainland Area. BCDM findings are based on research from *Geol. Survey, Canada*, Mem. 135, 1923; Dom. Dept, of Agriculture, Pub. 650, 1939, and by the Geol. Survey, Canada, Pub. No. 996, 1908.

In the Lower Mainland area both Interglacial and Recent clay deposits are common, although geological relationships are not as clearly defined as they are in the Vancouver Island area.

Stratified clay deposits, probably related to the Puyallup Interglacial deposits described on Vancouver Island, occur on the northeast shore of Howe Sound near its head, on the east shore of Anvil Island, at the heads of bays along the south shore of Gambier Island, and in a belt extending from Gibsons Landing to Sechelt along the main coast, at Welcome Point, and on the Thormanby Islands. The clay in these deposits is somewhat sandy and yellowish to bluish grey in colour and in most places contains fairly abundant pebbles.

The Anvil Island Brick Foundry used the clay from these islands of Howe Sound to make pipes for sewer systems and tiles.

1947 Gord Mitchell leans against a Fir from the east side of West Bay. Courtesy: Mitchell family.

Logging on Gambier Island

Tug hauling boom out of a bay. Sketch by Eliza Killam.

1919 Judge Harper relaxes on a cedar stump. Courtesy: Lynn Bell.

Logging on Gambier Island

I came to live fulltime on Gambier Island in 1968. Since that time, I have worked toward making a living from the land. Today, my woodlot on Gambier covers eight hundred acres and it is second growth with a few old-growth trees still standing. The second growth is now being logged and the woodlot is being reforested for third growth to continue the process. Around 2075, it will be ready for logging.

Our log home is a tribute to the fine quality of timber on the island.

1935 Taking a break. Courtesy: Jackson family.

1935 Log scaler accessing the quality of wood of this Douglas Bay log boom. Courtesy: Jackson family.

Loggers

The Squamish people were the very first loggers on Gambier Island. Cedar trees were used in all parts of their lives, most notably for totem poles for their home villages as well as for their permanent structures, and for their hand-hewn canoes.

There were also Japanese loggers on Gambier Island. They logged and brought their logs down by Cotton Creek and had their stables there as well. In these camps, I found opium, Saki, and beer bottles plus rice bowls and other artifacts that are now collectables.

Early settlers' objects from late 1800s to early 1930s. Courtesy: Bill Errico Jr.

Miss. Terfry mentioned to me that in the early days, when the old-growth timber was taken out, there were Japanese that died during the logging so there is a small cemetery on the back of the island. Remnants of their living sites such as the dump I came across while exploring the woods are evidence of their preference to live inland. In the land above Cotton Bay, I found rice bowls, and bottles and pottery with Japanese writing on them. One crock had marked on it: The Gold Seal Liquor Company, 722 Pender Street, now Vancouver, B. C. That date would have been 1902-14 before West and East Pender existed.

Timber was used for everything from fencing to docks and wharves to the construction of the many homes and cabins on the island. We know from the rings on the felled trees that logging of old-growth trees was at its peak between 1870 and the 1940s.

In West Bay and Centre Bay and on Gambier's west coast, land was pre-empted by loggers. Much of these claims were abandoned when the timber ran out. Some of these pre-emptors did stay. In May 1888, although their main intention was to log their land, Robert

Mr Beck and Rowdy step out on the Grennon Creek log bridge in the 1940s. Courtesy: Harper family.

Leatherdale, Joseph H. Gill and William Girr made improvements to their claim and received their Crown grant in October of 1889. The land along the storm-battered north-

eastern shore was pre-empted until 1908, but even though they were Crown grants, they were later abandoned.

1920 Joe Innes' first dwelling. Joe and bull pup sit on veranda. Originally built by Japanese loggers. Courtesy: Shirley Innes.

John Bernard Funke was an early pre-emptor who took up 175 acres on the south shore between Hope and Halkett Points on June 6, 1887 and received a Crown grant in 1895. Up to 1900, he was listed as "Lumberman" in the voters' lists.

Making it Work

Mrs. Terfry

The Anderson brothers, Jack and Ed, lived in Gambier Harbour. They brought a mill to the island in 1954 but had no idea how to use it. Les Terfry was a millwright and he set the mill up and showed them how to operate it. The Terfry and McKinlay

(Potter) houses were the first to be built from timber cut with this mill. The Andersons supplied lumber to the local people for many years.

Above: 1954 Jack and Ed Anderson with Less Terfry.
Left: Mr and Mrs Adkins, Jack Anderson and Less Terfry. 1954 Courtesy: Terfry family.

Note: In the 1905 Directory for Howe Sound it listed Albert Francoeur as "Logger and George W. Gibson as "Carpenter."

In the early days, horses were preferred for their speed but were replaced by oxen because oxen were stronger.

…equipment and supplies had to be brought by tug and barge to the shores of Gambier. Even the cook and bunk houses were towed to the island.

Top: Oxen hauling logs. Sketch by Eliza Killam.
Bottom: 1936 Tugs hauling logging camps. Courtesy: Jackson family.

Logging—Not for the Weak

Falling a four-foot-wide Douglas fir took a hard working team of men at least two hours. At other times, using double-bladed axes, two fallers could spent the better part of a day making the cuts for their springboards, and then the undercut into a Douglas fir—wider than they were tall. That says nothing for the time it took to strip the limbs and cut it into manageable lengths for transportation. All of their saws and axes needed a keen, clean edge. They used kerosene to clean the pitch off their saw blades.

1946 Gus Lund and Fred Stoddard cutting down a tree to build Bill and Kay Killam's camp at Druid Bay. Courtesy: Chris Wootten.

No matter, whether it was oxen in the late 1800s or in the early to mid 1900s with tractors, mine-towers or skidders, cold decking yarders, steel spars, log spars or grapple yarders, all of the equipment and supplies had to be brought by tug and barge to the shores of Gambier. Even the cook and bunk houses were towed to the island.

~54~

Once the crews were on the island, roads were created with logs laid cross-wise about six to ten feet apart set halfway into the ground creating the "corduroy roads" for skidding the logs – rough but functional.

For steep terrain, a spar was used. For this, they would top a very large tree, leaving it anchored by its roots and then attach a cable on the top with a block. The main line and choker's cable extended out to grab the logs on the steep area and haul them to the loading area.

From the early 1930s to the early 50s one of the methods used was a Caterpillar tractor and logging arch. An A-frame on two wheels, called an arch, was attached to the back of the Cat. A cable ran from a winch, through a pulley at the peak of the

Above: 1935 Logs ready to be taken from the forest. Courtesy: Jackson family.
Left: Ariel survey photo shows the sorting grounds of West Bay, Centre Bay and Long Bay on July 9, 1947. Courtesy: Pat Winram.

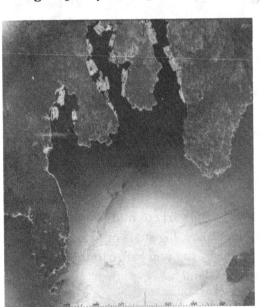

arch and down to the ground. At the end of the cable, chokers grabbed and lifted the front of the log to drag it. In this way, the log was not damaged and with less drag, it was easier to pull.

Gambier Island's coastline was dotted with independent and small logging companies and the products of the industry included many log booms anchored to the beaches. Of all the sorting grounds, Andys Bay was the largest.

Some of the companies that logged and/or

sorted and tied their booms around Gambier Island over the last century were: Burns and Jackson Logging Company, McLeod Timber and Logging Company, Hamburg Shingle Co., Inlet Timber Co., K & K Timber Co., R. McNair Shingle Co., Coastal Towing Company. Rivtow, MacMillan Bloedel, Cates Towing, Seaspan, and Weldwood show as the owners of some of the boom and sorting grounds on the following map.

Gambier map showing booming grounds over the last century. Crosshatch marks the sorting grounds. Parallel lines mark the log booms. Date of this map is uncertain.
Courtesy: John Cosulich

The bird and hexagon is a registered trademark of Rivtow.

My dad, Bill Errico Sr., told me, in between Mannion Bay and Steamboat Rock there used to be a long shoot running along the ridge of the bluff. It went quite a ways up the mountain and was for sending shake/shingle blocks down to the water.

Up along the same area where the shoot could be seen from the road, there was one of the biggest logging roads on the island. There are still sections that can be seen today. My Uncle Ernie said around the turn of the century, in the early 1900s, they had a name for that road, it was called Old Bridge Road.

Most of the logging was phased out from the 1940s to 70s, with only a few booms in 1995 in Long Bay and on the west side of the island and around Woolridge Island with Andys Bay an active booming location for logs transported from all over Howe Sound.

1944 Sir Thomas Lipton, *once a sailing ship this vessel was beached at West Bay to prevent the log booms from running up onto the beach at high tide.*

ForesTalk Resource Magazine Spring 1978

Snippets from Jean Sorensen's article:
"A Perspective on Forest Policy"
By Jean Sorensen

Part 1 1900 -77:

Forest Policy—A Towering Order

...at the turn of the century, a timber stampede started. Lumber prices in Eastern Canada between 1900 and 1909 had risen 53 percent compared to the previous 10-year period and 93 percent between 1890 and 1900 in the U.S....

...There was money to be made in BC's Forests.

By Foot and By Horse—They Counted Trees

...Not only were loggers and sawmill operators wanting more wood, but a pulp and paper industry was gaining momentum. Between 1909 and 1923, eight pulp operations had been opened on the coast. Harvest records for 1912 show that log production was 67 million cubic meters, but by the later 1920s, it had more than doubled to 141 million cubic meters.

Finally in 1937, 25 years after the inventory started, F.D. Mulholland issued The Forest Resources of BC, which recorded 26 million hectares of productive forest land.

Andys Bay Townsite. Moored alongside a log boom is the HMCS SS Givenchy. She served from 1910 to 1930 as a minesweeper. To the right is the 85 ft. A-Frame. Courtesy: Bill New.

Logging Andys Bay

B.C. Archives:
Milestone 1958:

> *"About 1919 to 1923 the area which is now the campsite at Andys Bay, was the site of a logging operation run by McLeod. It was a railroad show with approximately two miles of track down which cars were lowered by cable at a very steep grade…"*

Forties and Fifties

Andys Bay is located on Gambier Island's west shore. Only about 15 minutes from Vancouver by plane and a short boat ride across Thornbrough Channel from Port Mellon pulp mill. The bay is roughly three miles long with deep shoreline waters that remain free from the ravages of the Squamish winds.

Andys Bay was named to honour Captain Rasmus Andrea (Andy) Johnson in 1951. Captain Andy came to B.C. in 1895. He operated a tug business towing logs from coastal logging camps to mills in the Vancouver area. He discovered the bay, recognized it as a sheltered location to store logs that were on their way to the Woodfibre Mill, which began production in 1912. In 1924, he purchased the *St. Clair* with a partner and then acquired it for his own operating it until he retired.

Lumbering expanded along the west coast of B.C., including the Queen Charlotte Islands and to the west coast of Vancouver Island. Distance, weather conditions, and insurance, towing and service costs all added to the operating expenses of the logging companies.

In 1947, Oswald H. "Sparkie" New, President of Coastal Towing Co. Ltd. recognized the need to be prepared for modern marketing and established facilities on his property obtained at Andys Bay. His brother-in-law, Walter Morrison, relocated equipment from Thurlow Island. They set-up a sort at Andys Bay which "Sparkie" saw as a more logical location than Vancouver Harbour or the Fraser River for breaking down the Davis Rafts from around the province, and the storage of logs.

1950s Island Forester *and* EVAV, *a clinker built are tied to a Davis raft. Courtesy: Bill New.*

A Davis Raft was already waiting in the bay for them when they arrived to set up camp. The crew immediately established camp on shore, organized the sorting ground and set about learning how to break the raft down. In 1949, bunkhouses and facilities were built to accommodate the growing list of boom men needed to handle the increasing logging traffic.

The new company, Andys Bay Industries, contracted services to Alaskan Pine Ltd. Later, oil barges from Venezuela were purchased by Island Tug and Barge Ltd. and converted into log barges.

This 50-ton derrick nestles at the foot of rock cliff on the north face of Andys Bay. Courtesy: Bill New.

The Andys Bay sort facility was the first, and the only, fully equipped booming ground for this type of work on the B.C. coast. This location had raft-breaking and sorting facilities with a 50-ton derrick set into the base of a cliff. Its 108-foot boom reached out over deep water to efficiently load and unload log barges or ships that could land along side.

The derrick, so strategically placed at the base of the cliff at the north end of Andys Bay used its Murdie "50" winch and Chrysler Industrial engine to handle 500,000 to 800,000 fbm in a three to five day time span depending on the type of barge. A 32–foot tug with a 165 h.p. GM Diesel engine bag-boomed the derrick's production to the sorting pockets. It could easily build Davis Rafts using an assembly-line type system not seen anywhere else on B.C.'s coast. In this way, rafts of logs not marketable in Vancouver could be towed to a more marketable location.

The tug on the right is hauling the barge, once a sailing ship, named Powell II. *Courtesy: Bill New.*

The geographical characteristics of Andys Bay were key to the economical operation of this facility. There were no sand bars or other shallow areas which made its deep cold water, right along the shoreline, ideal for Davis Rafts, barges, etc., and the large tugs required to handle them. Some of the Davis Rafts drew 35 to 40 feet of water and the problems of handling them in enclosed places such as Vancouver Harbour did not present themselves in Andys Bay, as there was plenty of room for the tugs to maneuver.

Loggers wanting to sell their parcels of logs on the open market needed to be able to present their logs for inspection. Andys Bay provided a safe place to store flat booms in order to sell them in the standard way.

The entire salt-water operation and complex storage area was sheltered and as teredo-free as a sorting ground could be. The teredo worm/shipworm is a marine bivalve of the family Teredinidae. It bores into wood and is a threat to wood stored in water. The company maintained a constant vigil against the worm and halted all work to get contaminated logs out of the water if an infestation appeared. The bay, with its lack of debris on the steep shoreline, low temperature, and depth lessened the chance of floating logs being infected with teredos.

To get the logs to market for the least amount of expense, various methods of parcelling logs were created and then tested. Some tests succeeded while others failed adding to the costs to the loggers, the mills and the towing companies.

One of these methods was the use of Davis Rafts. A Davis Raft consisted of a mat formed from long logs interwoven with heavy cables, and had very large and long spruce 'sidesticks.' Once logs were loaded onto the mat more cables were strung over top of the raft and the load was securely tightened.

The most notable variation on the Davis Raft was the Gibson Raft, a predominantly valuable contribution to the industry. It was made of a separate log mat, was shorter, easier to use in tight quarters, and could be handled with limited equipment. Once the cheaper Gibson Raft was loaded with its bundle of logs and tied together, the raft could be towed away leaving the mat in camp. Due to its shorter length, the Gibson Raft with less-exposed tows was more seaworthy as the west coast swells would break up the big Davis Rafts of some 2,000,000 to 3,500,000 f b m of timber.

Flat boom storage at Andys Bay with a barge tied alongside. The townsite is at the far end of these booms. At the right of the far boom floats a group of loose logs held in place by a barrier of boomsticks waiting to be sorted. Courtesy: Bill New.

Around 1952, the Meighan Raft came into use. It was made up of about 6,500 board feet of logs held together by 'swifters' made of wire and fastened by a type (new at the time) of self-locking hook. The raft was built into sections, which in turn resembled a flat raft except it was bulkier. The Meighan Raft was a new idea in log towing at that time.

Boomsticks were held together by wire rope and self-locking fasteners without the use of boom chains. The lag-and-plate method and the Oregon dog method were some of the other parcelling methods along with log barges to bundle-booms, all of which to some degree combined the features of higher volume and increased security in each tow. With increased security came fewer headaches for tug skippers meaning cheaper tow fees, and secure loads reduced the insurance costs. Being able to travelling greater distances safely meant it was possible to store from two to two and a half times as many logs in one facility while they awaiting transportation.

Dumping logs off Powell I. *100 hp boom tug on right. Courtesy: Bill New.*

There were many variations on the Davis and Gibson type of rafts. Some designs resulted in complications in the processing of the rafts. Two rafts could look identical and hold the same amount of board feet but because of their different construction, one could take three to four days to process, while the other could take two to three weeks. The field men at Andys Bay were experts. In order to deal with these difficulties, a tremendous amount of different types of equipment was necessary.

Some of this equipment included two A-frames, one worked the rafts, its Mercury engine and Skagit B U 30 winch was used to clear areas of the foreshore in preparation for extensions to the camp. It was also used for some of the small logging jobs. Another, stationary A-frame was 85 feet high. The Davis Rafts were stripped of gear by the A-frame. Gibson Rafts were burned to break the parcel. Water-dozers and A-frame combined to break-up the stored bundles in preparation for sorting and booming. A spooling machine on the A-frame coiled the wire rope in order to return it to the owners. With bundle-booms, the tie-wires are cast loose after the sidesticks and swifters (log with cables attached to lie horizontally across the top of a bundle to hold it together) are released.

Sorting employed five to eight men and three boats: two Madill water-dozers—the one-man type powered by Chrysler marine engines and a small booming tug with a 100 hp Packard power plant. Any sized job could be handled in or from either end of the five double-ended, eight-section sorting pockets , allowing for tidal changes. Within-pocket sorting was also done with a swifter dropped in to separate the completed sort. Three men form a stowing crew. They put wire swifters on when a sort was completed and then moved to next pocket. The swifter machine with its Hayes-Lawrence 5-6 winch and Chrysler Industrial engine pulled log swifters into place to secure a boom. Alternately, a tug with deck-winches could do the job.

Creosote pilings in the hull of a barge. Courtesy: Bill New.

The float-borne chain saw with its No. 11 Oregon chipper chain on a seven-foot blade was driven by a 30 hp Wisconsin motor was an inspired piece of craftsmanship built by the crew to buck logs that were brought in. It was particularly handy to cut tree-length logs into selected pieces.

Logs were also brought to the booming grounds from camp by log barges. These large barges of up to several hundred feet in length were used extensively for a time. Log barges made mostly from salvaged, sailing ship hulls required the services of a tug and carried about three-quarters of a million feet. In comparison, the same tug that towed a log barge was capable of towing a Davis Raft of some 2,500,000 feet.

Early 50s. Andys Bay with townsite in the background. Courtesy: Bill New.

Andys Bay was originally laid out to unload barges, re-ship logs to purchasers and to break-up rafts in a time when the loggers were dealing with a soft lumber market. There was one set of five sorting pockets with plans for another set in the near future. This availability of storage allowed loggers a chance to turn market fluctuations to their advantage. They could deliver tree-length, camp-run booms sorted according to grade and species into the market as the demand arose while temporarily unwanted logs could stand by until pricing was more favourable.

In 1951, sorting capacity at Andys Bay was around 10,000,000 f b m a month and could be doubled as and when needed; the company's investment in equipment alone at that time was running at about $125,000.

Mr. O. H. "Sparkie" New, was president and managing director of Coastal Towing Co. Ltd. Walter Morrison was camp superintendent and together with Mr. New, breathed life into

the west coast of Gambier Island. The camp became a self-contained townsite with dining room, powder house, employees' residences, married quarters, cook house, bunkhouses and the superintendent's residence, and storage buildings. The original bunkhouse housed 28 men with a second bunkhouse planned.

The B.C. Government built a connecting road from Andys Bay to New Brighton to enable workers to drive to and from work and for married employees to live in houses located elsewhere on the Gambier. A school was proposed for the island rather than the Government school boat transporting children from Andys Bay to school in Gibsons.

1952 Mr. O. H. "Sparkie" New. From Harbour & Shipping 1952. Courtesy: Bill New.

The 80-foot wharf and float was completed in 1952 with the Standard Oil Company installing tanks to supply the need of this growing site. Water was piped to the wharf so boats could take on fuel and water without having to go to Vancouver. The head office was in Vancouver, communication between the camp and all the tugs was by regularly scheduled radio-telephone calls.

Mr. O. H. New was born near Liverpool, England. Oswald New came to Canada as a boy. He received his education here and passed his engineer's exams in 1926. With a love for the sea, he first worked as engineer on the Forest Service vessel *Hemlock*, served as master on fish packers and patrol boats and as engineer on fish boats, tug boats, government boats and passenger vessels. After obtaining a Diesel Engineer's Certificate of Competency in the early 30s, Mr. New held the position of chief on vessels of Harbour Navigation Company and on Union Steamship's costal vessel *Comox*. He then went on to be marine engineer for Northern Transportation Comp. in the McKenzie River district and then, in 1936, became marine superintendent for NTC, in charge of the shipyard at Bellrock, as well as the operation and commissioning of the company ships.

Mr. New was president, member and the head of several committees of the BC Towboat Owners' Assoc. He was also owner and operator of Coast Ferries Ltd. on the Mill Bay-Brentwood run with the ferry *Brentwood*.

He founded Coastal Towing Co. in 1937 with his 1937 *Hyak*, and acquired *Jessie Island VII* in '38, by '43 he owned *Beatrice*, *Fearless* and the *St. Clair* which he purchased from Capt. Andy Johnston—the namesake of Andys Bay. He also purchased the steam tugs: *Active, Petrel* and *Gleeful* from Canadian Western Lumber Company, and *Garrish* from War Assets Corporation. The tugs, *Black Raven* and *Celnor* were part of the fleet in the late 40s when Mr. New bought them from Towers Bros. Also reported as part of the fleet in the 50s were the tugs, *Tahsis King* and the S.S. *Sudbury* all of which were modernized and equipped to meet marine standards and to operate economically. The HMCS S.S. *Givenchy* was a minesweeper from 1910 to the 1930s. It was later scraped at the same time as the S.S. *Cecilia*, which served Gambier Island.

The Andy's Bay operation was a complicated operation and required a person with an expert knowledge of timber and rigging, etc. found in Mr. Walter C. Morrison, well known in

logging circles, he more than met these requirements. He was superintendent of the M&M Logging Company operation at Forward Bay on Cracroft Island for some time. He left to develop Thurlow Timbers Ltd. at Blind Channel, completed that operation and then became associated with Coastal Towing Company Ltd where he took over as superintendent at Andys Bay.

Mrs. Wilma Morrison, mother of Jerry Morrison, remembers Andys Bay in those early years. On

1959 Mr. Walter C. Morrison and dog, Trudy. Courtesy: Jerry Morrison.

November 1, 1948 with her husband and their children, they arrived on floats towed to the Bay. Mrs. Morrison was a registered nurse and as it was written in, *Andys Bay, Harbour & Shipping Magazine, October 1952* "has been fondly referred to as the "most attractive First Aid man" in any woods operation in British Columbia."

She not only looked after the health of the persons of Andys Bay, she took care of time-keeping, records, accounting, etc. As well as raising four children, in her spare time, she and

Walter frequently attended the Saturday Community dances at Port Mellon or Gambier Harbour.

Early 1950s Jerry ,Cathy, Clyde and Ken Morrison. Courtesy Jerry Morrison.

It took many qualified people to keep the Coastal Towing Co. Ltd. running at its best. Emmett Riordan was assistant to Mr. New. He was an experienced PLIB inspector and had thirteen years as an employee of MacMillan & Bloedel limited in log conversion and log trading.

Another person was W. D. "Bill" Mackintosh, the production manager, who joined Coastal in 1945 after serving seven years in the Air Force during WWII. His duties included ensuring that proper records were kept for approximately, fifteen hundred boomsticks, and around three thousand boom chains per month in addition to multiple tons of rafting gear: cables, blocks, etc. In order to carry

Early 50s Ken, Cathy, Jerry and Clyde Morrison. Courtesy: Jerry Morrison.

out the instructions from various customers, Mr. Mackintosh worked very closely with their log departments to ensure that the processing of their customer's logs was carried out.

Ed Cairns was one of the early employees at Andys Bay. The official "bull-cook," he was responsible for the camp buildings including their general cleanliness. In his spare time he built the rock retaining walls around the camp. He was 80 years old but still, his interest in the camp was an inspiration to the younger men. The appearance of the camp and the good work he did is a lasting tribute to him.

Above: Mid 50s. Ken Morrison. Port Mellon is in the background on the right. Courtesy: Bill New. Right: Late 50s. Clyde, Cathy, Ken and Jerry Morrison. Courtesy: Jerry Morrison.

Mr. W. Morrison, after working many years at Andys Bay passed away in May 1965. Jerry Morrison, son of Walter Morrison, grew up on Gambier Island and later became an employee of Western Forest Products.

The Andys Bay installation came together and provided a living and a way of life for many families because of the forward thinking of Mr. Oswald H. New and Mr. Walter C. Morrison.

Mike Fredea

Jim Thomson

Mike Fredea was a geologist born and brought up in Nova Scotia who spent half his year in Venezuela looking for oil, and the balance in a house he had built near a tiny creek in the big bay on Gambier Island just north of Steamboat Rock. He and his wife, Kelly, came and went in a small boat with an inboard engine which he had rigged with a clutch and reverse—an unheard of luxury. They had a cedar log float in the calm bay. He had a skid road cut into the side of the creek ravine behind his house, a path about 5 to 6 feet wide which led up through the shade under the alders to a large flat area well back from the water heading to a Japanese camp where there was a small creek with small trout in pools.

A small bridge planked with small cedar slabs crossed to the far bank. Working down the creek at the end of the pools you came into a long gravel stretch. Before long you could hear the murmur of the creek and would almost immediately come over a little shoulder and down into its tiny valley. On the walk back, there was a skid road branching off and running up the west side of the creek; it went up to the big camp.

The Government had stocked the lake on the bluff with rainbow trout.

1938 Union dock, Capilano, Lady Cynthia *and the North Van Ferry. Courtesy: Shirley Innes.*

Logging on Gambier's West Side

1. Gambier Creek
2. Gambier Lake
3. Third Lake
4. Fourth Lake
5. Douglas Lake
6. Mannion Lake

A. Pedenault Bros. of Hopkins Landing
   Fir & Hemlock by skidder–1960s

B. Truck & log chute
   Fir & Cedar–1920s

C. Bob Alsiger & Son of Gibsons
   Fir & Cedar–truck & skidder–1970s

D. Rolly Spencer of Granthams
   Fir–by truck–1950s

E. Plank Road & Cat with Arch
   Fir & Cedar–1936 –38

F. Inclined railway
   Fir & Cedar–1920s

G. Japanese Camp
   Cedar Skid Road–1920s

H. Bill Errico Jr. of New Brighton
   Fir, Hemlock & Cedar–by skidder–1990s

I. 1950 Jim's last ride with son, Ian on Cat

J. One man operation–1935

Map based on sketch by Jim R. Thomson.

Logging on the West Side of Gambier

Jim R. Thomson

My childhood summers from 1925 onward were spent at Hopkins Landing. Many of our hikes took us to Gambier Island. We also became acquainted with several of its residents because they came over to shop at the store in Hopkins and many of them were friends of my parents.

I was fortunate to personally see the old-growth being harvested. The last of the original forest growth consisted of some pretty magnificent trees—largely Douglas fir, red cedar and a little hemlock.

The logging of Gambier in the last one hundred years has determined the structure of the forest now covering the island. My knowledge of the early days is drawn from looking at the remnants of logging operations before 1936.

Prior to 1930, the area above Andys Bay (Bill Jr's wood lot (H) included) was logged for shingle bolt cedar. The bolts being dropped into the chute hit the water just north of the small draw which gave the loggers access to the area and was later the site of Mike and Kelly Fredea's house—the first and only settlers at Andys Bay, 1934 -50. There was a small cabin and a bridge across Mannion Creek, still standing about 1937.

1935 Log boom held in place with stringers across the surface.
Courtesy: Jackson family.

A large area between Andys Bay and West Bay (G) in roughly the same area as Bill Errico Jr's wood lot today (H) was the Japanese Camp. Cedar was logged by way of a skid road in the 1920s.

The timber above Andys Bay was removed by the inclined railway (F) which ran east up the bluff and ended close to the draw between the two peaks of Mt. Killam and Mt. Liddell. It was mostly fir and cedar. I'd put this show in the 1920s as that coincides with the date when Charlie Soames was injured while working on the site.

To the east of Ekins Point and north of Gambier Lake (2) fir and cedar (B) were harvested by truck and log chute in the 1920s.

The area above the inclined railway and up between the two peaks was logged about 1937 with a road punched up from the south end of Andys Bay. They planked the first section (E) up from the beach. When it proved to be too steep for safety, a caterpillar tractor and logging arch were used. They had a spar tree short of the very small pond in the draw between the two mountains. They were harvesting mostly large firs and some cedar. I saw this operation and rode up on the cat while they were working.

After the War, in the 1950's, Rolly Spencer out of Granthams extended a spur (D) from this road and switched back up the north-west face of Mt. Liddell. He logged fir by truck and then dumped at Andys Bay.

1946 Burn and Jackson home-built yarder on 1925 White Truck Chapman. Courtesy: Jackson family.

In the 1960's, the Pedenault brothers of Hopkins Landing cut a road at an impossible angle (A) up the gully of the northwest face of Mt. Liddell. The timber, mostly fir and hemlock, was taken out by skidder and dumped in a small bay across from Woolridge Island.

In the 1970s, Bob Alsiger and Sons of Gibsons extended the original road (C) around the northwest face of Mt. Liddell which is now the trail to the little lake and the peak. He drove the road as far as he could push his truck, logging as he went, and then built a bridge across a gully and using a skidder, he pushed up the east side of the setting and swung back to just below the peak. With the help of his son and one more man, they clear-cut the rocky side of the mountain. He too used the dump in Andys Bay.

I saw the operation in its early stages a year later, when Ian, my son, and I rode out on his last trip (I) with the skidder as he closed the operation down. This was the end of the cutting of old-growth timber on Gambier, just about 100 years after the logging of the first trees.

Bill Jr's wood lot (H) is a fine example of the harvest of this bounty. In the 1990s, he is logging the second growth of Gambier Island's forest.

Clear Cut to a Whole New Forest

Logging on Gambier was a main source of income as well as a main source of history. If it were not for the remaining stumps, one could never tell the area had been logged. Right now, we are working on the second and third generation of our forests.

Some of the mountain sides up the Sound were clear-cut in the fifties; in those days, there was no such thing as reforestation. When seen from the water or land today they are thriving young forests. Forests, like people, develop, grow, provide beauty, and replenish the earth, air and water.

Logging clears the land in much the same way as a fire does with the re-growth that follows being much the same. The land regenerates, starting with moss, ferns, berries, fungi, flowers and then deciduous trees reach toward the blue sky before they eventually give way to the towering evergreens.

Logging is also a boon for the population of deer on the island. The large cleared spaces become open meadows where the deer can graze. These areas are also home to rodents, mammals, birds, insects and reptiles, which play a vital role in the food chain, and in pollination and propagation.

Anywhere people go, to live and clear an acre or two; there is something that will grow under their feet. I can understand why some people talk of a logged area as being ugly. They may only see it once, but if they lived there, they would soon realize how the land recovers.

Here on the island, as the Crown Land is logged, it is reforested with new growth; all to continue the cycle of this rainforest.

On top of Gambier, looking out towards the Gap by Gibsons Landing. Logged in 1940. Courtesy: Errico family.

Residents Work with the Logging Companies

From Cotton Bay around to Andys Bay, large pieces of property used to be owned by people who had a house on the land and lived on about 50 percent of the property. Bit by bit, the big logging companies bought them out for foreshore rights for booming and sorting grounds.

Some of the owners were able to live there until they had to leave the island or until they passed away.

Mike Fredea owned one of these properties. Mr. Strachen did the same. Mr. Humber, Mark Jewitt's relative, also benefitted from these arrangements.

Tommy Austin, cutting his yearly wood supply. Courtesy: Shirley Innes.

Can Trees Talk?

What amazes me is how a tree can tell you its own history; a couple trees did that for me.

In the early days, the loggers cut notches as far off the ground as possible into the tree to hold the ends of their springboards. Standing on the springboards they used a crosscut saw to cut partway into the tree. Then using a double-bladed falling axe they would chip away the wood to make a wedge shaped undercut. An undercut was essential to help control the tree's direction, and make a clean break as it fell. Next, they would cut more notches for their springboards at the back of the tree and make a backcut to line-up with the undercut. As the cuts got closer, the tree would weaken and begin to fall, hopefully in the direction intended.

When I was young, I found an old-growth Douglas fir along Andys Bay road. It had an undercut in it but was still alive. Ten years later, when that tree finally came down from deterioration and age I cut a section out of the tree where the undercut was. I counted back the growth rings. It showed the undercut was made in 1894. It was then I discovered it had windshake in it and that is probably why the loggers left it.

Windshake happens when a tree is bent violently, as in a strong wind. Cracks can appear in the growth rings and pitch pours into these fractures in the wood to protect the tree from decay and insects.

A couple years later, I was reforesting an area within five to ten acres of that first tree when I came across an old-growth Douglas fir stump. Scars showed where notches had been cut into the tree. For some reason, after making the springboard cuts they did not take this tree. It also healed its wounds and grew around into the notches. I peeled back this part of the new growth. I cut it crosswise and counted the rings. I compared this to what I learned from the Douglas fir tree with the

A young woman stands in front of a fine example of an old-growth cedar stump. Courtesy: Jackson family.

undercut. This showed that the loggers came and notched the tree that is now a stump around 1870 but left it behind. Then they came back in 1894, made the undercut in the Douglas fir with the windshake, left it behind but harvested the tree that is now a stump.

This tells us the logging companies didn't just come to the island and cut everything at once. I would say one company would come and get the best and easiest, then another company, then another, repeating the cycle.

Now that is how a tree tells its story!

1936 Tugs leaving Douglas Bay after logging. Courtesy: Jackson family.

Steampot tug hauling a log boom. Courtesy: Jackson family.

Presence of First Nations Peoples on Gambier Island

The islands were once a part of the First Nations peoples camping and hunting grounds. On Gambier Island, there is evidence of their presence.

During the spring and summer months the First Nations peoples lived on the island, hunting, fishing, gathering roots and berries for food. They used a midden, usually at the mouth of a creek, as a place to discard the bones and shells of fish and shellfish. When the weather cooled, they left the Island until the following spring. A 1975 British Columbia Archaeological Survey uncovered evidence of nineteen sites of either camps or villages on the island.

The Squamish people named many villages, mountains and waterways around Vancouver. On Gambier, Port Graves at the head of Long Bay was known as Charl-Kunch, meaning "(long) deep bay."

I have heard of areas where there is evidence of the First Nations People. One is an area where thousands of First Nation beads were found. Studied by specialist at U.B.C., the estimation is at 3500-4500 years old. In addition, the head of a small statue is rumoured to be found and dating from the 1700s. I have also heard ancient paintings exist on Gambier, I look forward to finding them one day.

Native Americans sit in front of a tee pee. Sketch by Eliza Killam.

The Lady Cynthia *approaches New Brighton dock. Courtesy: Harper family.*

Cotton Bay

Mr. Humber

Mark Jewitt

He was a jolly old man, of course, I was just a young boy. He lived right in Cotton Bay. He owned a big portion of property that goes back to Andys Bay Road. Sea Span bought the property for the foreshore rights for log storage and there was an agreement that Mr. Humber could live there through his lifetime. Then Pacific Forest Products bought it, now Timber West.

Mr. Humber was one of the active members of the Army and Navy hall. Every Saturday he would walk to New Brighton and get a ride from there. At this time, his wife passed away so he was on his own but he did have a neighbour, Mr. Stracin and he was living on his own as well.

Finally, it came to Mr. Humber's last day. He went and joined a group of members at the Army and Navy hall drinking beer and chatting; then came the time to go home. Mr. Humber was dropped off at New Brighton wharf. At this time, he had a small boat with a Briggs and Stratton in it. When he left the bay, the boy could see him go around in circles singing away. No one thought much of it. As he was entering the log float—all it was, was two planks on one log—in front of Mr. Stracin, he was tying the boat up and slipped into the water. He went up and down a few times and ended not coming up again. Because of Mr. Stracin's age, he couldn't do anything.

There was a search for the next couple of days, nothing showed up. About a week went by and Mr. Humber surfaced. He was cremated and his ashes were buried beside his wife in his yard. When he died, family members came to tear his house down and take the material off the island for building materials.

Cotton Bay was named and Cotton Creek at the time after Mr. Cotton who owned the property. Cotton Creek (Mannion) comes right out into the center of the bay and is one massive clam bed. Mr. Cotton's house was at the edge of the high tide line on the right side of Cotton Creek. It was destroyed by fire and no one saw him after that day. Then the property went to Mr. Clarence Humber. The property was 150 acres that went right up behind New Brighton. Mr. Stracin owned part of this property on the other side of the creek.

HATOCO *Courtesy: Mark Jewitt.*

Norman and Irene Jewitt

Mark Jewitt

My folks, Norman and Irene Jewitt had talked to me about Cotton Bay on Gambier Island on a number of occasions. They had a float house there and had either owned or were thinking of owning property there in or about the time I was born in February, 1954. Just prior to my premature birth, Dad had almost lost his life there in an explosion on their boat, the *HATOCO*. When Dad finally got out of the hospital after a number of skin grafts etc. and after my Mother had given birth to me, they were finally getting things organized again. They had gone into Vancouver for supplies and returned to their home in Cotton Bay only to find it burnt, and the beach approach behind it burning. This was not the end of their problems. Mom had to return to hospital [due to illness] and I was fostered by Mrs. Wilma Morrison, and her family, [off island] until my mother returned. My folks moved from Cotton Bay to Twin Creeks on the mainland in or about the late fall of 1954.

My dad operated a log sorting grounds between Steamboat Rock and Andys Bay from approximately 1960 to 1965. This was where I learned about my dad's lifestyle. It was great. I would not have missed it for anything.

I purchased property near New Brighton on Gambier Island in or about 1980. As time went on even though it was a beautiful place to build, my work took me further and further North. We eventually settled at Cormorant Island, and the property at Gambier was sold in or about 1991.

My parents also told me that Clarence and Grace Humber, my dad's sister and her husband, also owned property at Cotton Bay. My Aunt Grace's ashes were secured in a brass box that I saw once at Cotton Bay. I do not remember ever hearing why they were placed there nor whatever happened to them, but when my wife and I visited the area in the early eighties, we could not find any indication of where they might have been nor did my folks know what happened to the brass box.

1938 The Innes/Holmes beach at New Brighton.
Courtesy: Shirley Innes.

New Brighton

Errico at New Brighton

Alfonso Errico 1979

On a beautiful summer day in July 1912, I was walking along Granville Street when I met George. He was not an intimate friend, but we spoke to one another when we met. This time he stopped me.

"Errico, I am going to my place on Gambier Island this weekend, will you have time to come with me?"

Since this was the slack season in my tailoring business I said, "Yes George, I would be glad to go." We made arrangements where to meet the next Saturday afternoon and parted.

We met at the appointed time on the dock on Vancouver's waterfront. The boat that was to take us to Gambier Island was small, with the capacity for about twenty-five passengers. We left on time at 1:00 a.m. It was a gorgeous day and the sailing was perfect. Soon we reached Point Atkinson where we entered the waters of West Howe Sound. If there was a Heaven, it was there. We continued about eight miles and then the boat rounded a point to a beautiful large bay. We proceeded another half mile and came alongside a small float where a sign read, "New Brighton."

After landing, we turned west on a narrow trail which was later widened and named "Austin Road." We proceeded about a quarter of a mile, and there we came upon a small cottage built on a knoll about twenty-five feet above sea level. We entered the cottage and there stood a man, about fifty-five years old and well built. His name was Thomas Austin.

"I want you to meet a friend of mine, Mr. Errico," said George. He had to repeat my name several times as Austin was hard of hearing.

We made ourselves at home, and sat outside for a long time admiring the view. Later, at suppertime, I cooked a meal. While eating, Mr. Austin made a remark of how good the meal was, "King George never had better," he said. We continued with our meal.

During coffee time, I was thinking how fortunate George was to have this lovely home. I said, "George, you have a nice piece here."

Mr. Austin, though being deaf, heard my remark. He sat up like a bullet; his face red as a beet and with an angry tone of voice said, "George, you are a stranger to the truth. You are a liar." He shouted, "Get out of my house and don't ever come again." I was never so surprised in my life. I thought Mr. Austin was looking after George's property. George picked up his belongings and left. He never went back again. When Mr. Austin calmed down, he said, "You will excuse my temper. I don't like liars."

I stayed the night, and in the morning, I cooked breakfast: potatoes and onions, bacon and eggs, toast and coffee. This was his favourite breakfast I found out. He was very pleased with my cooking, and he had a good appetite.

The time came too soon for me to go back to Vancouver. Mr. Austin came with me to the wharf. He said, "Mr. Errico, you are welcome to my place any time you like. The little room is for you." This was the start of our life-long friendship.

I continued to go to Gambier Island. I fell in love with the place; winter was just as enjoyable as the summer.

When Mr. Austin first settled there, he pre-empted a large parcel of land and named the location New Brighton, after Brighton City, a summer resort, and south of London, England. After living in New Brighton for some time, he decided to subdivide some of his waterfront acreage. The lots were subdivided on a North-South angle, sixty-six feet wide by two hundred and eighty feet long with one hundred and fifteen feet of waterfront.

1926 Alfonso Errico stands in front of the cottage. Courtesy: Errico family.

He was always after me to buy a lot or two. "It might be a place of refuge one day," he said. Finally, I weakened and bought one waterfront lot and two lots right behind it. I paid four hundred and fifty dollars for the front lot and two hundred and fifty for each of the back lots. The property remained idle for some time, and then the family began to arrive. My wife and I decided it would be ideal to build a little cottage on the waterfront lot and have a place for summer camping.

From then on every summer was spent there until the boys were through junior high. It was an ideal place for their health and their behaviour.

To build a cottage at that time at a place such as Gambier Island was not an easy task; however, our minds were made up. It was going to be built regardless of the ordeal.

Harriet and I began to make plans. I contacted my brother-in-law, Joe Alonzo, although he was a stonemason, he understood a great deal about building houses. We discussed our plans with him and he agreed to help us. By mail, I got in touch with Mr. Austin and told him of our plans. I asked if we could stay at his place while we were there building the cottage. He immediately answered my letter saying that we were more than welcome to stay at his place.

The following weekend Joe, my brother Jerry, and myself went to New Brighton to do some clearing. When we got to the property, Joe looked at me and said, "You should have your head examined, buying property at such a place." The lot was thickly wooded with large trees, many of which had to be cut down. Still, the weather was favourable and the clearing went without trouble.

The waterfront lot had a considerable slope to the beach, so a suitable spot to build was chosen, quite a ways back from the beach. Later it proved to be an ideal location as we had a splendid view, which we enjoyed for all the years we had the place.

1930s Bill Errico Jr's grandmother, Harriet Errico and his Aunt Alice Patterson. Courtesy: Errico family.

Errico at New Brighton – Alfonso Errico

I told Joe what we had in mind and he gave me a list of the lumber required as well as the other essentials. The following Monday morning I went to the lumberyard and placed my order. The man at the yard said he could not promise a fixed delivery date as the lumber had to go on a scow to New Brighton. It wasn't very long however, when I got a phone call from the yard saying that the shipment would be at New Brighton on a certain date.

Immediately, I wrote Mr. Austin informing him of the date the lumber would arrive as I had already made arrangements with him to receive it.

He wrote back that some help was needed to load the lumber onto a raft and then to tow it to our beach. I contacted my brother-in-law, Thomas Patterson, Wildon, my wife's brother and Jerry to see if they could come and help. They all agreed that they would. The agreement was to meet the following Saturday morning at the Vancouver dock. When the time came, no one showed up. They all had excuses. It was too late to ask anyone else so I went alone. Mr. Austin was waiting on the float when I got off the boat. Luckily, he had already assembled the raft with the heavy beams. When he noticed that I was alone he gave me one look and off he went, back to his home, I presume. Up to this day, I don't know why he took such an offense. I never mentioned it to him again and neither did he.

1926 After the cottage is finished, family and friends share watermelon. Courtesy: Errico family.

I could not waste any time, the lumber had to be on the raft and towed to our beach before dark. I laboured with the lumber for about four hours and although I had cotton gloves, my hands were all blistered and slivered. I could not think about my hands, the raft had to be

towed in. Mr. Austin had left his rowboat at least, and with it, the real ordeal started. The loaded raft was very heavy and the progress was very slow, I could only move it a few inches at a time. I cannot say how long it took me to reach the beach as I had lost track of time and it was pitch dark. The thing I shall never forget was that the tide was at its lowest of the year, for my benefit? I wonder. All night, I waited on the beach for the tide to come in, as I had to constantly pull the raft up the beach with the rising tide. When the tide was at its highest, I tied the raft to a large tree and went to Austin's place. I was tired! At breakfast, Austin never mentioned the lumber and neither did I.

I returned to Vancouver the same day, Sunday, and the first thing Monday morning I got in touch with Alonso and told him that all was ready to start building. I also told him the lumber was on the beach and couldn't stay there very long as it could be stolen.

He was very co-operative. "We can start at any time," he said. He hired a

Alfonso Errico at New Brighton with family and employees. Top left - Mother Asp, top right – Miss Donkersley. Bottom, left to right – Harriett, Alfonso Errico, Winnie and Frank Franco. Courtesy: Errico family.

Errico at New Brighton – Alfonso Errico

carpenter and with my brother, Jerry and myself, we all went to New Brighton, a day or two later. I had a lot of grocery shopping to do and other arrangements to make as I didn't know how many days I'd have to stay away from my business.

The plans for the cottage consisted of: a large room to be used for cooking and as a dining and living room, two bedrooms and a large veranda, wide enough to sleep outside when the weather permitted. We worked like Trojans, starting at daybreak and working until dark, as the carpenter could not stay very long. I was the cook, and it took nearly all my time to feed those hungry people. The climate out there makes one eat.

In less than five days, the cottage was ready for occupancy. Next, was to furnish it with beds, bedding, linen, dishes and all the things to make it liveable, including a wood burning stove, chairs and other knickknacks for a country cottage.

For the stove, I went to a second-hand store on Granville Street owned by the Wosks; that was their business in 1926. They had a large wood range made of cast iron and rust resistant. It was ideal for the place. My wife looked after the rest.

1927 -28 New Brighton. Ernie, Harriet, Billy Errico and guest. Courtesy: Errico family.

It was on the week of July 19th, 1926 the Errico family went camping, with Ernest going on four and Billy, one year old. Camping in those days was not as easy as it sounds. However, for the good of the children we dealt with the challenges. I must give a lot of credit to my wife

Left: *Alfonso Errico and Alice Patterson.*
Below: *New Brighton dock. Alfonso Errico is holding Bobby Errico. Harriet hugs her sister, Alice Patterson.*
Right: *30s Miramar and the boat house. Courtesy: Errico family.*

for putting up with a lot of discomfort; she was a good sport. To begin with, there was no electricity and no telephones. There were no inside toilets, no place to shop and last but not least, no drinking water. For water, my wife had to go quite a ways and draw the water from a well. As for the groceries, I looked after that part. I would travel from Vancouver to New Brighton every weekend. It sounds a bit odd to build such a place but the same conditions existed in many other camping places throughout Howe Sound. Still, it was pleasant for us and for the children it was a paradise.

I was always busy improving the property. In the fall of the first year, Mr. Austin dug a well for us near the house, and that made a tremendous difference the following summer.

Three years later, when we had Joe build the kitchen adjoining the living room and a fireplace; he had a different outlook about the place than what he'd had previously. He admitted that we had the choicest property that could be found anywhere.

When I retired, a decision had to be made, whether to live in the city or modernize the cottage and live at New Brighton. We decided on the latter. We moved to New Brighton and lived there for a while like primitives, with the wood stove for cooking and heating, and

1958 Harriet, Naomi, Janis and Alfonso Errico. Courtesy: Errico family.

kerosene lamps for light. There was a lot of work to be done of course, improving the property and wood to be cut. When we first went there, there was no such thing as a chainsaw; we had to use the old-fashioned crosscut saw. The logs were cut in stove-length blocks, split, cut and stacked to dry; this procedure was all done on the beach and after the wood was dry it had to be carried up to the woodshed. But, once we got power on the island, I built a track from the beach up to the woodshed for hauling in firewood.

We remained in New Brighton until 1967. My wife and I enjoyed every minute of those thirteen years. Of course, everything comes to an end.

Advancing age comes to all of us, as does a time when you cannot carry on any longer. Today, the Erricos still remain on Gambier Island. Our three sons have taken over, for them it is a paradise, so it is.

"Styles come and go but human nature remains the same." *Alfonso Errico, 1978.*

Mr. Austin

Alfonso Errico

Mr. Austin's Request

Mr. Austin was quite a character. He used to row his double-ended rowboat from his place over to the wharf singing away to himself and his voice was so loud that people across the water at Williamson's used to say they could hear him singing on a clear morning when he was out in his boat. Mr. Austin had an old dog by the name of Bugs. Later on when the road was constructed from Mr. Austin's place to the float, it was called Austin Road, at this point I heard it has been changed.

Mr. Austin approached me one day and said, "Alf, I don't know how long I will be able to care for myself here, when the time comes that I cannot, will you take care of me? If you promise me that you will, all my property in New Brighton will be yours." I was taken aback for a few seconds, when I regained my senses I said, "I'm afraid that will not be possible Mr. Austin." Our conversation ended abruptly, Mr. Austin did not take my refusal as an offense, and we remained friends as much as before. He did make a similar request to another New Brighton resident, and when the time came that he was incapable of taking care of himself, his benefactor put him in a hospital at Marpole. Periodically, I went to the hospital to shave and trim

1930 Harriett Errico and Mr. Austin's niece, Mrs. Nellie Yates. Courtesy: Errico family.

his hair. I asked him how he liked the place, if the grub is good. "King George never had it as good," he replied, the food is what interested him. He died soon after.

His Brush with the Law

Mr. Austin was summoned to court for having an affair with that young girl staying with his nearest neighbour. He was very fond of reading, most afternoons he would lie down on top of the bed with a pillow propped under his head. The girl in question would come in his room and lie down beside him. When he told the judge that he was old enough to know better, he asked the judge what he would do in a similar circumstance. The judge considered his age and let him off by paying the cost only.

He Came to Gambier Island

Mr. Austin originally came from Bolton Longshire, England, he came to Canada during the latter part of the nineteenth century. He was a coal miner by trade and was employed by the Marpole coal mines in Nanaimo. He had a family in Vancouver but for some domestic reason he left his family. He went to a merchant that he knew in Vancouver and asked to be, "Grub Staked" as he called it. When that was settled, he bought a small boat, which he called a "dinghy" with a pair of oars. One day in 1898, he left Vancouver for the unknown, paddling his way to Pt. Atkinson skirting the shores of the Strait of Georgia. He stopped when he felt tired, at the same time looking over the place to see if it was good enough to settle on. He continued his paddling all through West Howe Sound, keeping his eyes open for a place to settle. Finally, he reached Gambier Island; still he kept on paddling until he reached a point where he turned into a large bay. Immediately, he decided to make that his home. I never asked him how many days it took him to reach the place where he made his home.

He remained in his beloved place until he was not able to look after himself. He was taken to a hospital for the aged in Marpole, in Vancouver, where he died in 1946.

Mid 1920s Union Steamship Capilano *approaching New Brighton. Courtesy: Shirley Innes*

My Gambier Island Days as a Boy

Ernie Errico 1998

It all began in the summer of 1926 when I was three years old and brother, Bill, was only one. You may have heard he learned to talk on Gambier Island.

Dad, Alfonso Errico, first came to the island in 1912 on the Marine Express. He came to visit Thomas Austin with a mutual acquaintance. Austin and Dad became good friends and shortly after the war ended in 1918; he purchased three properties in the area which Austin had recently subdivided. In 1925, he built the cabin on the waterfront property with the help of Uncle Jerry (Dad's brother), Uncle Joe (his brother-in-law) and a professional carpenter.

I remember when Gambier Harbour was called Grace Harbour, Grace Islands were called Twin Islands and Mannion Creek was called Cotton Creek. The two mountains in the center of the island, Mount Killam and Liddell, were called Peter and Paul, and Mariners' Rest was called Steamboat Rock. In these days, what is now referred to as Gambier Lake was called Linfoot Lake, and the first lake reached when hiking from Mannion Bay was called Douglas Lake.

1940 Ernest Errico, Maurice Anderson, George Frost and Bill Errico. Courtesy: Errico family.

I shall write about the people I remember in the early days of my boyhood; starting from the west side of New Brighton. There were Joe and Lila Innes and their family, including Shirley. They had two cottages, which they rented over the summer months. For several years, Joe Innes had a herd of goats, which supplied milk for many of the campers. In the late twenties and early thirties, Mr. and Mrs. T.V. Clarke rented the upper cottage for the summer with their teenagers, Sid and Muriel. Later, they purchased property on the east side of the wharf. Other summer-time campers who rented the cottage included the Charles Jeffrey family, the Bob Jeffrey family, the Cliff Caroll family and the Liddell family, including Edna, Gladys, Bob and John.

East of the J. Innes property, was the Thomas Austin residence and his house, woodshed and chicken house was located on a ledge directly behind the present Symons location. He had a steep winding path down to the beach, up which he packed his winter supply of wood and his daily supply of water from a well, located above the beach. He lived there contentedly during the twenties and thirties with his dog, Bugs (who was blind and deaf) and cat, Betty, before fire destroyed his house in the early forties. Mr. Austin also had a cabin on the beach where the present Symons' house is located. He rented this out to his niece,

1940 Mr. Tommy Austin. Courtesy: Harper family.

Nellie Yates and her daughters, Evelyn and Audrey.

Another summer camper was Mrs. Terry who was known for her fishing expertise. She could catch salmon with a rusty spoon, cotton line and make-shift weight as long as brother Bill and I were rowing the boat. On one occasion, she caught a salmon too large to gaff and it had to be landed on the beach.

Next to Thomas Austin, the Shottens resided. Mr. Shotten was a retired cabinet maker and Mrs. Shotten was known for her fabulous cooking and gardening. Her home was surrounded with flowers. Mr. Shotten had two boats (Clinker-built) with outboards which I believe were the first on the island. They were started with a wind-up knob on the top. He also had one of the first battery operated radio receivers on the island, which he used to listen to "Mr. Good Evening" of the daily *Province* 6 p.m. news. The Shotten Property was later purchased by the Whites, and then by the Liddells.

Mr. Wise owned the next property to the east; he erected a cabin on the beach in the early twenties. During the thirties, he rented to Mrs Eldridge and a nephew, Thomas Slater. Henry and Clara Moore and son Telford eventually bought the Wise property and owned it for many years. Henry was an enthusiastic fisherman and was the person who initiated the concept of the Gambier Island fishing derby. The W.H. Moore trophy was named after Henry.

Mother and Dad's property was east of Mr. Wise's. The property next to them was

Mid 40s Capilano. Courtesy: Errico family.

originally owned by Mr. and Mrs Dan MacDonald, and their daughter, Jeanette. George Frost later acquired the MacDonald property. George Frost, a WW I veteran and former scout leader was quite active in organizing activities among the teenage boys in the area. He loved to hunt and fish and always had hunting dogs named Major. He was the one who arranged rowboat camp trips for us boys around Gambier Island or up McNab or Bear Creek. On these occasions we would be out for two or three days and would camp overnight using a single blanket. He also enjoyed playing the card game of Hearts and on rainy afternoon would organize competitions at which he would sometimes treat us to a pancake eating contest.

Harry Hay owned the next property, after which it was purchased by Mr. and Mrs Ben Fox.

Mr. and Mrs. Johnston and children, Mary, Florence and Don owned a large piece of property east of the Austin lands. Along with Shirley Innes, Don Johnston was the full-time summer camper with whom Bill and I associated. Don was also a great fisherman as well as a banjo player with a repertoire of novelty songs. At our many bonfires, Don would accompany us on his banjo.

Judge and Mrs. Harper owned the property next to the wharf along with their children, Andre, Josephine and Arthur. Art was well known for his bright red speedboat, the *Miss Fire*, which he built and operated.

Mr. and Mrs. Wheeler Lawrence lived in the home presently occupied by Mrs. Negroponte. Mrs. E. H. Lawrence was the official postmaster from 1919 –1940 and her husband, Wheeler, was the courier until his death. Mrs. Lawrence always had the appearance of a stern and serious person, partly because of her appearance (she wore her hair drawn back in a severe bun) and partly because of the way she handled the postal services. She reminded one of the old time actress, Marjorie Main. In the summer, she had a firm ritual for distributing the mail. Wheeler would pick up the mail from the Union boat and deliver it to the rear of the house. Mrs. Lawrence would then dutifully stamp each piece of mail with the official New Brighton post office stamp. She would then come out to the front porch where all the patrons were waiting, some seated on the wide railing and call out the name of the recipients for letters, parcels and

1926ish Harpers, Mr. Johnston, Don Johnston, Betty Burchell and friends. Courtesy: Shirley Innes.

newspapers. She would not allow anyone to deliver mail to a neighbour unless she had received express permission from the recipient. The receiving of the mail in this fashion was a daily ritual, except on Sundays when the post office was closed.

After Wheeler died, Mrs. Lawrence herself picked up the mail from the Union Steamship in spite of the fact she had a great fear of water and did not like to go down to the wharf, which at most was only a float. In spite of her rather serious demeanour, Mrs. Lawrence was basically a kind lady who had a fondness for us children and was very good to Mother and Dad. In the late twenties and thirties, the Lawrence's had two cows which would often be resting and chewing their cud on the trail between the two crab-apple trees near the present barge ramp. I remember Mother being a little nervous about the cows but they were a source of milk for two or three summers.

Mr. and Mrs Don MacLean and their daughters, Elsie and Donalda rented the Urquhart's place just east of the wharf, which later became the Matheson's place. There was a huge field behind this property where the older teenagers would practice softball, usually with a broken bat and torn ball. Bill and I were a little young but enjoyed watching and acting as bat boys. Some of the members of this team were the Harpers, Clarkes, Don Johnson and friend, George Pearson and others visiting at this time. Since they would play teams from the Y camp and other church camps in the area, they called themselves the New Brighton Pagans.

1945 Elizabeth Beck and Rowdy, Al Kingston's horse. At Helen Negroponte's house. Courtesy: Helen Negroponte.

Other residents on the east side included Mr. and Mrs. Singleton-Gates, her mother Mrs. Drage and her ward, Johnny Cox. The Clarkes eventually built their own cabin at what was the end of the road on the east side of the wharf. Further residents who lived behind Mrs. Lawrence, or on the road to West Bay were Al and Elsie Kingston, Charlie Power, Tommy Burns, Vimy and Cappy. Al Kingston, who owned a horse called Rowdy, was a logger, and for a number of years he took out alder and maple for the Hammond Furniture Company which was then located on Venables Street in Vancouver. Tommy Burns (who lost an arm in the First World War) lived in a cabin next to the Harper property, adjoining the Lawrence Property. Charlie Power owned a double-ender rowboat which he would row standing up facing the bow.

Many things which occurred during my childhood still remain in my memory. For example, I can still feel the sense of excitement when we were preparing for camp and when we arrived at the Union dock early in the morning and saw all the steamships lined up to leave for their various destinations. Of course, our steamer was always at the end of the dock! The ship would leave Vancouver at 9:00 a.m. and would take four to six hours to arrive at New Brighton after stopping at various ports of call in West Howe Sound. We were always dressed in shirt and tie and could hardly wait to get into our camp clothes upon arriving for the sense of freedom we felt. I remember the scent of the cedar v-joints in the ceiling of our cabin, getting water from the well on the beach and the smell of the kerosene lamps at night.

The big social event of the day was the arrival of the Union ship whose time was always unpredictable. However, we could estimate the time by watching the boat as it called at various ports in the Sound and by listening for its whistle. Regardless, we would be down there one half hour ahead of time. The ships that served the sound were the *Capilano, Lady Cynthia* and on weekends, the *Lady Evelyn*. The *Lady Evelyn* was taken out of service in 1935 and the *Lady Cynthia*

Mid 30s Alfonso, Bobby, Harriet, Billy Errico, Alice Patterson and Ernie Errico. Courtesy: Errico family.

then served on weekends. The *Lady Pam* joined the *Capilano* for weekday service shortly after. The *Lady Rose* was brought out from Scotland in late 1937.

Mother spent the whole summer alone with us, from the end of June until the end of August. Dad would come up Saturday afternoons laden with food and flowers. The *Lady Evelyn* left Vancouver at 2:00 p.m. and arrived around 6:00 p.m. It would leave New Brighton Sunday night at 5:30 p.m. Sunday night, and the wharf was usually very crowded. People would start to arrive about 4:30 p.m. and although we could see the ship as it came down from Seaside Park and called at Williamson's Landing and the YMCA camp first, people were always at the wharf early. The Saturday afternoon and Sunday evening sailings were often called the "Daddy Boats." Sunday night was always a very lonely time for Mother. She would watch the *Lady Evelyn* as it stopped at the various ports from Hopkins to Gibsons and finally steamed out the Gap at dusk on its way back to Vancouver.

In the mid-thirties Union Steamships instituted a Friday night boat to West Howe Sound, where the ships left Vancouver at 7:00 p.m. Friday evening. Although, at first, the run did not include New Brighton, the first port-of-call was Grace Harbour where the time of arrival was 9:00 p.m. When Dad felt he could afford to take time off from the shop Saturday morning, he would take the Friday evening ship. Bill and I would walk to Grace Harbour to meet him. Sometimes, however, as we grew older, we would row to Avalon Bay then walk to Grace Harbour to meet him. On these occasions, I remember stopping at Ormie Cambie's General Store located on the Avalon Bay Trail just west of the Grace Harbour wharf to buy ice cream bars, shipped up that night, all packed in dry ice. As at that time, there was no daylight savings time; these trips would be made in the dark.

Mother would always make two trips a summer to visit Mrs. Heay at West Bay, who had a garden full of flowers and baking always on hand. When Mrs. Lawrence gave up her cows, Mother would bring back milk from Mrs. Heay. Frank Heay, her husband, worked in some official capacity on the large booming grounds which were then located in West Bay. Another trek we would make every summer was to visit Mrs. Black who also lived in West Bay. Mrs. Black was a very sad lady who related her tales of woe and tragedy to Mother throughout the visit.

Our main and often only supply of milk was from tins, except when we were able to obtain milk from Mrs. Lawrence or Mrs. Heay. However, around 1933, Joe Innes brought a herd of goats to the island and for a number of summers we literally lived on goat's milk.

I should point out that none of the milk was too palatable because it was not ice cold. We had no refrigeration. Mom and Dad did the best they could to preserve perishables such as butter, eggs, milk, cheese and bacon by dropping them in the well cavity in a bucket. If Dad brought up meat Saturday, it was eaten Sunday. In fact, most perishables were eaten immediately. Our staple food included pancakes, bread and strawberry jam, pork and beans and lots of vegetables and fruits. These latter were obtained from the gardens of the local residents.

From time to time, we would have a bread delivery service. Art Harper provided this for one or two seasons and Arthur Lett from Grace Harbour did so for several summers. They would take Mother's order one week and deliver it the next. Mother stored the bread in large lard tins, but keeping the mould away was always a problem. Needless to say, we had lots of bread pudding!

I remember well, the one Christmas we spent it Gambier. This was 1930 when I was in Grade 2 and Bill was only five. The purpose of the trip was to burn a huge stump, which was located near the front stairs. Dad was already planning to build the kitchen addition on the east side of the cabin. I remember Mrs. Lawrence killing one of her prime roosters so Mom would be able to cook an appropriate (and delicious) Christmas dinner.

The addition and fireplace were built during the summer of 1932, after Bob was born. Dad took the summer off and Uncle Joe came to do the masonry work. It rained almost every day that summer. The Union Steamships delivered all the supplies to the wharf so Dad built a makeshift raft at the wharf using part of the lumber intended for the addition. He piled the rest of the lumber, bricks and other supplies on the raft and towed it by rowboat to the beach where it was uploaded at high tide. It took hours. I can

1930 Peggy Jeffery and Ernie Errico. Courtesy: Errico family.

still see Dad towing this raft in the pouring rain, dressed in an old oil slicker and a sou'wester hat. Poor Uncle Joe went out of his mind trying to get the brick mortar to set while building the chimney and stone fireplace. Some sections had to be rebuilt two or three times.

The main recreational activities were swimming, boating, fishing and hiking. We would spend all afternoon in the water. Mother would never let us swim until an hour after eating. Often a gang of kids would gather at Innes's Beach where we would swim and sun and play word puzzles such as geography and spelling games. As for boating, rowing was the only means of transport. We thought nothing of rowing to Grace Harbour, Hopkins, the Y camp and even Seaside Park. When hiking up to the lakes, we rowed to Fredea's camp north of Steamboat Rock and took the old logging skid road from there. Often there were bonfires in the evening and various beaches where we roasted wieners and marshmallows. This was when Don Johnston would entertain us with his banjo playing and would lead us in the singing of campfire songs. One other event was Mother's annual taffy pull for the teenagers. It would take Mother days to clean up sticky candy after the party.

These were happy times; before the advent of electricity, telephones, television and indoor plumbing and just some of my memories of my boyhood days on Gambier Island.

Mid 1950s On the beach in front of Holmes. Right front- Bobbi Pearson, beside her is Joely Symons. Left front to right – Mrs. Jeffery, unknown, Shirley Symons, unknown, Peggy Errico. Behind unknown – Leah. In front of log – unknown, unknown. On log – Mable Clarke. Courtesy: Pearson family.

My Early Years on Gambier

Bill Errico Sr.

When Bill first asked me to write of my early years on Gambier, I thought that I would compose a narrative of epic proportions. But now that I have started, I am beginning to think differently. I ain't no Hemingway. What I will do, will be to just try and record some of my memories of the wonderful growing up years at New Brighton.

I think the first memory that I can come up with is one about strawberry jam. It all started after school closed for summer vacation. After leaving our Kerrisdale home at about 7:00 a.m., we walked, carrying our supplies, from 50th Ave. to 41st Ave, to catch the #7 streetcar to take us to the Carrall St. dock of the Union Steamship. There, amongst the hordes of summer people, we boarded the West Howe Sound Boat, (probably the *Capilano*) for a 9:00 a.m. departure. As nearly all the boats for the other routes left at the same time, the confusion and chaos was overwhelming, especially for a wee tot like me whose wonderment and curiosity would result in my losing my mother and the rest of my family for a few frightful moments. Then came the most exciting time of the day, after boarding the boat, Mother went to look for a suitable seat while Ernie and I, full of anticipation for the trip to "Camp," headed for the boat rail to watch the departing procedures. The last of the freight was winched aboard with a big clatter, the gangplank was hauled on board, and the lines were thrown off the bollards on the dock. The ship started backing away from the wharf with three long, loud blasts of its steam whistle. You can imagine, with three or four other ships all doing the same thing, it was quite a spectacle.

Now, it was our time to explore the boat. The best part was sneaking down to the hold with all its wonderful sights and smells. There might even be a cow or horse down there along with stacks of hay. It was a dangerous place especially since the great doors, where the freight had been loaded through, stood wide open and the wind that rushed in could pluck us up and carry us off the ship. (Look closely at the *Capilano* photos.) Next, we ran to the stern where we could watch the seagulls diving for the scraps of food thrown out by the cooks in the galley. The restaurant was off limits to us, as it was for the rich people. We were quite happy with the picnic lunch Mother provided for us.

After a couple of hours, the ship would start calling in at its different ports-of-call. If I remember correctly, it went something like this: Eastbourne, Long Bay, Centre Bay, West Bay, Grace Harbour, Gibsons Landing, Grantham's Landing, Hopkins Landing and then New Brighton. As soon as the whistle announced each one of these ports-of-call, it would find us kids at the railing again watching the seamen throwing the heavy lines, and then the Captain warping the boat to the dock; the lowering of the gangplank, unloading and loading of passengers, unloading and loading of freight with those magnificent cranes and steam winches, and then dragging in the gangplanks, throwing off the lines and going astern with those whistles blasting out three times again.

1935 Capilano sailing into New Brighton. Courtesy: Errico family.

It would be early afternoon before we reached New Brighton, (probably three or four clock) depending on the amount of freight at the other stops. Then poor Mother had to get everything organized to leave the boat. After leaving New Brighton, the ship would continue on to the Y Camp, Williamson's Landing, Hillside, Port Mellon, Seaside Park then back to Vancouver.

Upon disembarking, we walked with all our luggage to the cottage where our house is now. The first thing we did, was to make a quick inspection of the property, including the outhouse to find out what damage was done over the winter, then Ernie and I were handed a couple of pails and instructed to fill the water pails, two large and two small which survived the winter sitting upside down on a bench at the back door. Unfortunately, the well was down at the beach and by the time we had the water pails full we were pretty tired and hungry.

This is where the strawberry jam comes in. Mother sliced up some fresh bread, put a big plate of butter on the table (I loved butter) and opened a new tin of Elmer's (Empress) Gibsons pack strawberry jam. I don't think anything ever was, or ever will taste as good as that bread slathered in butter and gobs of fresh strawberry jam.

It wouldn't be long—usually about the time mother was cleaning and filling the oil lamps—when we would hear singing out-back. On looking out, we would see this bandy-legged, squat, old man sauntering down the trail towards the house. He would yell, "Thought I saw smoke coming out of the chimney, just came over to see what was going on." This was Tommy Austin, our nearby neighbour and the original inhabitant of New Brighton. He yelled because he couldn't hear very well. He also couldn't see worth a darn, had no teeth, false or otherwise (the story was that when he got a toothache he would pull the tooth himself with a pair of pliers until they were all gone) and chewed (or gummed) walnuts which stained his heavy moustache permanently. He said, "They toughen my gums." After all the pleasantries were dispensed with, Mother would ask if he would like to stay for a "bite of supper?" His immediate response would be, "Don't mind if I do—don't mind if I do." And then he would make himself at home.

Thus was how we started a complete summer without shoes, worries, or commitments that lasted until Labour Day.

Now here is a rundown of all the local residents of New Brighton as I remember them. Please be tolerant with me as I might not get my facts straight. I always did think my memory was not the best ever since I had the knock on the head as a youngster. At the furthest west part of New Brighton lived Mr. and Mrs. Joe Innes. Already I have forgotten Mrs. Innes's name. I want to call her Dolly because she looked like a little porcelain doll to me. Oh yes, her name was Lila, the same as one of her daughter's. The present Shirley Symons (nee Innes) was another daughter and Joley Switzer is her granddaughter. The property they lived on originally belonged to the Malcolms of "Malcolms Best Foods" and the original house still stands on top of the hill. Word has it that at the turn of last century, shake cutters occupied that house, and cuts shakes on the island after it was logged. I don't know if this was pre or post Malcolms.

At one time, Mr. Innes decided to raise goats and for a whole summer, us kids only had goats milk to drink. I did sort of get used to it but it wasn't the same as cow's milk. He had his goat sheds up on the bluffs beyond his house and allowed the goats to roam free. They did prove to be a bit of a nuisance especially when they wouldn't allow you to pass on the trail. I think Mother wasn't scared of them. She would shoo them away with a wave of her hand and a scowl on her face. Eventually Mr. Innes's prize doe hung herself on the branches of a tree she was browsing and I think that discouraged him in his goat raising scheme.

They also used to rent their cottages to summer visitors; the original one at the top of the hill and one they built on the bluff near the goat sheds. One of these annual renters was the

Jefferys and their daughter Peggy, who became Ernie's childhood sweetheart and then his wife.

The Innes's beach, considered the best beach around, became the gathering place for all the kids on a hot summer afternoon. With its small smooth pebbles, it was an ideal place to lie in the sun. Another bonus was that Mrs. Innes was always around to dole out tender loving care for all the scrapes and cuts we received during our water activities. Shirley's dad also had two magnificent double-ended Clinker-built rowboats which were the envy of the locals. They were Mr. Innes's pride and I was never allowed to row one, much to my chagrin.

Other renters at the Innes' were the Clarkes with son and daughter, Sid and Muriel. They were a little older than I was so I didn't know them that well. Muriel went on to marry Jack Pearson and begat Donna, Bobbi and Leah. Bobbi and her husband Kevin now own the property next to ours. Donna has a house behind us next to my daughter, Carolynne's. After

1949 Bobbi, Jack, Leah, Donna Pearson and Mrs. Clarke. Courtesy: Pearson family.

they had rented for a while, the Clarkes bought property on the east side just beyond where Dodie Errico's (nee) Myers family cottage was.

Just east of the Innes's was Tommy Austin's property, which he pre-empted around 1895. The story was, as I understand it, Tommy, after a separation with his wife in Vancouver got in a rowboat and started rowing until he reached this part on Gambier Island. He thought it was "God's country" and settled in. I think his first pre-emption was acreage located behind the farm as old maps show the location of his house and fruit trees. When he moved down to the beach remains a mystery, but he was there in 1912 when Dad first visited him with George Darby. In 1910, he named the place New Brighton, after his favourite resort, Brighton Beach, New Brighton, Cheshire, England. It was from this property that ours was subdivided about 1925.

Tommy had a ramshackle old shack on the top of the bank, at the end of Austin's Road, about where Joley's new house is now. It had two rooms on the west side, the kitchen in the middle, and Tommy's bedroom on the east side. It also had a long narrow porch across the front. I can remember that when I left the house by the front door I had to be careful not to fall off the porch as it was so rundown and had such a slope to it. The two rooms off the kitchen were for quiet and storage; the rear room was full of chicken feed etc. At times, there were even chickens in there. His chicken coop was just to the right as you left by the rear door. There was a blackberry bush across the back. This blackberry had the variegated leaf and was planted there. I don't remember there being any of the Himalayan blackberries we have now. We also had a loganberry bush that never seemed to do very well.

Tommy always did his own cooking (except when he could sponge a meal) and even baked his on bread. His bedroom was also off the kitchen but on the east side. It was very sparse with a dirty unmade bed with a side table and shelves of books at one end. His meals were usually quite simple and he always had fried potatoes and onions for breakfast. I remember one incident when he was making bread. I was watching him knead it on a board on his kitchen table. A large black spider started to walk across the board. I saw it walk right into the bread dough he was kneading. I guess it I should have said something but I never did. As he was nearly blind, I suppose lots of other things ended up in that bread.

I don't think Tommy thought much of doctors as he was always doctoring himself. His favourite remedies were slippery elm poultices and burdock tea. They must have worked as I don't ever remember him being sick. His original job on the island was cutting shakes, and then later he became the original road foreman.

Tommy also had a cottage on the beach, below the old shack he lived in. He rented it out when he could. One of his first renters was a Mrs. Terry. She was an avid fisherwoman and used to get me to row her boat so she could catch the fish. She was usually lucky and could catch fish on the proverbial bent nail.

Besides chickens, Tommy also had a goat for a while, which he kept in a shed up behind his house. That didn't last long though; he probably had as much luck as Joe Innes.

When we first knew Tommy, he had a dog; the name escapes me now (Lady maybe) but I do remember that whenever she had pups he would put them in a gunny sack, weigh it down with stones, then row out in the bay and dump them.

I remember that about once a week you would see him on the beach, in the water, summer or winter, with a bar of soap. He would lather himself up and then go for a swim doing the breaststroke. Sometimes he would swim across in front of our place, heading for the wharf.

Another passion of Tommy's was playing dominoes. Ernie and I would spend much of our spare time sitting at his small kitchen table playing with him. We would only have to mention "dominos" and his eyes would light up and he would "fetch" his wooden box of ivory, double-nine dominos and dump them on the table to begin the game.

Tommy subdivided his pre-emption sometime around 1925 and gave Dad, Alfonso Errico, the first chance to buy the lots of his choice. Dad took three; the waterfront lot for which we paid four hundred and fifty, and two hundred and fifty for two lots behind it. Dad started to build our cabin about 1926.

Next to Tommy, where the Grays are now, lived an elderly couple, Mr. and Mrs. Shotten. Mr. Shotten had an enormous gibbous on his upper back and was therefore not very active. Mrs. Shotten was a very nice lady. As I remember, whenever Mother took us over to visit them, Mrs. Shotten would have a big jar of candies, usually the Scotch mint—you know the kind—with the soft caramel in the center. She knew the way to a child's heart.

The Shottens were not permanent residents but did spend a lot of time there. Mr. Shotten had a boathouse on the beach with a homemade hand-winch out behind so he could pull his boats in.

Mrs. Shotten always had a beautiful garden and she would save all her seeds to spread along the trails. Whenever the foxglove grows in the spring, I always think of her and wonder if she had anything to do with them. I first saw them mixed in with Sweet William, wall flowers, and Snap Dragons growing along beside the road where she had thrown the seeds.

Next to the Shottens and next door to us was the Wise's cottage. I don't remember them but they used to have renters there every summer.

Another renter was Mrs. Yates, a friend of mothers, who had two daughters, Evelyn and Audrey (they later changed their names to Shirley and Brenda). She was a niece of Mr. Austin and the wife of Captain Yates. They also had a son, Lawrence who was older and never came to Gambier.

On the other side of us lived a Mrs. McDonald, a thin sour faced old biddy that

1940 George Frost and his dog, Major. Courtesy: Errico famly.

had no use for kids. She lived in a house that was located on the hill above the beach. I had nothing to do with her until she brought up a First World War veteran, George Frost to live with her. Mother wanted nothing to do with him (living in sin and all that) but he and I became good friends—like Tom Sawyer and old Jim. I think George had more influence, except for family on my growing up than anyone else. He was the one to take me hunting, fishing, hiking, camping, exploring etc. He taught me honesty, integrity, sportsmanship, respect for other's property, and was in all a good friend.

I remember one time when we were out fishing. He was rowing the boat and I was sitting in the back holding on to the hand line—a length of cutty hunk with a one hundred and ten pound test gut leader and one pound weight and a #5 diamond spoon. We were just crossing in front of the mouth of Cotton (Mannion) Creek when something yanked the line out of my hand. Fortunately, we always secured the line to the rowboat seat. Whatever was on the line started to pull the rowboat backward and I was unable to pull the line in. George traded places with me and I can still see him standing in the back of the boat pulling the line in hand over hand. He was stripped to the waist and was actually pulling the boat backward. When he finally pulled the line in, I looked over the side and saw a salmon about the size of a barrel roll over, and take off. He never stopped and broke the one hundred and ten pound test leader. I think that was the only time I heard George swear. He estimated that the fish weighed between fifty and sixty pounds. The largest he had ever seen, and that ain't no fish story.

George was always doing things for the kids. Every summer he would have a pancake eating contest for the boys. Then he would organize a two or three day camping trip, when we would row around the island: ten points if we saw a seal, twenty points if we saw an eagle, and fifty points if we saw a deer.

Another incident occurred when he asked me to help him top a tree in his yard. I was up the tree and had just finished chopping a notch (no chainsaws then) and I stuck the axe in the tree underneath me, so I could start sawing. George was under the tree picking up limbs. Just as I looked down the axe came loose and started to fall directly towards George who was bending over underneath. I yelled and George looked up just as the axe caught him across the side of the neck. Fortunately, he sustained only a superficial cut. I expected him to be mad as Hell, but he never said a word. He just went to his house, bandaged the cut and came back to work.

George always had a dog called, Major, his first was a Pointer which was purebred and was quite high strung. Later he had a Springer Spaniel, which was a lovely dog.

George also gave me my first rifle, an old 44/40 with an octagonal barrel…. Unfortunately, Mother didn't like guns so George kept it at his house for me. Then tragedy struck; George's, I should say Mrs. MacDonald's house burnt down and I lost my gun. I also lost a friend; George never seemed the same after that. Mrs. MacDonald died after the house burned down. He lived for a while in a boathouse on the beach with a woman named Mae. But we had lost our old camaraderie.

He also had a Dupreytone's contracture in his right hand and it got in his way every time he rowed a boat or fired a rifle. The only other thing I remember about George was he was from the Isle of Mann and that he thought that Winston Churchill was an opportunistic drunken bum.

Next door to George lived Ben Fox. The house he lived in previously belonged to Hay's. The Hays had lost a son by drowning off the beach in front of their house and they lost interest in the place. Ben was an ex-logger who loved to tinker. He was an excellent mechanic and could sharpen a crosscut saw so it would pull a two-inch curl. Ben had the first rowboat with an inboard air-cooled engine (Briggs &Stratton) that I had ever seen. Ben was a quiet soft-spoken man who was liked by everyone. I can hardly remember his wife, as she was so reclusive.

Across the road and on the next acreage lived the Johnsons. He was a retired high school principal and spent his summers there with his wife, his son, Don and daughters Florence and Isabelle. Don used to hang out with us kids but Florence and Isabelle were a little older and we didn't see much of them.

The last time I saw Don was at HMCS Cornallis, Nova Scotia where I was taking basic training for the Navy. Don, who was sub-lieutenant, and I spent a weekend together at Wolfville, Nova Scotia at a girls college that was used by the Navy during the summer months.

Old Mr. Johnson owned the first outboard engine I ever saw and we used to see him sitting for (it seemed) hours in

1931 Art Harper cruises the waters aboard his bright-red speed boat, Miss Fire. Courtesy: Harper family.

the back of his boat, pulling on the starting cord of his balky engine and sucking his pipe.

The Johnsons had quite a nice orchard and we as kids used to take advantage of the fact. There was a small creek that ran through their property—Johnson's Creek or Joker Creek— where as a youngster I used to catch small salmonoid fish, which I thought were trout to put in our well. As none of them ever survived, I am thinking maybe they were salmon fry and not trout. I never did actually see any salmon spawning in the creek, but that doesn't mean that there wasn't any.

Next, along the shoreline, were the Harpers. Now, I don't have to say much about them as their history is well documented and they are well represented in the present population.

I will say though that I really liked old Judge Harper, and I always wanted gold teeth in front like he had, and then there was that "smart-alecky kid" Art, who used to roar around the bay in his speedboat, *Miss Fire*. He had his uses though; he did bring milk over from Hopkins at times. When we first started to live on Gambier, it seems that there used to be a bachelor called Charlie Powers who lived in a shack near where the beach house is now. He may have worked for the Harpers.

Then there was, Mrs. Lawrence. She lived with her husband, Wheeler, where Mrs. Negroponte lives now. Mrs. Lawrence was our Postmistress and every day after the steamship left, everybody would walk up to her place to sit on the porch and wait for her to sort the mail. This was about our only source of social intercourse.

After a while Mrs. Lawrence would appear at her door, "harrumph" a couple of times, adjust her spectacles and start reading off the names and handing out the mail, very officious and without a smile on her face. It used to be quite a thrill to hear your name called out and to receive a letter, or better yet a package.

It's amazing how appearances can be deceiving. Mrs. Lawrence looked just like a witch with her long chin and nose and her toothless grin, but she had a heart of gold and was a good friend of Mother's. Mother tells the story of one time when we were on the island for a holiday (Christmas or Thanksgiving) and we had no meat, Mrs. Lawrence showed up at our door with a large haunch of venison. Wheeler kept pretty much in the background. He spent his time looking after the garden and his cats (I think he had about a zillion).

The only other people I can remember from this time were the Burns and the MacLeans. Tommy Burns was a one-armed war veteran who lived with his wife and son, Connie somewhere on the bluff between the Harpers and the Lawrence's. We saw very little of them as they seemed to disappear into the bush for weeks at a time. Connie got his education by correspondence, and I remember Tommy "rowing" his boat by sculling from the rear with one arm.

The MacLeans were one of the originals and built the house that the Mathesons have now. I believe he was another school principal and had two daughters. They were a lot older than I was and I didn't know them very well.

Every summer, at least once, Mother would take us for a walk to visit Mrs. Heay or Mrs. Black in West Bay. To visit Mrs. Heay was fun, because she had cows, chickens, and she used to tame deer. In fact, we used to get milk and eggs from her, but to visit Mrs. Black was another story. She was always crying and whining and a real pain in the... Mother always felt sorry for her as one of her children committed suicide and her husband was a drunken bootlegger, but that didn't help, and it used to be an afternoon "hard spent." She didn't even give us any candy.

Out on the point towards Avalon Bay there was a small bay called Burgess Cove. A Mr. Burgess lived there; he was a retired chief engineer off the old Empress boats. And one of his sons, Johnny, had a beautiful hunting dog, a Rhodesian Ridgeback. One time, after I had just bought myself a brand new Cooey single shot 12 gauge shotgun for fifteen dollars, Johnny offered to take me hunting with him and his dog. One morning, before light, we went to the Ladner Marsh to shoot ducks. We sat in the blind all morning and never saw a thing. We then spent all afternoon combing the fields with the dog looking for pheasants, nothing, then back to the blind for the evening flight. It was just getting dark and I figured I wouldn't have a chance to initiate my new gun when we heard a faint, "Quack, quack, quack." There—way up in the air was a flock of ducks. Johnny said, "Don't bother, they are too high," but since I was

determined to shoot my gun, I let fly. I knocked three ducks out of the flock. Needless to say, I was the hero for the day.

1933 Ernie, Harriet and Bobby Errico. Aunt Alice Patterson and Billy Errico. Courtesy: Errico family.

The Hebbs lived at Avalon Bay and the Killams on the point. Mr. Graham lived on Twin Islands (Grace Islands).

The foregoing are some of my earliest memories of Gambier residents. Later in the post-war years, people like the Kingstons, the Drages, Johnny Cox, Vimy, Singleton-Gates, and an old bachelor veteran who lived in the shack across the road from where the Higgins are now, came to Gambier Island. The Kingstons built the house where the animals lived. Al Kingston had a horse named, Rowdy.

Perhaps this would be a good time to tell of the first time I got involved in island politics.

Al and Elsie Kingston along with George Frost were having a feud with Francis Drage. I think it was about the time Francis (who considered himself the self-appointed mayor of Grace Harbour) wanted to take the post office from Mrs. Lawrence and move it to Grace Harbour which he renamed Gambier Harbour for that purpose. I happened to be with George when I heard him talking with Al and Elsie, planning to "get even" with Francis. The plan went like this; Elsie was to confront Francis on the wharf at Grace Harbour when the Union Steamship came in while everyone else was on the dock, and try to start a fight. George and Al were then going to step in and "defend her honour."

Everything pretty well went to plan. I can remember Elsie going up to Francis and the next thing I saw was Elsie smashing Francis over the head with her purse. Poor pudgy-faced Francis looked quite bewildered and put his arms up to defend himself. That was when George and Al walked in and started beating on Francis. Nothing serious happened apart from maybe a bloody nose and a lot of confusion.

But that wasn't the end of it for me. Francis brought charges against George et al., who in turn subpoenaed me as a witness. I was in a hell of a dilemma, if I told the truth I would be speaking against my friends. I was supposed to say that I saw Francis put his hands up to "strike" Elsie. I don't think they remembered that I was there at the planning stage. Fortunately, I was not called on to testify. The judge put them all on a five hundred dollar bond to keep the peace for a year.

Old Mrs. Drage (Francis's mother) lived in Clarke's house at New Brighton and looked after little, bug-eyed Johnny Cox who lived in a shack on the property.

Vimey was a shell-shocked veteran of the first war. I think he was a veteran of Vimey Ridge, hence the name. He lived in a shack just at the junction of the Grace Harbour and West Bay Roads. He was a sorry sight and I used to visit him to try to cheer him up.

Singleton-Gates built the house just south of the MacLeans on the beach. About the only thing I can remember about him was his English accent.

It was about this time the Moores arrived on the scene. They took over the cottage next to ours where the Wises were. They had a son, Telford. W. H. (Henry) Moore was an avid fisherman and was always able to come home with a big salmon. He always named his boat the *Halcyon*. He was also the originator of the salmon derby. The trophy is named after him.

Other things about this pre-war era were our hikes to Lynnfoot Lake (Gambier Lake) which was in the valley between Mt. Peter (Liddell) and Mt. Paul (Killam). The names of the mountains were changed to honour two air force lads who were killed in the war. In the area between the mountains, we had to pass through a virgin forest that was spectacular; it was a park-like setting with magnificent trees. Also near the first small lake was an old logging camp with the shacks still standing. On the way to the lake we had to find our way along ancient logging roads as there was no Andys Bay Road. The better one was known as "The Old Bridge Road" which still can be seen just west of the Mannion (Cotton) Creek. This area had a large number of blue huckleberry bushes. I can remember once George and I were hiking the area and he showed me the remains of an old flume that he said was used by Shingle-bolt Cutters. It was up on a broken trestle and was pretty well dilapidated at that time.

A daily ritual was the meeting of the Union Steamship. When we heard that familiar two long, one short, and one long blast of the whistle we would take off at a gallop so we could be the first ones there to catch the heaving lines. On Fridays, we were lucky because there were two boats. Every Friday evening there would be a "Daddy Boat" that would leave Vancouver at 7:00 p.m., bring the Daddies that had to work all week to visit their families at "Camp." Our daddy would arrive with a large black club bag just bulging with goodies. Especially welcome was the huge bag of cherries (in season) that he would pick from our tree on Angus Drive. We would sit on the front porch and gorge ourselves, spitting the pits over the railing. For a while Ernie delivered the *Sun* newspaper which was sent up on the boat. I used to help him, and we covered quite an area.

1935 Billy Errico Sr. on New Brighton diving board. Courtesy: Errico family.

Quite a few Union ships made the West Howe Sound run. I can remember the *Capilano, Lady Alexander,* captained by Captain Yates (who would become my first chiropractic patient), *Lady Cynthia, Lady Cecelia, Lady Pam,* and later the *Lady Rose.* We would identify each one of them by their whistle before they came in sight around Twin Islands.

The first wharf I remember was a float attached to the shore by a series of long floats with a plank stretched between them. As a youngster, these planks seemed quite formidable, especially if one was missing. The next wharf had a long approach on pilings, similar to the present one, but the shed was on a float stabilized by groups of pilings so that it would rise and fall with the tides. It was attached to the approach by hinged ramp and the shed to this one is still on the farm.

Mother said that when she first came to New Brighton the only trail to our house was across behind the Harpers and the Johnsons. The road along the shore wasn't there until the Johnsons and Harpers gave an allowance in exchange for the surveyed road between these properties.

One of my favourite pastimes as a youngster was to still-fish off the wharf. I would go down at the change of low tides, catch some shiners, bait my set-lines, and spend a couple of hours fishing. I always came home with two or three nice blue cod, which Mother said she liked better than salmon. I used to catch a variety of other fish too: dogfish, skate, ratfish, flounders and sole and a lot of sun-starfish. Once while I was fishing, George came in all excited and had a couple of "fangs" in his pocket. He told us of an encounter he had had with "the ugliest creature I have ever seen," in the shallows in Cotton Bay. It turned out that his "monster" was a large wolf eel; the first ever seen in these parts.

Another of my favourite memories was when "Uncle Tom" and "Aunt Alice" would come to visit. Uncle Tom would always take us fishing. He would get us up before daybreak and we would row either to Steamboat Rock (Mariners' Rest) or Twin Islands. His favourite trick was to spit on the spoon for luck. We usually did pretty good.

I would be in remiss if I didn't mention that during this time Ernie and I built the "dangedest" boathouse on the beach in front of our house. We collected all the planks from the flotsam that came up on the beach and cut the three-foot shakes ourselves. Actually, we did a pretty good job and it lasted quite a few years. We kept our ten-foot Clinker boat and various

1958 New Brighton. Right – Fisherman's hut. Center – Now existing store. Land owners: Carmels, Potters, Nash, A Luc, Bob and Sue Tigar. Dick Atchison Jr. is the shadowy figure on the right bottom. Courtesy: Dick Atchison Jr.

items of junk in it, and used it for a dressing room to change into our bathing suits.

Another job Ernie and I had to do was to cut wood for the kitchen stove. We would use a two-man crosscut saw, a bucksaw, axe, and sledge and wedge. It was during these sessions that my wonderful big brother used to marvel at how strong I was and exclaim that I could saw so much better then he could, and praise my skill with an axe. Of course, I used to "bust my ass" to show him how right he was. It wasn't 'til years later that I figured out I was being "Tom Sawyered.". But the wood got cut and I guess that's what mattered.

An annual event was the West Howe Sound Regatta. It rotated from Gibsons, to Granthams, to Hopkins, to Camp Elphinstone. Mother used to take us over every year with Ernie and I rowing double with two sets of oars. Who would think of rowing to Gibsons these days?

Top: October 1964 Garth Errico – Ernie Errico's son, Aunty Alice Patterson and Jamie Errico – Bill Errico Sr.'s youngest child.
Right: August 1956 Darrel Errico – Garth Errico's older brother – Jeffery Errico's younger brother. Courtesy: Errico family.

Top left: late 40s Don Johnson and Tom Parker –
brothers-in-law. Tom married Florence Johnson.
Right: 1960s Bill Errico Jr's cousin, Francis Errico and
Bill Errico Sr.
Bottom: 1964 Yvonne Errico in doorway, Bill Errico Sr.
on porch with Jamie Errico sitting in front of him,
unknown person on the stairs. Photos courtesy: Errico
family.

The Boy is Now a Man

After all those years of wonderful summers, 1942 was to be the last for about seven years, as I was occupied with the Navy, and college in Toronto. When I got back to the island with my family in 1949, things had changed drastically around New Brighton.

➢ The Innes's had taken over Tommy Austin's property.

➢ Bob Holmes had the Innes's Property.

➢ The Liddells had taken over the Shotten Property-Edna-Gladys Gray.

➢ Harold and Marie Woods built their house.

➢ Mr. Humber lived in Cotton Bay.

➢ Atkinsons built a house where my daughter, Carolynne is now.

➢ Smarts built a house on the beach on MacDonald's property.

➢ Parker's (nee Florence Johnson) were living in the Johnson house.

➢ Johnny Knight had moved a float house onto the shore below the Harpers and was living there.

➢ The Burns had gone.

➢ The Negroponte's were where the Lawrences lived.

➢ Orville Becker's aunt, Mrs. Kselby lived up the Andys Bay Road, which had been built in the meantime by Francis Drage to bring workers from Andys Bay to the pub at the newly built Army and Navy hall at Gambier Harbour.

➢ Orville Becker and his family lived on the road just past the junction, toward West Bay. His father lived just across the road. Orville had a water taxi, probably the first on the island.

➢ The Mathesons took over the MacLeans farm.

➢ Old Breacher lived as a recluse up the Andys Bay Road with his horse.

➢ The Boyds arrived on the island and started a store.

➢ The Bowers and Fosters built on the East shore.

➢ The Anderson Brothers had a sawmill in Gambier Harbour.

➢ Mrs. Atchison (Dick Atchison's wife), Vic Pearson and Gus Lund lived on the Gambier Harbour Road. Mae and Marie Woods cut ferns for a florist company—Gambier was supposed to be the best source for ferns on the coast.

➢ Tommy Austin was gone; consigned to the Marpole infirmary.

➢ George Frost had disappeared.

➢ *And* the Errico's started a new phase in their life by starting to build a summer cottage on the back property.

These last few pages chronicle my early life on Gambier, a place that means a great deal to me. After all, I took my first steps on Gambier, and with a little luck, maybe I'll take my last.

Learning to Love the Rock

Yvonne Errico
New Brighton, July 2009.

In July 1947, as a newlywed of six months, I came to Vancouver to meet Bill's family and ended up at his parent's cabin in New Brighton. Part of my initiation to Gambier Island was a very long trek up a rough trail between Mount Peter & Paul, which turned out to be an all day climb. It was so hot and so tiring; I was soon exhausted. This was supposed to be a treat but it was hard to pretend that I was thrilled, not to mention that I completely destroyed my strappy sandals. Talk about a novice! We returned to the beach and home about nine hours later, thankfully, dinner was waiting.

1947 Peggy, Ernie, Bill and
Yvonne Errico on hike to the big
lake, Linfoot/Gambier Lake.
Courtesy: Errico family.

I was only 18 years old and a bit naïve so I found it difficult to understand why anyone would leave all the modern amenities in Kerrisdale and come to holiday on a rock with outdoor toilets and no running water or electricity. But maybe, I thought, the allure was the beachfront; however, upon investigation I noted near the shoreline there were crabs that looked like giant black spiders that crawled sidewise. I didn't think I would ever go to the beach, let alone into the ocean to swim. In spite of all that I became acclimatized and less traumatised, and even ignored the giant crabs that summer. It took a little longer to adjust to the outdoor plumbing though.

We went back to Toronto where Bill graduated from college in 1949 and then moved to Vancouver with our six-month old Carolynne. We spent that summer in New Brighton and by this time I was a little more prepared for "Life-on-the-Rock," as I jokingly called it.

We built our own cabin in 1953, 54, 55, 56 and on and on…. By this time, we had three more additions to the family: Bill Jr., Janis and Naomi. The children and I spent every summer at New Brighton. Lucky for me, my sister, Hazel came from back-east with her husband and three children, and her husband, Art, helped build the cabin during the summer of 1953.

From then on, my sister and I, and our seven children spent every summer at New Brighton. I don't think I could have done this otherwise but with her company, it was fun. By the time the men returned on the weekends we had dropped at least two pails down the well.

All building materials were delivered to the island on the Union Steamships and

1954 Billy, Yvonne, Janis and Carolynne Errico sit in stern of the Putt Putt. *Courtesy: Errico family.*

we spent much of our spare time carrying buckets of sand for cement, and 2 by 4s up from the beach to build the cabin; it was a never-ending job. Much of the laundry was done on the beach with linens and diapers spread out on rocks to bleach in the sun.

We warned the kids, if they didn't behave, we'd plan a trip for the next day. We planned the long hikes hoping the children would sleep longer—it didn't work, but we kept trying anyway. The kids named these hikes "death marches."

I had a reputation for not caring much for this life on Gambier. I think I voiced my grievances jokingly and I was quoted many times, "I'm being sent to the Rock for the summer." But in spite of the drawbacks—I loved those summers, most of the time. Bill's mom reminded me so many times that it was good to get the kids out of the city and "Its evils." So what could I do?

By 1959, Jamie was a welcome addition to the family, which made eight children, and then another sister, Myrna joined us for the summers. With her daughter, Linda, we ended up with nine kids—all under 12 years old. But the children were getting older and could take on some of the responsibilities, like looking after the younger ones. We packed large, interesting lunches and directed the older ones where to go with the hope it would give us time to do the chores. Alas, instead of being gone for two hours, they were back in half an hour with the food all gone. The fact that they ate breakfast before they left and had numerous sandwiches and treats and drinks didn't seem to matter. Nothing ever worked for us in that department. So after numerous tries we gave up on that tact.

Most of the activities were fun; the children loved to walk to Mrs. Boyd's store to buy penny candies. One very big attraction on the island for the adults was the Saturday night shindigs, all the good dancers loved them, and later came the children's Christmas parties. By this time, I loved Gambier but because of my early complaining I could never redeem myself, now, thank goodness, that's all forgotten.

Grandpa Alfonso Errico was instrumental to the advent of electricity, and everything changed in July '61, but it came too late for the beach laundry as Jamie was already out of diapers.

The whole family and friends still congregate at New Brighton, at summer holidays and for family birthdays and all the other holidays.

There's nowhere else I'd rather live.

Early 50s Putt Putt, Bill Errico Sr.'s first boat is anchored in front of the Errico property. The house in the photo belongs to the Smarts family. Courtesy: Errico family.

Camp Stories of the '50s

Carolynne Errico 2010

All year long, we looked forward to summer. As soon as school was out our family piled into our little putt-putt boat loaded down with supplies, and headed for the cabin at New Brighton on Gambier Island. Grandpa, Grandma and the bottomless cookie tin lived there in a little blue cottage on the slope to the beach, with our cabin just a hop, skip and a jump behind them.

Upon arriving at New Brighton, we all had to be loaded into the rowboat and ferried to the beach. After many trips to the house, all the supplies were piled on the porch and the well was checked to make sure the little speckled trout still swan in its depths. The well was our drinking water and our refrigerator. Perishables were loaded into a bucket and lowered into the cool water.

Inside the cabin, the clean-up was underway. Drawers and cupboards were cleaned and mouse nests discarded with the children rescuing the little pink baby mice and tenderly caring for them, keeping them warm and feeding them warm milk from a medicine dropper; all to no avail, year after year not one survived.

Coal oil lanterns, the wood stove, and the outhouse were checked and readied. Bunk beds were made up and chamber pots placed under them for children too frightened by the dark to make the trek to the outhouse in the night.

1952 Carolynne and Billy Errico. Courtesy: Errico family

That first morning at camp, we would awake to the sounds of the summer forest with birds singing, squirrels chattering and scolding and hopefully no sounds of rain on the roof.

We would lie awake in our cozy bunks while the wood stove cracked to life; one brave soul having hurried over icy floors to light the nest of newspapers and kindling. Slowly the cabin would start to warm.

Outside there were forests and beaches to explore, clams to dig, berries to pick, fern forts to build and hikes to find fungi, upon which Mom would chronicle our adventures with pictures and poems written with a nail.

On a very hot day and looking for a Popsicle, we might walk to the store, which perched precariously on the edge of the bank where the road met the wharf. Padding along in our bare feet, the warm dust squishing between our toes, we tiptoed past the beach house not wanting to alert the little dog that lay in wait ready to dash out and nip at our heels as we made our final run to the safety of the store.

We would check the big sign at the end of the wharf, which reminded the community about the most important social event of the summer—the yearly Fishing Derby! Kool-aid, hot dogs, doughnuts and fishing for shiners and cod off the dock with the hand lines that Dad put together for us while he carefully got his own gear ready for the big day! Kid's heaven!

1954 Billy and Carolynne Errico, Barbie Symons. Courtesy: Errico family.

A visit to Mr. Negroponte might be next. Married to Mrs. Negroponte the postmistress, Mr. Negroponte, a kind man was tall and very thin. He always seemed so genuinely pleased to see us traipse through his gate, a long line of happy children looking for a handful of raspberries and a carrot plucked carefully from his garden and washed under the garden tap.

As Friday neared, the perishables in the well perished and the food stocks ran low. Soon Dad and the other fathers would be rounding the point in their various boats. We just had to listen for the putt-putt-putt sound to know our dad was on the way. As we raced to the beach to meet him we knew he would be bringing our weekly groceries, a small toy picked out for each of us and of course, always the giant watermelon!

Dad would look us over and decide which of us would have the great responsibility and honour of carrying the watermelon to the house. The one selected would solemnly receive the precious fruit into out-stretched arms with Dad's reminder, "Are you sure you're ready for this? Don't drop it!" Although handled with great care the watermelon somehow was always dropped. The real question was how much damage would occur. Would it reach the house with a small dirt-filled crack or would it be splayed open on the porch, unrecognizable? Whatever the outcome we would still devour its red juicy fruit swallowing a little grit and a few seeds with it.

1958 Janis, Carolynne and Naomi Errico. Courtesy: Errico family.

Beach bonfires, listening to scary stories in the dark, roasting marshmallows, and laying on our backs gazing into the Milky Way were all part of our summer fun, as was swimming in the golden phosphorescence on very dark nights then stripping our bathing suits off in the dark boathouse sending sparks flying in the water droplets.

Alas, the days would get shorter and the mornings and evenings took on a chill. Soon it would be time to pile back into the putt-putt boat for the ride back to the city and a new school year.

Little feet that had been free all summer would be stuffed back into tight leather shoes and little bodies into desks.

We longed for summer to rescue us again.

Growing up on Gambier Island

When I was a boy, our family lived in North Vancouver and my father's parents lived on Gambier Island. My father, Bill Errico Sr., had a clinker-built boat with a putter motor in it. I remember going out from Horseshoe Bay, around the point and on past Garrow Bay. It would take us two hours to get to Gambier Island, which we called, Camp.

Coming from a city into a forest is like breathing new air and is a different world all together. Father built our summer cabin on Gambier, not far from Camp.

A good time of the year was spending Easter with my grandparents. When they invited me, I got away from the horrors of school and my teachers.

We were "Summer People." My Grampa told me he remembered when he was "Summer People." He said there was a community meeting at the Harper's in their large living room. The "Residents" sat on one side of the room and the "Summer People" sat on the other side of the room. He said he could see the red line down the center of that room.

In July and August the "Summer People" would come. They were quite different from the residents. We didn't worry much about them as they would be gone soon. But, there too, there seemed to be a red line in the sand between "them" and "us."

My siblings and I spent most of our time outdoors building forts with our cousins. Some days we needed exercise to burn up our energy and on those days, Mother would take us all for a picnic, which usually meant a major hike. She would lead us down to Cotton Bay, up Cotton (Mannion) Creek and then back down Andys Bay Road—an all-day project.

1958 Errico cousins - Jamie on Billy's shoulders, Carolynne, Jeffery holding Garth. Front row – Darrel, Naomi, Richard and Janis.
Courtesy: Errico family.

Many times, as we explored the woods, I would find glass and broken rice bowls. That is when I really got started collecting bottles, rocks, tools and artifacts from the old camps.

As I grew older, we would take hikes and walks into the forests. At the mouth of

Johnson's Creek on Johnson's Beach, where the ramp is, there was an old apple tree. It was 100 years old when I was little. I was told there used to be two but no one could tell me how they got there.

Sometimes, we picnicked down at Mannion Bay where there was a large old tug grounded on the beach. We would spend a good part of our time being deckhands or the captain.

A few years later, I built forts in the trees and on the ground. When I was deemed old enough, I actually spent the nights camped outside. Once or twice a week, we would hike up to Mannion/Cotton Creek, follow Andys Bay Road, and stop at the falls that made pools of water

1956 -57 Billy Errico Jr. Courtesy: Errico family.

where we swam. You could see the brook trout swimming, darting back and forth. We saw lots of wildlife, much the same of which is still carrying on today.

There were old growth trees up on the rock ridges of the creek. We'd hike down to the creek, have our picnic, and then hike to the north end of the beach, and then head back along the trail that returned us into New Brighton.

Other days, we would spend time rowing around and doing some fishing off the wharf, in, and around the bays. The hard part was pulling the old, clinker built boat back up to the boathouse. There was never something you couldn't do, from cutting firewood for the cooking stove, bringing in buckets of water, and preparing the coal oil lamps. You could have running water if you had a well dug further back on the property and then siphon it down to the house. You could even have electricity and indoor bathrooms instead of an outhouse but with those luxuries, it's not real camping.

Another thing that was fun to do was going to the orchards—climb the fruit trees, picking apples, plums and cherries—anything left on the ground was for the deer to have a good meal.

We spent a lot of time on the beach collecting hermit crabs and bullheads from the pools in the small rock bluffs on the beach. Once a week, we collected horse neck clams for

Left: 1967 Yvonne, Billy Jr., Janis, Naomi, Bill Errico Sr. Courtesy: Naomi Errico.
Below: 1956: Naomi, Carolynne, Janis Errico. Courtesy: Errico family.

Opposite page.
Upper: 1958 Carolynne Errico – Billy Errico Jr's oldest sibling, Aunty Alice Patterson.
Lower: August 1962 Aunty Alice Patterson's grand nephews – Jamie and Garth Errico.
Courtesy: Errico family.

clam chowder.

Time went on and even though it took us a couple of the years of thinking about it, Father and I made the big decision to clear some of our property for pasture land. At that point, all we had was a beaten-up chainsaw that worked when it wanted, axes, sledge and some light wedges. We worked our butts off, enjoying ourselves—most of the time.

We had people thinking we were nuts. One person came up to us, took his hat off, and shook his head saying, "What the hell are you doing this for?"

Every weekend and holiday we could, we came up to Camp to work on the land. After many blisters, bruises and sore muscles, we finally realized it wouldn't hurt to look for a small piece of machinery. We found an old D2 Caterpillar tractor. It did make a big difference after all that time of breaking our backs, and believe me, the way we were using dynamite I'm surprised any of us are still alive.

The average old growth was 3 to 4 feet in diameter, mainly Douglas fir and R the AS home stop ed Cedar 100 to 175 feet in height and, there were some even bigger.

When we had it logged, we traded the timber for help with the land clearing. When we were

finished burning a clearing, we put in a big fence. With most of those big trees gone, we saw a lot of wildlife because there were more bushes and shrubs in the open fields for them to survive on.

Next, came the cattle—four Herefords. We brought them on a float as close to the beach as possible, they jumped off the float and swam to shore. One went head first into the water and I thought that was it was dead but it was fine.

When I finally finished school in 1968, I came to live on Gambier.

Dad and I would spend a lot of time together from boating, exploring, working, hunting and land clearing. That is why I am as far as I am today.

1934 On the right side of the photo a tractor with Caterpillar treads makes its way up the hill. Courtesy: Jackson family.

Gambier Island Residents and Visitors

Our small community was made up of many "characters." One of our neighbours was an older lady and every time I saw her, I would stare because she had big whiskers on her face and I was sure only men had whiskers.

The Alexanders:
The Alexanders lived in Gambier Harbour. Mrs. Jean Lee is the Alexander's daughter.

The Anderson Brothers:
The Anderson brothers lived in Gambier Harbour. I remember them as good guys and easy to get along with. They also had a liking for their booze. They did a lot of mill work. Some of the machinery they used was so big and heavy I don't know how they moved it to the places where they worked.

They sold their place to the Dickeys, and then it was sold to Dave Langley and a partner, Dan.

Hughie Mowatt,
Ed Anderson,
Jimmy Boyd,
Jack Anderson,
Dick Atchison Sr.
and Girly, the
dog.
Courtesy: Dick
Atchison Jr.

Mr Austin:
Mr. Austin used to look after the roads in New Brighton before the roads went to West Bay and Gambier Harbour they used to be just trails. After Tommy Austin left the island Mr. Bradbury took over, then Mr. Bill Wesslen, then Mr. Bill Reynolds, and now Mr. Phil Richardson is in charge of roads.

Mr. Orville and Mrs. Pam Becker:

Mr. and Mrs. Becker came to the island after his father. Orville's father, Oliver did mainly building and carpentry work. Oliver and the Anderson brothers built the bridge that used to cross the creek down by Mrs. Negroponte's.

Orville Becker's house being built. In phase one. His father is helping him build it. Courtesy: Bryan Becker.

Mr. Ernie and Mrs. Jenny Bowen:

Mr. Bowen was an ambulance driver, one of the first. Mrs. Bowen was a nurse and retired in New Brighton. She had emphysema.

Their house was sold to Fred and Sally Grant.

Mr. and Mrs. Boyd:

Mr. and Mrs. Boyd were a couple that came to New Brighton around 1945 with a son, Jimmy Boyd. He was born in North Vancouver 1941. Father Boyd worked for the tugs while Mrs. Boyd worked in the store. They lived in the place before the Boyds. They left the island in the mid-fifties. Jimmy lived there for another five years mostly logging on the island.

Mr. and Mrs. Clegg:

Mr. Peter and Mrs. Joyce Clegg owned her father's place—that was Mr. Matheson. The house was built in 1911.

Mr. Drage:

I never did meet Mr. Drage but I've heard so many stories from people I feel like I was there in those early days. I did meet Mrs. Drage during my younger years. She was a very sweet person. Mrs. Eva Julien Drage and Mr. Drage lived two lots up from the wharf in Gambier Harbour. Eva, known to some as Elizabeth, operated the Post Office until August 24, 1965.

Mr. Drage and Mr. Lett owned the store at the same time. Mr. Lett went for the mail.

In World War I, Captain Francis Drage served in the Imperial Army. During World War II, Captain Francis Drage was the commanding officer of the 119th Company Pacific Coast Militia Rangers known locally as the Gambier Island Rangers. Due to his rank as Captain, he most likely got a grant to help build the Hall. Other members of the P.C.M.R. were Joe Mitchell, Thomas Burns, Art Yule, W. S. Bradbury, and C. A. Lett. After World War II, a log and frame memorial hall was built by volunteer labour with material donated by the members of the P.C.M.R. Unit 276 of the Army, Navy and Air Force Veterans of Canada. It was dedicated on September 21, 1947.

1937 On the trail to West Bay. Roy MacLaren, Tony Pringle, Marie and Owen Houston. Courtesy: Houston family.

When Captain Drage wanted to create better access to the Hall so more members could make it to the Hall, he was able to get a grant to create more jobs and to build a road to Andys Bay. He got a big old Cat about the size of a D6 and put roads all over the island that were mainly walking trails and he did not stay on road allowance either. If another spot was easier, he cut through there instead, even if it was on private property so there are a few pieces of property that are cut in odd pieces. When they got about half finished that dozer hit a snag and the top broke off and hit Mr. Drage, killing him instantly. Mrs. Negroponte can remember when they brought him down past her place in a wagon with a blanket over him in the 1954. The monument of rocks is still there on the side of the road where he was killed. But that did not stop the rest of the group from continuing the project.

After the road was finished and as the time when on, the members from Andys Bay petered out and the road was never maintained. They were mostly "corduroy roads," that is logs placed one after the other, so that it could be driven on because they did not have access to gravel. I got involved about 25 years ago and I have maintained the road ever since.

When I was old enough to go in the Hall, I found a picture of Captain Drage that was taken outside of the Hall. He was in his uniform and held a baton in his hand with the active members standing up straight as if they were still in the army and of course, you sure would think Captain Drage thought so, too. This was Remembrance Day.

The Hall was active on summer Saturdays. If you wanted to get in, an active member had to sign you in. All of the staff volunteered: bartending, looking after the games, pool and shuffleboard, hauling beer from the wharf, supplying firewood, and doing the bookkeeping. We had someone playing records for dancing and that really got things going as well as at parties. A supply of water had to be kept on hand in case the well or the lines froze or lost siphon. Eventually, they had a well drilled.

Mr. and Mrs. Foster:

Mrs. Foster's parents used to live in Eckman's place.

Mr. and Mrs. Foster were retired. Mr. Foster used to work for the RCMP. When we were kids, I remember the girls visiting Mrs. Foster for candy and cookies. Their children were Sid and Jack. The original cabin belonged to Mrs. Drage's parents. The Fosters added on to it and added on to it and then when the Meyers owned it, they added on to it. Now Dave Burton and a friend of his own it.

1960 Jack Foster on New Brighton Dock. John Knight's place on the shore in background. Courtesy: Harper family.

The Higgins:

The cabin that Higgins own used to belong to Miss D. Poore's aunt and uncle named Notman. They were retired.

The Wishing Well:

Off the road going past the junction to West Bay and Gambier Harbour there is a small piece of property off the road where there was a well with an arch over it and the kids called it the "wishing well."

1928 Art Leatherdale, Dolly Leatherdale, Shirley and Joe Innes on porch of Innes' #3 house. Built by Japanese settlers at the turn of the century. Courtesy: Shirley Innes.

Mr. and Mrs. Innes:

Mr. and Mrs. Innes retired and came to Gambier. They had owned their property before they built their house in 1920. They had an interesting outhouse. It was made from a hollow cedar stump. All they did was build a roof over it.

Mr. Innes raised goats and he sold the milk. Some of his customers even made cheese from it. He would let the goats wander where they wanted but at night they would have their own stall and go to the same one each time, all fourteen of them. Every now and again, he would row one of them in his boat to Keats Island to get it bred.

Before he retired, he owned a shingle mill where he had a Chinese crew working for him. The mill burned down before he had a chance to use it. After that, he filed blades for other mills. In his family, he had four girls and two boys. He had chickens, rabbits and sold vegetables out of his garden on Gambier.

He rented out the one cabin he built and the one that was already there. The one that was already there nobody knows when it was built, most likely late 1800s, he rented to the Clarkes. They are related to Donna Pearson. The one on the bluff was rented to the Jefferys, my Aunt Peg's uncle. It was built with a lot of shake wood. Mr. Innes cut a lot for fencing, wood sheds and cabins. Mrs. Innes had two sisters. Mr. and Mrs. Innes are related to Ralph and Shirley of Symons.

Later the Holmes' owned the land.

Japanese Settlers:

There were two Japanese immigrants that were living on the island at Cotton Creek by the falls. After WWII they left the island and have not been heard from since.

The Johnsons:

I never met the Johnsons but they had a nice place with an opened area where they had an orchard right by the creek on the beach. Every one called it, Johnson's creek. The house is now deteriorated. After Mr. Johnson died, his daughter took over and her married name was Parker. The place was sold in the early sixties and now belongs to Mr. and Mrs. P. Roeck.

Mike and Helga Kselby:

Mr. and Mrs. Kselby were a quiet, retired couple that lived on the island. Mrs. Kselby was Orville Becker's aunt, his father's sister. I remember a mentally handicapped boy named Harold who lived with them for a while. Helga made maple burl tables. Mr. and Mrs. Kselby were born on Bowen Island.

Tommy Medforth:

Around 1956, Tommy Medforth supervised the building of the concrete dam and put in the main line to supply water for all the houses on the Harper property. He and John Knight built the kitchens, and moved all the gravel up for the dam and to replace the old wooden dam. They used a little Caterpillar tractor with a small blade to make a road and to put the main line down the middle of the road.

1940 Tom and Florence Parker. Courtesy: Parker family.

Cliff Burton was a great friend of Harpers. He came to the big house on weekends and holidays and eventually bought property at Gambier Harbour.

1949 New Brighton Across the road from Mrs. Negroponte's. Mr. Kingston's horse – Rowdy. Hugh Brimacombe – Dulcie's uncle, unknown, Dulcie, Barbara, Leiani Brimacombe. Courtesy: Dulcie Brimacombe.

Mr. Kingston:

Mr. Kingston was one of those guys that pulled dirty tricks on other people. The cabin where he lived is now Annals place and the cabin was a little smaller at first. It was originally built on Negroponte's property and then dragged over to where it is now. He was a beachcomber and a hard worker. Mrs. Negroponte said she can remember him walking by her place and most of the time he had an axe over his shoulder.

Mrs. Negroponte:

Mrs. Negroponte came here in 1945 and one of her main jobs was collect eggs from her 100 chickens and send them to be sold in "town." Mr. Wheeler built the house when it belonged to Alex Beck, Elisabeth Beck's father. It was later sold to Mr. Ted and Mrs. Helen Negroponte.

Mr. Rauh:

The house that now belongs to Dr. Rauh was sold to him by Mr. Al Fox and his wife, who got it from his dad, Ben Fox, old timers who bought it from the Heays in 1917.

Mr. Urquhart:

Mr. Urquhart owned the Matheson property before 1910 and he worked in a liquor store.

Deer on Gambier Island

Bill Errico Jr.

It is interesting how the deer thrive on Gambier where there are no predators. I recall a couple of years in the 1960s when there were quite a few carcasses scattered here and there. As time went on, I figured out why. There was a point, after decades of interbreeding that the deer contracted a liver disease and then they started dying off.

Once in a while deer will swim across from the mainland bringing new blood to the island. I have observed that when this "new blood" is introduced into the herd, the deer seem to be healthier. I have also noticed that after warm winters, the deer are having twins and after a cold winter, they have only one fawn.

With logging, the forest floor is opened up and animals have more areas where they can find different kinds of plants to eat. This difference in their diet helps with their survival.

Just before 2000, I logged an area that was a blow down, and a year later when I reforested it, I was surprised to see hawks and birds I had not seen on Gambier before. I realized when there was old growth, that there was not much growing on the forest floor for the animals to survive on much like today. After the sixty years I've been on Gambier, 2010 is the first year I've seen deer with such healthy colour and shape.

Believe it or not that logged area is starting to turn into a whole new forest as third growth.

Twin fawns – Bucky and Doey. Courtesy: Dorothy

Miramar II: Gambier Island's History

The Stores

The first original store in New Brighton was at the bottom corner of Mrs. Negroponte's property by the creek. The Community Association helped out with it and Mr. Kingston ran it. It was part of Mason's house and is now Fitz-Martyn's place.

The first store, down by the wharf, had living quarters and was owned by Mr. Eaton. He sold the store to the Woods, Harold and Marie. Harold was a fisherman and lived on the island. Then the store went to the Boyds and was used as a post office before it burned down. The word is that the fire started because the ash box was so full plus there were ashes on the floor and the stove pipe was packed solid.

Mrs. Negroponte ran the post office from 1957 to 1967.

From a *Coast News* clipping from the 1986 **30 YEARS AGO**

"New Brighton (Gambier) Post office and store were burned down completely on Friday morning [1956].

Mr. J. B. Boyd had gone to the jetty when he noticed smoke pouring from the doorway. He rushed into the store but the smoke was too heavy. He tried ...then opened the door of the downstairs store room. 'Then there seemed to be an explosion," he said. "Windows were blown out and everything became intensely hot all at once. I was unable to save anything.'

Two tugs from twin Creeks came with hoses but by the time they arrived the frame building was gutted."

Above: 1944s New Brighton Association Community store. Courtesy: Mrs. Negroponte.
Right: New Brighton wharf. At the head of the wharf is the Harpers boathouse that Art Harper turned into a store.
Courtesy: Harper family.

Gambier Island - Where the World's Problems Solved Themselves in Just One Hike

Naomi Errico 2010

My memories of summers on Gambier Island are still very clear and wonderful. Our cabin, near the end of Austin road, New Brighton, was finished the year I was born, 1954. I can truly say I've been here all my life.

1958 Billy Jr., Naomi, Janis Errico on Errico's beach. Courtesy: Naomi Errico.

I remember long, hot summer days in New Brighton, playing on the beach or in the forest behind our house. Evenings or dark rainy days, we played giant hopscotch or giant checkers on the game patterns that my dad had made with the squares of the linoleum flooring. We had no electricity, so we used kerosene lamps at night, our milk was canned or powdered, and the perishable food was kept in the wooden cooler with mesh doors on the back deck. Our wood stove or the fireplace kept us warm.

Each summer, the five of us would get one pair of thongs (flip-flops) each. After several pieces of wire and a good stiff bobby pin or two had been put into service in an effort to hold them together, but no longer could, we would have to admit they were spent, and we could finally go barefoot. The wonderful grass strip that ran down the center of all the roads that led to New Brighton to Gambier Harbour and to West Bay afforded us a cushion path for our summer feet. We could travel a greater distance with only a few sharp rocks to curse along the way.

I always looked forward to my summer visits with those true characters of Gambier. Old man, Breacher was a good character who lived off Andys Bay Road about half a mile. He would welcome a visitor with black tea poured from a metal pot and served in dainty porcelain tea cups full of dark cracks, and a slab of meat from the ball that hung from his kitchen ceiling. Breacher would then play his organ for us; he was very good. It seemed odd, an organ so big and beautiful in a shack in the middle of the forest. We would then feed his horse and be on our way.

1962 Naomi and Jamie Errico. Courtesy: Errico family.

There were many orchards that dotted the island landscape, but my favourite was old man Fox's (Ben Fox). His orchard was in New Brighton, top of the Austin Road hill. Fox's apples were good and plentiful, but he had a salt rifle; all the kids knew about it. We had to be fast, and it had to be dark. One fateful night, my sister, Janis and I, decided to sneak out to visit Fox's orchard—the apples always tasted better when stolen. We snuck out successfully, climbed the fence, climbed the tree, picked two apples each, and then the screen door opened! We leaped out of the tree and ran like the wind for the fence, apples in hand. I cleared the fence and ran, but Janis was not behind me. I stopped when I got to the bush to see Janis in the moonlight swinging on the fence top by her nightshirt. She hung quietly while Fox searched for us. Thankfully, he did not find her. After fifteen minutes, I helped her down, trying not to laugh too loud. We laughed all the way to the New Brighton dock where we sat and ate our prizes.

I remember Bob Holmes AKA Homsey, and his grand old boat *The Chispa*. Homsey lived on the far west end of the New Brighton beach. He moored his boat out front of his waterfront home and when he saw a seal climb onto his precious boat's swim grid, he would take out his rifle and shoot at the seal. I don't think he ever hit a seal, and as far as I know, he never hit his boat 'cause it seemed to stay afloat.

Our beach was in the middle of New Brighton, and it was perfect. We had a grass strip to play on, and the beach always had sand at the top. My grandfather, Alfonso, raked it every morning. We had our own dock to swim off; my big brother Bill made it all on his own. We also had a rope swing that dropped you in the ocean at high tide. We were never less than 8 to 10 kids at a time, with cousins and friends, so the fun never stopped. We would all sit on that beach every Friday evening waiting for Dad to arrive. I still remember the excitement I felt as Dad's boat rounded the point at Avalon Bay.

Miramar on Gambier—the best place in the world!

Up to approximately 1965

1930s Avalon Bay, "Where Mother kept her boat and where we went on our picnics and swam in the quite water in the bay." Courtesy: Houston family.

Ormie Cambie

Wendy Graham

Ormie was the son of Mrs. Mary And Mr. George Ormond Cambie who built a home right next to the Brian Anthony's. Mrs. Cambie was the sister of Mrs. Enid Stoddard and Mr. Fred Stoddard. Ormie inherited the house and property from his parents.

For something to do Ormie opened a makeshift store on Mrs. Lett's property on Gambier Road which was named Ormie's store. He sold soft drinks, chewing gum, chocolate bars, etc. to the summer people.

Ormie Cambie. Courtesy: Wendy Graham.

Eventually, he moved to his own property and finally due to lack of business had to close down the store and eventually sold his property to the Ray Cromptons and moved to Vancouver. This property is now owned by Pat and Cliff Burton.

1945 Back row: Owen Houston, Jack Hibberd, Jack Ridley, Ned Larsen. Front row: unknown, Betty Ridley, Marge Bullard – Betty's cousin, Ormie Cambie. Courtesy: Betty Ridley.

Ormie Cambie

–Bill Errico Jr.

At 10:00 p.m. one night in Grace/Gambier Harbour, Mr. Drage and Mr. Lett with lanterns in their hands, were going to the wharf thinking the Union Steamship was docking but it was only Ormie Cambie who could do a perfect imitation of its whistle. It was even funnier to see the look of astonishment on visitors' faces when he imitated a train.

Days in the Lives of the New Brighton Girls' Club
Plus Andy H., Jimmy B., Teddy & Jimmy S

Donna Pearson and her sister, Leah

In the late 40s through the 50s, New Brighton was populated by so many girls that when one of the Union Steamship boats came in, the crew wanted to know what girls camp was there. We were together because many of our moms were friends who formed a service club called "Gemm Oui" when they were at U.B.C. Several of the Gemm Oui families had summer homes in New Brighton and we spent many happy holidays together. We were Shannie Harper (nee) McJannet, Joyce Matheson (nee) Clegg, Lea Macdonald, Donna and Bobbi Pearson (nee) Kennedy, Lynn Snetsinger (nee) Bell and Joley Switzer and Barb Symons and Roberta Grey. And oh, yes, Andy Harper, Jimmy Boyd and Teddy & Jimmy Simpson were occasionally allowed to hang around. Graham and Susan Clarke were also sometime members of our group.

Early 1950s Back row: Jimmy Boyd. Middle row: Shannie Harper, Donna Pearson, Joyce Matheson, Leah Pearson. Front row: Bobbi Pearson, Andy Harper. Courtesy: Donna Pearson.

We would spend most days together hanging-out in our bay, not often venturing forth by well-used trails to the other bays, or by boat along the shoreline. It seemed most summers were sunny, so we would start the mornings playing in the woods building forts, eating licorice roots, climbing bluffs, picking fruit or doing chores like bringing in wood for the stoves, baking and making trips to the store. Our forts were built in the woods behind the Big House and along the beach between the Symons and Holmes houses, using moss, ferns and leaves for beds and seats, and wood chips, shells and other "finds" for dishes, books and whatever else we needed. Leah was usually the leader because she was oldest, but the rest of us did as we were told—most of the time.

Climbing the bluffs took off from the Goat House at Mr. Holmes' that was sometimes occupied by Mr. & Mrs. Jeffrey (Peggy Errico's parents). We had many routes, but the challenge was to remember where they were, and then how to get back down to the water to make our way home from Cotton Bay. When we went further back on the bluffs, we found lots of trees with moss and licorice roots in the damp forest.

Mid 50s Graham Clarke, Lynn Snetsinger, Donna Pearson, Jimmy Boyd, Leah Pearson, Susan Clarke, Shannie Harper. Courtesy: Donna Pearson.

Shannie, Lynn and Joyce rowed in three boats to Pearsons to play kick the can or cards on days when the morning tides were low. Sometimes before heading home for lunch at noon, we'd decided we all needed a swim to cool off. We never remembered swimsuits, but the Pearsons came to the rescue—they had a big box of suits in the bedroom and we could have our choice. Often during the visit, the tide would come in and Uncle Jack Pearson rescued the rowboats before they floated to Cotton Bay or toward Gibsons.

After very high tides, we picked washed-up bark for bonfires or our kitchen stoves. Saturday night was for bonfires, usually at Pearson's. As the tide started to drop, Mr. Pearson would build the fire and we'd all find a spot with our blanket to settle down to sing, talk, roast marshmallows (before the days of Smores) and throw on more wood to keep the flames flying high. Before it got too late (9:30), the brave ones would go for a quick swim, sometimes even skinny-dipping if only the girls were there, and then finish up with hot chocolate.

　　We had three weekly mail days at Helen Negroponte's and we would meet in her garden or at Mrs. Boyd's store, where the barge landing is now. Fridays were special as we could get fresh vegetables or raspberries from Negroponte's wonderful garden so our mums could make great meals for the dads who arrived for the weekends. Sometimes, we would pick ferns for Mrs. Atchison (Dick's mom) and Siddie Foster that they bundled and sent to florists in Vancouver. Whenever the *Lady Rose*, *Lady Alex* or another Union Steamship boat would come to New Brighton, we would be on the dock to see what provisions or new furniture had arrived and to inspect the new group of boys going to Camp Elphinstone.

Mid 50s Left to right: Jimmy Boyd, Lea Pearson, Teddy Simpson, Donna Pearson, Shannie Harper, Jimmie Simpson, Andy Harper, Bobbi Pearson. Courtesy: Donna Pearson.

　　We would go home for lunch, which was the "big" meal of the day, so that we did not have to put on our wood stoves to cook in the evenings. All the meat and potato meals were cooked for lunch so we would be well-filled before our afternoons of adventures. It meant we could spend longer hours on the beach, just lazing in the water and swimming to the wharf, the rafts, or to some different beach.

These afternoons were often spent at the beach by the dock below the Harper Big House or in front of Holmes', Symons' and occasionally the Clarke's. This was before the age of suntan lotion and skin cancer, so we would simply pour on the Baby Oil to cook up a tan. Of course, you had to burn first on the early days of summer, then peel—and most of us just tanned after that! Who would believe that now, but we thought the sun was safer then.

At the beach, we would swim to the dock, or swim off a raft that our dads built every year from scrap wood and logs found in the water and on the shores. It was a special treat when the mums came onto the wharf and we could dive off the lower wharf and swim to the beach. Leah, Donna and Lynn, and sometimes others, made the annual swim from Pearson's beach to the wharf, at high tide, when the waves were gone for the day. Or we would play with some of the row boats that were around. (Did you know that if you turn over a rowboat, lift it and then place it upside down on the water, an air space is created underneath under the boat that you can swim into and have a secret conversation?) Our afternoon break consisted of Freshie or Kool-Aid drinks and cookies, and then it was back into the water. Days that were especially hot would consist of 10 or 12 swims, with a tanning session for talking or reading between each "dip."

On special days, we got to surfboard with both feet on a board, (before water skiing began)

1940s John Knight's place just put in. Ray Leatherdale in Dreamer.
Courtesy: Harper family.

behind the *Shandy* (Harper's boat) or the *Dreamer* (Symon's boat). We would wander home about 6:00 p.m., exhausted but having had our fill of fun and vitamin D. Amazingly, we had no serious accidents to deal with, just a few slivers in bums when we would slide down the ramp. Once, Andy tipped over his "speed" boat, but that was the worst we had to deal with.

Those rare (as we remember them) rainy days, we would often meet at the Harper house as it was huge and central and had a great deck where we could play games. Crazy 8's would last for hours (probably a little cheating going on!), or Rummy or a game of "Store" where we would create money and products for sale! Sometimes, one of us had new comic books which meant our mums had some peace as we found beds and cushions where the books could be enjoyed. My favourite was Archie. Other homes had board games, which kept us busy for hours, or even days.

As the summer progressed, we picked transparent apples at Shasta Lodge (the Big House), huckleberries for meals in our forts and blackberries for the famous New Brighton blackberry pies and jams. Our scratches were testament to the hard work this job was, but the results were enjoyed in town during the winters.

Sometimes, when we could see the shrimp boats, we would row out to get shrimp and come home, prepare it and have a feast. Or we would take the annual walk to West Bay to watch Mrs. Heay feed the deer by her creek. At that time, the road was not as we know it today… it was barely a walking trail. So we would hike to Gambier Harbour to swim at the beach by the dock. Other special events included days the boys from the Y Camp came to hike up to the lake, or a charter water taxi would bring a dad or special guest for one of our families.

Some of our dads had their own boats and so could come and go whenever, but for others, dads would arrive on the *Lil' Pete*, and later on the Mercury boats, on Friday nights with supplies of fruit, vegetables and treats for the week. It was great to see the boat come around the point. We would race to the wharf to meet Dad and weekend guests. Often, it wasn't a

1955 New Brighton wharf. Left to right: Susan Clarke, Dennis Wood, Donna Pearson, Ted Simpson, Shannie Harper, Jimmy Boyd, Joyce Matheson, Leah Pearson and Lynn Snetsinger. Courtesy: Pearson family.

restful weekend as there would be wood to chop, repairs to make and inspection of our new achievements in the water or on the beach by our dads and all the gathered guests. For a treat on Saturday nights, the parents would head to the Army and Navy Air Force Veterans' Hall in Gambier Harbour. That would leave the kids to have a sleepover at the Big House to be watched over by Grannie Harper and Nana Clarke.

On Sundays, probably as a bribe from our folks, Siddie Foster would have us over for Sunday school. Auntie Siddie had many stories to tell every week while we enjoyed sandwiches and cookies. Not only did she tell great stories, she baked delicious bread. The aroma greeted us as we came along the trail to the kitchen. We couldn't wait to have a piece with butter and some of her delicious berry jam.

Her husband had been the Chief Engineer on the *St. Roch*, the boat that made the first trip from the East coast to West coast through the Arctic Ocean and the Northwest Passage. There was a picture of this boat and crew in a Socials book we used at school, and on Foster's wall. We all felt very attached to this picture! After our food, we would entertain Siddie and each other with songs, dancing and skits we had practiced during the week. It was a fun and different thing for us to do, a break in the routine and a time that was loved by our folks I am sure!

Some of the moms were square dancers during the winters in town, so they decided to teach us some dances for all to enjoy. We were short on boys, but we managed to get four couples to make a square. With our own caller –Donna Pearson, and a wind-up gramophone, we had music to dance to. We even got skirts and shirts made. It was something new to learn and a different way to spend parts of our day. The dock made a unique dance floor and we had fun entertaining everyone on the community fishing derby weekend. The girls aren't sure that Jimmy, Teddy or Andy enjoyed it, but it did create memories for us all.

We spent the evenings playing cards or board games, reading by the light of the coal oil or gas lamps or listening to the radio. We finally got electricity in 1962, and all of us had to get our houses wired. But it just wasn't the same without the lanterns. Many of us took several years to get electric stoves, so our wood stoves preserved the old traditions.

As we got older, we went on longer rowing cruises, often in the evenings to the Y Camp at Elphinstone to join their campfires or perhaps to talk with some of the boys! Or we would row to Avalon Bay or Cotton Bay to explore the sunken tug boat or to swim off the log booms. Now we have become even older and these tales will remain memories to those who lived them.

Home on the Island

Shirley Symons (nee) Innes

Mr. Innes took his goat over to Keats to get it bred. Part of his income was from selling the vegetables in his garden. People would row over from Keats to buy them. One of his main vegetables was potatoes, the purple ones, and the berries were, raspberry, boysenberries, Logan berries. He asked people, if they caught dogfish, to bring them to him, and he would plant them in his raspberries.

When Mr. and Mrs. Innes would row to Hopkins or Gibsons, they kept their eyes open for driftwood to avoid hitting it with their double-ender rowboat. They always took a sail with them, just in case the wind came up but it would never work that way coming back. He had rollers on the ramp to get the boat back up and out of the water.

1938 The Innes house. Shirley Innes and Peggy Jeffery. Courtesy: Jeffery family.

He had rabbits and Bantam chickens but they didn't last too long. He raised goats and of all his goats, Daisy Bell, his favourite goat got her horns caught in some limbs and hung herself, and that was it for goats. Daisy May's kid was chocolate brown and white named Little Billy and Shirley would sleep in the hay with him. Unfortunately, they had to put Little Billy down since he was a male and they didn't want him around with all the females. He tanned the hide, and Shirley had it for years.

Mr. Innes rented out two of the cabins on his property for the summer. He cut wood for each cabin. Shirley's brother, George helped build the house on the beach. She remembers the times he would take her out in the boat and she'd splash him, using an oar.

The family did have a radio to beat the long hours in the winter.

Shirley's nephew, Ray loved it on the island. He had polio so he had a hard time getting to the beach, and had great ways of getting into the boat—that was why they called it *Dreamer*. He was a happy guy and one day swam from the wharf. He died young.

Mrs. Innes, Shirley's mother, was married at 16-years-old. Shirley was born in 1921.

1928 Shirley Innes sits on branch between her mother and father, Eliza and Joe Innes. Courtesy: Shirley Innes.

Shirley's brothers were George and Joe. Joe left the island at 17 and moved to the States, he would visit once in a while. Shirley's sisters were Eva, the oldest who reluctantly visited Gambier Island. The second oldest, Mary, lived back east. Dolly, the third oldest spent most of the time on the island. Dolly was Ray's mother.

Shirley's mother came from Bolton, England. Her father was from Woodstock, Ontario. Mr. Innes' family came from Elgon in Northern, Scotland. There is a house there called the Innes House.

George and Shirley's mother would row from Vancouver to get to New Brighton and would bring back the odd piece of furniture with them.

In those days, there was all sorts of fishing going on but now one would be lucky to catch anything worthwhile because there aren't that many left.

Kids in the fifties would go to Sunday school at Mrs. Foster's. Tommy Austin bought property from the Malcolms.

Lady Cecilia with the Gibson's Gap in the background. Courtesy: Shirley Innes.

Harper Memories of New Brighton on Gambier Island

Art Harper 1995

The Harper family, Mr. and Mrs. Harper and my sisters, Jo and Andree and myself, (Arthur) first went to West Bay on Gambier Island in 1916, when I was just two-years-old. We rented a cottage owned by Mrs Angus. Mrs. Angus had two sons, Gordon and Stanley. We spent the summer of 1916 at West Bay, and while there got to know quite well a Mr. and Mrs. Frank Heay, who lived at West Bay permanently.

Mr. Heay was the "boom man" at West Bay, they had a small farm there, and I can recall that they had three cows and the names of the cows were Queenie, Muggins, and June. My father was taken by the name "Muggins" and thereafter he used to call my sister, Andree, Muggins in sort of a joking way. The Heays were very good to us. When my father and mother went to town, they would leave the three Harper children with Mr. and Mrs. Heay for a day or two. We used to enjoy roaming and playing around their farm. One interesting thing about the farm was, what is known as a 'water ram'. The Heays had a creek running through their property but it was a problem to pump the water from the creek up to the level of their house. This ram was worked by the force of the water, and as I recall it, for every two gallons of water used in pumping the ram, one gallon of water was pumped up to the tank from which Mr. and Mrs. Heay obtain their household water.

Also, at West Bay, we met a Mr. Mitchell, who had a son, Joe. Mr. Mitchell was a Mauri from New Zealand and his son, Joe was a very husky young man who later on in life, moved and lived in Long Bay and most everyone on Gambier Island got to know Joe Mitchell.

The next two summers in the years, 1917 and 1918, we rented the Urquhart's cottage in New Brighton; it is now the Matheson house. The old Urquhart's cottage had been built in about 1911; there was a ramp and a float running out into the water in front of the place, which was then known as Urquhart's Landing.

Shannon has an old picture of the beach in front of Urquhart's and one of the pilings of the old ramp can still be seen in that picture The picture was probably taken in the twenties and the pilings were disintegrating then. At that time, there were three big maple trees in front of the Urquhart's house and I can recall that my mother used to have people address their mail to New Brighton, to ourselves, and the address was "333 Maple Avenue." When we rented the Urquhart cottage, there was quite a cleared field up in behind the cottage, and in this field, Mr. Wheeler Lawrence used to tether his cow.

Mr. and Mrs. Lawrence lived at New Brighton permanently, and their house was the home now owned by Mrs. Negroponte. Mrs. Lawrence, whose name was Lizzie, had at one time been a maid for the Urquharts and then she married Wheeler Lawrence, who I think had been a logger in the area. The Lawrences had a cow so that we were able to buy fresh, raw milk from them during our summer stays at New Brighton.

I think it was the year 1919 that the big Harper house was built. I recall that my father contracted with a Mr. Richards, who built the house, but others in the area, particularly Joe

The woman leaning on the cow is Ellen Harper. On the right is Lizzie Lawrence. The Harpers bought milk from them. Courtesy: Lynn Bell.

Mitchell, did a lot of the bull-work. However, my father fired Mr. Richards when he found out that Mr. Richards was selling some of my father's lumber to Arthur Lett over at Grace Harbour.

The Johnston family had a cottage at New Brighton at that time, and it was D.B. Johnston who had originally suggested to my father that he have a look at New Brighton as a suitable place for a summer camp. D.B. Johnston was a schoolteacher who eventually became principal of King George High School. Mr. and Mrs. Johnston had three children, Florence, Mary and Donald..

1920 The Harper "Big House." Judge Harper, Jo, Andree and Arthur Harper. Courtesy: Lynn Bell.

I remember that behind the Urquhart cottage there was a cleared pasture where Wheeler Lawrence tethered his cow. The pasture was large enough to use as a playing field. At that time, Miss Florence Urquhart owned the house. She was related to Mr. D.B. Johnston. Mr. Johnston owned the property west of the Harper lot and east of the H.H. Hay property. The children of New Brighton, both boys and girls, used to meet in the pasture behind the Urquhart property for a softball game. We didn't have enough players to make two teams but we would have four or five to a side and play in the field which wasn't completely flat but served our purpose. Some of the players I remember were my two sisters and myself, Sid and Muriel Clarke, Donald and Elsie MacLean, Bill and Betty Burchell, Shirley Innes and Don Johnson. The MacLean family would spend part of the summer in the Urquhart house as did that Burchells. On other occasions, we would have enough players to form a team and we would play other teams, mainly at Hopkins (where there was a real playing field) which required a trip by boat, rowing of course, to Hopkins Wharf. The brand of softball was not great but it was a lot of fun and created a fun outing for the New Brighton young folks.

My father had bought our ten acre lot from a Mr. Fisher who was a friend of Wheeler and Lizzie Lawrence. The Fishers had a daughter by the name of Myrtle.

When the Harper house was ready for occupation, it didn't have any running water, or any inside plumbing and I recall that my sisters and I used to walk over to Johnston's creek with pails and pack back the household water.

We used to walk over daily to the Lawrence's house to buy fresh, raw milk. Then in 1920, a Mr. Brooks from Gibsons built the fireplace in the "Big House" and I can remember going with Mr. Brooks out to Gower Point to pick up some round, smooth rocks for the facing on the fireplace.

In those early years, the only people living at New Brighton permanently were Wheeler and Mrs. Lawrence and old Tommy Austin who live near the point leading to Cotton Bay. The only other houses that I can recall when the Harper house was finished where the Johnston house, the house of H. H. Hay and the house owned by Mr. Innes which was over near Mr. Austin's house.

It might be wise for me to just talk about each house and comment about things I can remember about the owners. First, the Urquhart's house which was owned by Florence Urquhart, a maiden lady who was a schoolteacher and was related to D.B. Johnston and family. The Urquhart house used to be occupied by Miss Florence Urquhart and the MacLean family. Mr. MacLean was a teacher who had two daughters, Donalda and Elsie, and from time to time, a family by the name of Burchell, who were also related

1920 John Knight and Art Harper after some time spent fishing. Courtesy: Lynn Bell.

to Miss Urquhart used to come up to occupy the Urquhart's home. Mr. and Mrs. Burchell had two children, Bill and Betty. One thing about Mr. Burchell, is that he used to make whistles for the children out of alder sticks. Next, is the house of Wheeler and Lizzie Lawrence.

My father and D.B. Johnston lobbied the government to have the post office at New Brighton and Mrs. Lizzie Lawrence became the postmistress in the mid 20's. I can well recall Mr. Lawrence picking up the mail bags from the boat whenever it came into the float, and after packing the mailbags up to the house, Mrs. Lawrence would insist upon all the people gathering on the front porch, where we used to sit on the railing, and she would bring out a pile of letters, and call out people's names and they would go up and receive their mail from Mrs. Lawrence in a very formal sort of way. Lizzie Lawrence was a very dominant character and her husband, Wheeler, was a kind, gentle man.

Beyond our house was the Johnston home. Mr. Johnston was known as the keen fisherman of New Brighton. He would spend hours in the bay fishing for salmon, and he never came in empty-handed. Johnston's had a friend by the name of Miss Fletcher, who was also a schoolteacher, and may have been related to them, but in any event they were

Top left: Art Harper and Jo Knight.
Above: 1920 Andree Harper. Courtesy: Lynn Bell.

very kind to her and they built her a separate little cottage between their house and the Hay house. In later years, they built a house in behind their own home for Miss Fletcher. The Johnstons had quite a nice orchard and they had two lovely cherry trees as well as apple and pear trees.

The next house was that of H. H. Hay. Mr. Hay was a representative of Marshall Wells Ltd. and he traveled up and down the coast for that company. He had a lovely boat called the *Nahleen*. The Hays had three children, Dot, Tim and Buff. The Hays did not live at New Brighton the year round, but they seemed always to be around during the summer months. I recall Mr. Hay had the initials HHH tattooed on his arm with a circle around them and he used to always tell me that that stood for Happy Harry Hay. He was a great swimmer and many times he would dive off the float and swim underwater for great distances. Sometimes he would even dive off the float and swim under the logs, coming up on the other side, while everybody on the float wondered where he would come up and when they didn't see him, they would start worrying as to what had happened to him. It is ironic that Mr. and Mrs. Hay, in spite of the fact that he was such a good swimmer, were both drowned many years later when their boat, *Nahleen*, got into difficulties and was swamped up the coast. They found the boat floating half full of water and they found Mrs. Hay's body close-by with a life jacket on, but they never ever did find poor Mr. Hay. The Hay house was eventually taken over by Ben and Mrs. Fox who had a son, Al. Then I believe it was purchased by a chap by the name of Wiggins and is now owned by Dr. Jurgen Rauh.

Tommy Austin, who lived at New Brighton all year round, occupied the next house. I was always under the impression that old Mr. Austin came from Brighton, England, and that he named our bay on Gambier, New Brighton, however this may not be so. Mr. Austin was quite a character; he was deaf as a post. He used to row his double-ended rowboat from his place over to the wharf singing away to himself, and his voice was so loud that people across the water at Williamsons used to say that they could hear him singing on a clear morning when he was out in his boat. Mr. Austin had an old dog by the name of Bugs. Later on, when a road was constructed from Mr. Austin's place to the float, it was called Austin Road. Mr. Alfonso Errico was a good friend of Mr. Austin's, and used to visit at New Brighton, and of course eventually built a house here himself.

Then later another house was built just east of Mr. Austin's and was occupied by Mr. and Mrs. Shotton. The Shottons were a very fine couple with us children; they had a dog by the name of Keeper. I can remember as a child, my sisters and I would throw bits of wood for Keeper who would always retrieve them. Mr. Shotton was a cabinetmaker and was badly crippled with arthritis. He was still able to do wonderful woodwork. He made two benches for my father and mother constructed of oak wood from leaves out of the table. I believe the benches are still up at the Big House. Mr. and Mrs. Shotton were always very kind to the local children and I always remember them having a good supply of chocolate, which they gave to us from time to time.

Just east of the Shotton house, Mr. and Mrs. Wise built a house down on the beach which was later purchased by Henry Moore, then taken over by his son Telford. Telford tells me that his father was related in some way to May Wise, who was the daughter of Mr. and Mrs. Wise. The Shotton house was eventually purchased by the Liddell family, and is now occupied by George and Gladys Gray.

Another good friend of Mr. Austin was Captain Lawrence Yates of the Union Steamship Company. Captain Yates also had a son by the same name of Lawrence, who I think became captain a local tugboat.

Returning to old Tommy Austin –I can recall when I was a young boy, I used to go over to Tommy Austin's house and read the funny papers to him. I don't know whether he was able to read or whether his eyesight was bad, but it's a thing I'll always remember.

1920 A series of floats connected the wharf to the shore. The shed on the shore was the Urquhart's boathouse.
Courtesy: Art Harper.

Later on, I will make a few comments about other houses that were constructed, but I thought I might comment on some of the things I remembered about the 20's. When we first went up to New Brighton, there was a wharf with the shed on it where the boats would come in, and connecting the wharf to the shore were series of floats. The shed on shore was our boathouse. It was built for us by Mr. Lawrence (the shakes on the roof having been cut out of the cedar Mr. Lawrence felled in and around New Brighton). Years later, I turned this boathouse into a store from which I sold cigarettes and candies in the early '30s. The floats in that snapshot are to the east (the Matheson side) on a large rock which one can still see on the Matheson side of the dock leading out to the present wharf. During the '20s, we would all meet down at the float in the late afternoon and have a swimming session: the Johnston family, the Harper family, the Hays, and later on the Clarke family.

In that first store (which I operated for only one year), I also supplied New Brighton with fresh milk. I think it was the year 1933 or 1934; I used to run over to Hopkins every

morning about 5:30 or 6:00 a.m. to pick up 10 gallons of fresh, raw milk from a man by the name of Lockhart who used to bring it down to the Hopkins Wharf for me in the morning. I would take it back in two 5 gallon cans, stopping at Killam's on the way, and then I would walk around New Brighton filling up the quart bottles with fresh

Early 30s John and Jo Knight on Harper's wharf. The boathouse on the shore was turned into a store. Courtesy: Art Harper.

milk which I sold for 15¢ a quart, or 2 quarts for 25¢. The Harper family always took 2 quarts so at the end of my rounds, we'd hoped there would be 2 quarts left, and during the course of my rounds, the cream would rise a little to the top and we would always get fairly rich milk because ours would be the last out of the can.

For several years after that, Mr. and Mrs. Boyd ran a store at the head of the wharf. Their son Jimmy grew up with our children. Jimmy now works as a welder at Mannion Bay. Mrs. Boyd was a very kind lady and her husband, Jim Boyd served in the Canadian Navy during the Second World War.

Mr. Lawrence built a cow-raft built because there was no bull on Gambier Island, and he would periodically take his cow over to Hopkins to have it serviced. As a young lad, I often wonder why Mr. Lawrence was taking his cow out for a ride on the cow-raft over to Hopkins. Perhaps Jo and Onnie knew but they never told me!

Left:1920
Right: 1924
Left bottom: 1928
Bottom right:
Andree, Muriel
Clarke, unknown.
All photos
courtesy: Lynn
Bell.

Andree Harper

Above: Waiting for their ship to come in. Lynn Snetsinger's mother is at bottom left bottom row. Andree and Jo sit beside her.
Left: John Knight's playful side shows through.
Below: Rod, Mike and John Knight continue the fun. Photos courtesy: Lynn Bell.

When I was a child at New Brighton, every now and then, an old Indian dugout would float up on the beach, which of course would be cut out of a cedar log. I can remember two in particular, one was a lot smaller than the other, and I have a photograph of myself in the larger dugout, which I named *Safety Last* and into which I fixed oarlocks. I painted the name *Safety Last* on the sides of the dugout and I think the other one was *Amen*. My guess is that I was about 12 years of age. These Indian dugouts floated up on the beach every now and then, but we never knew where they came from. I also remember the bridge games.. Wheeler and Lizzie Lawrence, the Harper family, the Johnston family and the Burgess family would gather every now and then, rotating between houses for a bridge evening. In those days, we played "auction" bridge (not contract bridge) and I can remember that old Wheeler Lawrence was a fine bridge player but Lizzie was not. However, in spite of this, Lizzie (who was the dominant person in that family) was always criticizing old Wheeler about his bridge game; he was a very patient and fine old man.

In my childhood regattas used to be held every summer at Gibsons, Granthams and Hopkins (rotating). There were swimming races, boat races, etc. Mr. Oxley comes to mind, he was from Granthams. He used his very loud voice to make announcements at the regattas.

I spent many hours of my childhood at New Brighton with a man by the name of Dawson. He was the brother of Mrs. HH Hay. Mr. Dawson taught me how to play cribbage, and he and I used to sit for hours and hours down on the float playing crib.

After the post office was established, people would have to walk over to Mrs. Lawrence's house to collect their mail, and the only path for the houses that were to the west of the post office came right across in front of our house. In the early days, we had steps leading down from the front of the house with the division leading to the west and to the east. People walking over to the post office used to have to walk up one side of our steps and down the other as this was the only path that led to the Lawrence home. Then, after my mother had planted Shasta daisies in front of the house, the path led between the rows of the Shasta daisies and people would walk along the path rather than walk up and down our steps. Later, when we fenced the place, the path led along the waterfront. This land was actually private property but both Mr. Johnston and my father allowed people to walk back and forth so that it eventually became a public road. The road now cuts in front of an old tree which grew from an acorn my mother obtained from England and of course, the large oak tree up near the house was from another English acorn my mother planted.

Other houses were built from time to time. One of these was between our place and Mrs. and Mr. Lawrence's, built by Tom Burns. In about the mid 20s, Mrs. Lawrence made an arrangement with Tom Burns agreeing that he could build a house on the corner of her property and he could live in it for 10 years. After the end of the 10 years, he would vacate it and the building would become the property of Mr. and Mrs. Lawrence. Mr. Burns married a girl by the name of Lillian Ship, and after they had built their house, they lived permanently

Above: Jo Knight sits with dog. On her right is Muriel Clarke and Andree Harper is her on left.
Left: Lynn Bell (nee) Snetsinger) is in the bow, center – unknown, A. Pearson is at the stern.
Lower right: Donna, Leah Pearson with Lynn Snetsinger at back, Andy Harper is in the boat, on the right side is Bobbi Pearson.
Photos courtesy: Lynn Bell.

at New Brighton. Mr. Burns was a veteran of the First World War and was badly shell-shocked. Because of his war injuries, he always had a bad time whenever we had a thunderstorm. Evidently, the thunder resembled the noise of the cannon, and whenever this happened, he would have to leave the house and go out into the woods. Mr. Burns was a very kind man and was a great hunter and fisherman as well as an accomplished writer. Mr. and Mrs. Burns had one son, Conrad, and I believe Shannon has a picture of Con Burns in a rowboat down at the wharf when he was a year or a year-and-half-old and the picture was taken in 1926. After the 10 years was up, Mr. and Mrs. Burns left the house which was eventually bought by Al Kingston, skidded down and then erected up behind the Lawrence house. Mr. and Mrs. Burns then built a home on the waterfront over at Gambier Harbour – once Grace.

I mentioned earlier the Burgess family. Mr. and Mrs. Burgess had a house in Burgess Cove, which is now owned by the Gardiner family: Tony and May and their children Kent and Sarah. Mr. Burgess was a Canadian Pacific steamship engineer and there were three children, Pattie, Johnny and Terrence. In the late 20s or early 30s, the Burgess home burned down and he rebuilt it. Strangely enough, after his place was purchased by a man by the name of Derrick, it burned down again.

I also mentioned Mr. and Mrs. Alfonso Errico, who were great friends of old Tommy Austin. Mr. Errico had three children Ernie, Bill and Bob. Ernie became a school principal, Bill, a chiropractor, and Bob, a lawyer; of course now a judge. Mrs. A. Errico had a brother by the name of Wilden Asp. He used to come to New Brighton often as a visitor. A Dr. and Mrs. Patterson were great friends of the Erricos and visited at New Brighton from time to time. I recall too that Mr. A. Errico had a brother, Jerry.

Another house was built by Mr. and Mrs. MacDonald. They had a daughter named

1934 John and Jo Knight. Courtesy: Lynn Bell.

Janet. Later George Frost, who was a friend of Mrs. MacDonald's spent many summers at New Brighton. George became known at New Brighton as the "Great Fisherman."

Another name I should mention is that of Charlie Power. Charlie was an old logger who fell on hard times, and my father built a small house just to the west of the Big House in which Charlie lived and acted as a sort of caretaker. Charlie used to cut firewood for us, and unfortunately, once, when he was working in the woods, a tree fell on him and broke his leg. He never really, properly recovered, and I think he passed away in about 1929 or 1930.

In about the year 1933 or '34, Mr. and Mrs. Singleton-Gates came to New Brighton from Akron, Ohio, and built a house just to the west of the Urquhart house. Marjorie Singleton-Gates was the sister of Francis Drage. Rupert Singleton-Gates was an Englishman who I think had served in the First World War and was not accustomed to "roughing it" as he had to do when he came to New Brighton. However, he adapted himself to the new

environment and did a lot of the bull-work in the building of his new home at New Brighton and he lived there all year round. Mr. Drage, the father of Marjorie Singleton-Gates and Frances Drage, had a small house built to the west of the Singleton-Gates place and a friend of mine by the name Don Crocker contracted to build a house for Mrs. Drage for $19.00. This figure

Above: 1940s Inside Mrs. Clarke's kitchen. Courtesy: Joyce Clegg.
Lower right: Goods that would have been common in any kitchen during this time period. Photo: taken at Anne Northrup's house on Twin Island by Scott Young.

covered only the labour, with Mrs. Drage supplying all the materials.

The T.V. Clarke family started coming New Brighton in the 20s and for several years, they rented one of Mr. Innes's cottages over on the point. The cottage they rented was the one up the hill. There were two children, Sid and Muriel. Sid married a girl by the name of Marion Grant and Muriel married Jack Pearson. The Clarkes eventually built a house to the east of Mrs.

Drage's home. Jack and Muriel Pearson's children, Leah, Donna and Bobbi all became very attached to New Brighton, and I understand that Bobbi is now occupying Jack Pearson's placed on the beach. The Singleton-Gates house was eventually taken over by Sergeant and Mrs. Jones, Sergeant Jones having retired from the RCMP. His son-in-law, Jack Foster then took over the house to the east of the Jones's house, and Jack and Sid Foster lived at New Brighton for many years, Sid being very popular with the young people of New Brighton. Jack Foster was one of the crew of the *St. Roch* when it took the Arctic trip in 1942 from the West Coast to Halifax.

John Knight and my sister Jo, built a house on the beach below the old Harper house, and as I recall it, John purchased a small house and had it towed by floats around to its present site and added to it from time to time on his retirement. John and my sister lived in retirement at New Brighton for a number of years during which time John became the wharfinger and operated the water taxi service until they moved to Gibsons where they now reside.

The Hebbs and the Killams build houses out on the point and of course, Mr. Graham (a bachelor) had always owned and lived during the summer months on Twin Islands.

In the early days, the YMCA camp was situated at Hopkins Landing and the names of George Ross and Gordon Stevens come to my mind, along with Bill Hood and Reg Wilson, who were great friends of the Harper family. In those days, the YMCA camp had two large war canoes, each of which would hold possibly 30 or 35 canoers and they would often take excursions to New Brighton from Hopkins Landing. Later, the YMCA camp moved to its present site near Williamson's Landing.

A word about the old boats that used to call in to New Brighton, the first boat I remember was the *Marine Express* owned and operated by the Merle Thomson. It was a three cylinder, gas engine boat which used to run into New Brighton with passengers and supplies. Billy Errico Jr. has a picture of his grandfather, Mr. Alfonso Errico, (see Dedication in *Miramar*) getting off the *Marine Express* at New Brighton, after the First World War before Mr. Errico had been de-mobilized. After the *Marine Express*, the Union Steamship Co. serviced Howe Sound and the boat that we knew best was one called the *Capilano*. She gave good service to Howe Sound, calling into Williamson's (if necessary) and would then tie up at Seaside Park before her return trip.

My two sisters, Jo and Onnie, along with Muriel Clarke made lemon pies for the crew of the *Capilano* and in return, they often hopped on the boat at New Brighton, take the trip up to Seaside Park and then get off at New Brighton on its return trip. The girls became known as the "Three Lemons" and were treated by the officers and crew of the Union Steamship boats, mainly the *Capilano*, to trips to Seaside Park and back.

Other boats that serviced New Brighton were the *Lady Evelyn*, *Lady Cecelia*, *Lady Cynthia*, the *Chilco* and after the war, the *Lady Rose*. The *Lady Rose* was a little diesel vessel brought out from Scotland and is still in use in the Alberni Canal. Captain Lawrence Yates, who I mentioned earlier as a friend of Tommy Austin, was captain of the *Lady Evelyn*. Other names I remember are Captain Lawrie and Captain Harry Roach.

From time to time a bunch of us would go up to Seaside Park on the Union Steamship boats and have a ballgame in the park before the return trip. There was a hotel at Seaside Park at that time, which had rooms and a beer parlour, and in old days, the CPR used to run

1948-49 Harper's House now McJannet's House. Courtesy: Lynn Bell.

excursions from Vancouver to Seaside Park on a fast boat called the *Princess Patricia*.

After the war, we built our house (now occupied by the McJannet family) on the west side of the Harper property, and then my sister Onnie and her husband, Doug Snetsinger, built the house between our place and the old house which is now occupied by their daughter Lynn's family.

A few more names have come to mind. Mr. and Mrs. Notman were a very fine elderly Scottish couple who had a house on the West Bay trail. They were kind to everyone and were liked by everyone. Their home is now owned by the Higgins family (Ed, now deceased, Marion and children).

Mr. and Mrs. Adamson had a home on the trail leading to Innes's Point, on the other side of the road from the Errico house. Mr. Adamson was a carpenter and I can remember when we were building 830 Fairmile Road (1953), there was a carpenters' strike. Mr. Adamson came and worked on the house in West Vancouver, found another carpenter. He went by the name "Frenchy" and helped to get that house finished in spite of the strike. Both Mr. Adamson and Mr. Notman gave Doug Snetsinger and myself a hand unloading the barge we brought in with all the building supplies

1949 Art Harper rides Betsy at Johnston's beach. Courtesy: Art Harper.

on it, including "Betsy" (the metal wheeled tractor) for our old home. I believe Jack Smart also gave us a hand in unloading that scow.

Mr. and Mrs. Jack Smart built the house, which is now owned by Bobbi and Kevin Kennedy, Bobbi being the youngest daughter of Jack and Muriel Pearson. It is on the water, just to the west of the Ben Fox/Jurgen Rauh home.

The Original New Brighton Wharf

When the old float was installed, in the 20s, a paddle wheeler named the *Sampson* was in charge of the installation. I remember the *Sampson* coming into shore in front of our place and lifting up a large rock (about the size of the one still there) with chains around it, and using it as one of the anchors for the float.
Art Harper 2003

Above: Judge Art Harper and the catch of the day.
Above left: 1919 -20 Sampson. *A paddle wheeler dredge. Courtesy: Art Harper.*

Joyce Clegg (nee) Matheson

Joyce Clegg: 1950

They stayed in the big house for three years and then rented Urquhart's house for two years. They built forts in the woods or would go over to Pearsons in the morning. They'd sometimes row or walk over for lunch, and at Holmes' there was a box of bathing suits they could put on

In front of Holmes': Ricki, Danny, Bob, Dorothy Pearson – Donna Pearson's cousins. Judy Dewolf, Leah, Jack and Muriel Pearson. Bob Matheson – Joyce Clegg's father. Courtesy: Joyce Clegg.

to go swimming before going home for lunch. When the phosphorus would come out, they would go swimming off Knight's deck. Sometimes they would have bonfires and go swimming with the G Boys when they would come to join them.

The taxi named *Little Pete* would come out of Horseshoe Bay. The food in the early fifties would come up in little cases on the big steamers. The recipients would start opening these boxes right on the dock while onlookers looked at all the cooking and food with big eyes.

Jim Scott had an old fishing boat, the *Emu*. He hung around Gambier for quite a few years. He was a First World War veteran. He would take people over to Gibsons and pick up bread and groceries for the local store, and they would be sitting on the rear end of the boat drinking. Jim ended up living on his boat at Andys Bay. He finally died and the boat *Emu* sank right after he died.

Joyce and Shannie would clean out the store. They would find old cranberries on the shelf and dried out bugs here and there.

South Grace/Gambier Harbour Peninsula

Ruthie Massey (nee) Killam

Ruthie Massey

Camp

In 1928, Lawrence and Edith Killam looked for the right place on Gambier Island to buy. We camped on the trail near Avalon Bay by the stream. I remember Masu (our cook) and her daughter Shizu being with us. In 1929, Lawrence and Edith bought 30 acres from Louis Dalamere, bordered by the Shaws, the Johannsens, and Bill Bailey.

The men at Woodfibre were idle because of the Depression so Father put them to work building the main house camp and tent platforms. There was one for the maid, one for Lol & Bill's tent, a family tent down by the beach, and a platform for the circular army tent near the back porch for the cook. They tried digging wells with no luck; there was no water so they hired a water-diviner and water was found at the bottom of "The Bowl" but it was somewhat salty, so they dug further up from the beach and found excellent water, which is still depended on.

We soon had boats, a large rowboat, and an eastern canoe, which was extremely safe. We used to sail it at times with the use of sideboards, and we could even use a small outboard on it at times. The covered bow was a bonus for our Irish Setter. He would stand on it as I paddled. In 1936, Father bought an outboard motor.

Then gradually "the boys' house" (a Sears garage kit) was built by "the boys," the yellow house, a studio for Edith Killam, the woodshed, and the boat house. The old army tent had come to the end, so a minimal sleeping house near the kitchen was built. Finally, the Snobbery was built for Grammy. It was called the Snobbery because it looked down on the others.

The Hebbs

Dr. Hebb taught at U.B.C. with Father. They became great friends, the Hebb and Killam families. We regularly spent Sunday's together, and any other time we could manage. They had a summer place at Granthams and Bill became very fond of Kay. Bill could often be seen canoeing over to visit her. Kay was one of five daughters of Thomas Carlyle Hebb, who founded the Physics Department at U.B.C. In the course of these visits, in 1932, Bill Killam persuaded Dr. Hebb to purchase 12 acres on Gambier, adjoining the Killam Property. The Hebbs built a cabin on the SW point of Gambier, which later burned in the early 1950's, along

*Above left: Kay and Bill
Killam newlyweds on Union
Steamship.
Above right: 1959 Evelyn Hebb
Killam during construction at
Avalon Bay.
Right: 1945 -1947 -Kay Hebb
Killam in Putt Putt.
Courtesy: Bunker Killam.*

with a sleeping house which overlooks Twin Islands.

Not only did Bill Killam subsequently marry Kay in 1933, but two of my brothers, Lol and David also married two of Kay's sisters, Evelyn and Elizabeth. Three Killam boys married three Hebb sisters! David, an enlisted naval officer, married Elizabeth in 1943, and received the Distinguished Service Cross for a highly dangerous attempt to rescue stranded British officers under fire on a French beach and destroying German installations. He was however killed in action in the English Channel in 1944 while commanding a torpedo boat. Subsequently, Mt. Killam, on Gambier Island was named in his honour.

Late Night Rescue

Ruthie Massey

Yvonne, (Mrs. Ralph Killam), and I were at camp during the summer of 1948. I was 24. I was expecting friends to arrive in a sailboat so I prepared beds for them everywhere. The only bed left for me was in Dave's house – a humble shelter near the water. I went to sleep exhausted and woke at 1:00 or 2:00 a.m. to loud shouts for "Help" coming from the water. Thinking it was my friends, I was cross at them for being alarming. Anyway, as it was raining, I quickly gathered raincoats for them, and a lantern—the only one I could find had a small wick, and was nearly out of kerosene, and hastened down to the boat. The next call for help was very faint, so I figured that they had gone behind Twin Island in their stupidity and I was about to steer over there when I saw a light straight out towards Keats, so I headed toward the light. As I advanced, the light gradually faded, and when I was about three miles out, having shouted periodically for them to shine their light—with no response—thinking I was a fool to be sitting there in the wind and rain in my pajamas, I just thought that I would shut off the engine to see if I could hear their call.

They were right beside me!

I reached over and touched their boat! The boat was full of water, and around it in the sea were four drunken young people who started ordering me around. I pushed one obstreperous young man off his feet to the bottom of my boat! Anyway, we left their boat drifting and I took them to Granthams Landing where they lived—they had no light!

The police were alerted because of the abandoned boat, and the press. Then I received many letters and tales of similar "miracles at sea." I also was presented with an award from the Humane Society.

I must add that I went home to the main house, lit a fire in the fireplace, and went to sleep in front of it. Yvonne got up in the morning and found me there. She scolded me for sleeping in "that leaky little house," and I told her to leave me alone as I had been out rescuing people all night – she laughed and told me not to be silly.

Ruthie Massey (nee) Killam

My Life as a Washerwoman

Ruthie Massey 2008

As a young child, I was responsible for my clothes at the camp. We had little water, so we were provided with "salt water soap" and washed are clothes in the sea. When our own children were young at Hermit Island, they had to do the same, but on our way home [leaving the island] we chucked them in the sea as rags trash.

When I was 16, I had the job of being cook housekeeper at camp. I was paid two war bonds for two months work, worth a total of $50.00. The wash had to be done two or three times each week: sheets, tablecloths, clothes etc. I would carry the laundry down to the bottom of "The Bowl" and get water from the lower, brackish well, carry it up to heat on the stove, then carry the hot water down the steps to the well, the wash tub, and the scrub board. Before he went to war, there were Dave's white socks—terribly hard to scrub clean after he had been fishing up Cotton Creek or wherever. Then I carried the wet wash up the steps and through the house to the wonderful clothesline that was strung from the veranda to the huge tree by the boathouse—what a glorious invention!

Killam main house before the kitchen was closed in. Edith Killam is standing on the porch. Ruthie was standing on this same porch when the bullets whizzed over her head. Courtesy: Maud Killam.

The sun and wind made the cotton crisp and filled with ozone—Bliss!

We had a secondary line from a pine tree across the rocks facing the beach, and one day I was hanging the wash there, a small boat load of hunters shot at me and bullets whizzed over my head when I'd lean down to get more wash from the basket.

Another memory of those wash days was that my mother's linen overalls had to be ironed, as well as the sheets and tablecloths. We had to have a good fire in the stove for baking bread, and we heated the irons on top of the stove, put a blanket, then a sheet on top of the kitchen table, and ironed there. I, no doubt, had some lovely jazz records playing on the wind-up gramophone.

Old wharf in front of Killam property. Lady Evelyn passes between Rose Island, and Bowen Island which in shadow. Courtesy: Maud Killam.

The Union Steamships serviced West Howe Sound. They brought freight and passengers on six days of the week. We used to write a list and send it to Spencer's store, and a few days later it would arrive at Grace Harbour wharf. Our bananas came by the stock in a wonderful hexagonal crate. As small children, we were not allowed near the crate as it was being opened because there might be tarantulas in it!

Francis Drage

Francis Drage and his wife came to Grace Harbour during the early days of the war with Japan. First of all, he took over the little store that Arthur Lett had started, enlarging it somewhat. He soon made himself "Captain Drage" and organized a unit of the PCMR, the Pacific Coast Militia Rangers, using the permanent residents, with headquarters at the store. He made little John Cox "the runner." John was a harmless person who was born mentally challenged. There was Ormie Cambie who was also not very bright, and Arthur Lett, slow and obliging. The only private was Fred Stoddard, a true gentleman, with all his marbles. Fred was an honourable, clear thinking gentleman. His sister, Enid was a well-known portrait painter from Australia.

Francis Drage kept us in constant fear during the war, telling us that balloons were found on the back side of the island, and that submarines have been sighted, etc. He said that the Japanese were going to land on Gambier in order to take Vancouver. Most of us didn't believe him, but it did lend an air of caution. He kept ordering more and more guns from the war department until the basement was jammed with them.

Ruthie Massey (nee) Killam

There was another gentleman, who lived just west of Professor Larsen, who was not a member of the PCMR, but was their secretary. One day he was told to write to the Ministry of Defence and say that all the guns had been distributed and that they needed another shipment of guns and ammunition. He knew that the basement of the store, (Drage's store), was filled with more undistributed guns than the island could use already, and refused to write the letter whereupon he was fired as secretary, and several times after that accused of using his little outboard more than necessary, and disobeying the blackout, (which we all doubted he did).

John Cox was the PCMR runner, who was to run all around the island to alert everyone when the Japanese landed. John was a remittance man, a simple man. One day, Ned Larsen and I were hiding up in the rafters of the little house on the wharf and Drage came in to pick up the bag of mail that had arrived on the boat. He reached in and examined the mail that had come, and he opened an envelope addressed to John Cox. There was a remittance cheque for John, which Drage took and put in his pocket, and he then resealed the envelope and put it back in the bag. Was this because John had refused to write yet another letter asking for more guns?

The police were called quite often by Drage for imagined infractions, but they did cut off this poor man's gas ration.

A year or so later after the police had been called so many times unnecessarily, one of them said to me, "There's going to be a murder around here someday and I don't care who does it!"

Fate did finally step in one day. It was on a windy day a while after the war, when Drage was putting in the road to Andys Bay so more customers could get to the Hall in Gambier Harbour. The Cat was pushing a dead snag when the top half broke off and it fell on him and killed him.

It was Drage who suddenly changed the name "Grace Harbour" to "Gambier Harbour." His feeble excuse was that there was another Grace Harbour somewhere.

Sketch of Killam wharf by Ruthie Killam.
Courtesy: Bunker Killam.

Ruthie Massey (nee) Killam is the youngest daughter in the Lawrence & Edith Killam family. Grandchildren with camps on Gambier today include Bunker, Maude, Peter, Jamie, Ricky, Tom and Elizabeth Killam Wootten.
Ruthie Massey (nee) Killam passed away in 2011.

GAMBIER GUMBOOT DAYS

Don Benson

When my grandfather Gustav "Gus" Lund retired to Gambier Island nearly seventy years ago, the island soon came to represent for me a special time and place that summed up all the good things it meant to be an adventurous boy.

Gus and his second wife Margaret McCormick Lund retired to Gambier in the early 1940s, when both Gambier Harbour and New Brighton Harbour were thriving little communities, each with a little grocery store, a post office, and convenient Union Steamship transportation right to the foot of Carrall Street in the heart of downtown Vancouver.

Gus Lund was born in Norway in 1886 and immigrated to a Norwegian farming community in Minnesota as a youngster. As a young man, he had the wanderlust, and over the years, his impulse to travel found him at the San Francisco earthquake in 1906, wrestling a tame muzzled black bear in mining town saloons, selling boom-time real estate on the Canadian prairies, trapping furs in the Rockies, working for the CNR and then logging on the B.C. coast.

In 1912 at Sylvan Lake, Alberta, he married my grandmother Nellie Tingstad, whose ancestors were also from Trondheim Fjord in Norway. Gus took jobs with the CNR Railway, first as a section hand near Mount Robson, then as a contractor falling and bucking timber for railroad ties. Some winters he ran a trapline. By 1930, Gus was logging on the B.C. coast, first at Harrison Lake, then at a series of bays, inlets and islands along the Inside Passage until the early 1940s.

I first recall my "Grandpa Gus" in the summer of 1939 when I was taken as a six-year-old, on the Union Steamship *Venture*, to stay at his float camp near Echo Bay along the Inside Passage. That was my introduction to our magnificent B.C. coast, and I was spellbound by hand-falling and timber-bucking, A-frames, donkey engines, float houses with gardens, boom sticks, rowdy

Gus Lund 1936. Courtesy: Don Benson.

and boisterous loggers, salmon, eagles and bears, lapstrake row boats and endless isles and inlets waiting to be explored.

Gus and Margaret retired to Gambier Island halfway between Gambier and New

Brighton Harbours to a distinctive little cabin made of vertical logs, and I believe it is still standing. For me, that began several endless summers of hiking, fishing, swimming and running down to one harbour or the other to check out what was unloaded onto the wharf by steam-winch, and who arrived from Vancouver, or who headed "to town" on the Union boats, and why.

Hydro electricity had not yet arrived on Gambier, and those with hand-cranked telephone service shared a single iron-wire telephone line that ran from tree-to-tree along the trails tied to glass insulators on side-blocks. All stoves were wood stoves and lighting was by kerosene lamp. A few folks owned a battery-powered radio, but the dry cell batteries were expensive, and used almost exclusively for the CBC evening news and weather reports.

All cabins had a similar aroma in those days, and I wish we could have bottled it. The perfume was a blend of wood-smoke, kerosene oil, aromatic cedar kindling, pitchy-fir firewood, canvas "bone-dry" rain gear, moth balls, baking bread and sometimes home brew or wet dog.

When electricity did arrive on the island, the first thing Gus bought was a toaster. Before that, bread was toasted on the kitchen range after the surface had been rubbed with waxed paper. When dial telephone service arrived, all the ladies on Gambier wanted a coloured telephone, and having one became a status symbol. Gus didn't see any sense in spending more money for a coloured phone, but Margaret held out, and they ended up with a red one.

There was no road between Gambier Harbour and New Brighton in those days. But

1940 Gus and Margaret Lund with Don's brother, Bobby Benson. Courtesy: Evelyn Benson.

there was a trail from Gambier Harbour to New Brighton that today's road follows, and just east of Gus's cabin the trail wound its way around two huge fir trees, with just enough room for a wheelbarrow to get through.

To supplement his government pension, Gus felled and bucked firewood using a cross-cut saw and double-bitted axe, and did odd jobs as a carpenter and handyman, pushing a wheelbarrow of hand-tools along the trails from job to job. Gus and Margaret Lund had magnificent flower and vegetable gardens all surrounded by a tall fence of cedar stakes to keep the deer out.

Gus Lund was a water-dowser of some distinction, who was often hired to locate underground water where others had failed. He travelled light with only a sharp jack-knife and a few sticks of dynamite carried in a small army-issue kit bag.

Americans would sometimes buy coastal property or little islands but then couldn't find fresh water, so they'd send for Gus Lund, and sometimes I'd go with him. As a kid, I thought everyone could dowse water except Americans. As an aside, it turned out that in our extended family, I have had some success locating water, and I believe one of my first cousins has the same "gift."

During World War II, beginning in the spring of 1942, Gambier Island men of all ages volunteered to join the local "patrol group" of the Pacific Coast Militia Rangers. The Rangers were established to provide a local defence against the threat of Japanese invasion. Age was not a factor in joining, as it was ruggedness and knowing the terrain that counted most. Importantly, belonging to the Rangers gave a sense of purpose to men who were too old for military service, or had been rejected on medical grounds when they tried to join up. Their presence also helped to diminish the unease felt by Islanders when the Japanese began sending hydrogen-filled balloons with incendiary bombs attached across the Pacific on the jet stream.

1940 May Atchison (nee) Lund holds Don Benson. Courtesy: Evelyn Benson.

On joining the Coast Rangers, men were issued a rifle, a handful of cartridges and an armband. The standard rifle for the Canadian Army was the British Lee-Enfield 303, but the Rangers were each issued a Model 1894 lever action Winchester 30-30 carbine, 'the gun that won the west' because it was the most popular rifle on the coast, and the islanders were totally familiar and comfortable with it. Following the War, Rangers were permitted to buy their rifle for five dollars if they wished.

As a ten-year-old, I recall the Rangers marching and drilling near the Hall at Gambier Harbour, and my recollection is that they were a grizzled and ragtag looking crew by Hollywood movie standards. There were a couple of World War I retired army officers living at Gambier Harbour, and they were in their glory barking stern commands. I believe one was a retired colonel and the other a retired major, and there was a much posturing and strutting on their part that had the regular chaps, mostly down-to-earth loggers, stump ranchers, fishermen and beachcombers, rolling their eyes.

In the mid-1940s one of Gus' daughters, my mother's sister "Auntie May" and her colourful and fun-loving husband Dick Atchison moved from Crescent Beach to Gambier Island and settled on the 10-acre parcel adjoining and to the east of Gus' 10-acres. The property is still in the Atchison family. Dick Atchison Senior worked intermittently at logging shows around Howe Sound, while May came up with one challenging enterprise after another to help supplement the family income.

May was an entrepreneur, a tireless worker and an incurable optimist. Over the years, she cut ferns and leather-leaved salal for florist displays, raised chickens, and angora rabbits with long, soft hair, operated a bakery and ran a shake-camp. Eventually she drove her own Case tractor with box trailer to transport the road gang to various work sites. When one enterprise failed, she'd go on to the next without once losing heart, or losing stride.

In the late summer and fall of 1949, I worked with Dick Atchison Senior and three of his brothers, logging at Douglas Bay on Gambier. During the week, we lived at a float camp tied up at a little creek around the point from Douglas Bay, so I got to know Dick pretty well. He was our rigging slinger, and famous around Howe Sound for his colourful and extended string of cuss words when a log on its way to the cold deck got hung up on a rock ledge. Orville Becker of New Brighton also worked at the camp. Dick and those from Gibsons Landing went home weekends, transported by Jimmy Scott, a colourful old reprobate, in his unpredictable boat, the *Elmy M.*

One time Dick's brother Huckleberry Atchison was setting chokers for the yarder when a huge fir log inexplicably started rolling and bouncing toward him. Huck, who had a gangly build, started running frantically down the steep hill with his arms and legs flailing wildly, and I swear, everywhere Huck scrambled to, the log followed like it was tied to him with an invisible line. It was uncanny, and had to be seen to be believed. Finally, exhausted, Huck fell flat on his face, and the log bounced over him and continued on its way down the hill. It wasn't really funny, but for weeks after, whenever we looked at Huck, those of us who witnessed the incident, burst out laughing.

1952 Dick Atchison Sr. strolls along Columbia Street in New Westminster, B.C. Courtesy: Don Benson.

A dinner at May Lund Atchison's place was a meal to be remembered. Most of the ingredients came from the two acres she had carved out of the wilderness and fenced with

1947 Dick Sr. and May Atchison.
Courtesy: Gordie Mitchell.

cedar stakes, and from the nearby forest and ocean.

Fresh or canned chicken, salmon bartered for home-baked bread, or canned venison possibly shot from her doorstep in or out of hunting season, and potatoes and other vegetables from the garden was all topped off with berry pie or canned "preserves," and steaming hot coffee from a big old battered coffee percolator.

May had a canning machine to seal all the bounty she harvested in tin cans she labelled carefully. But if you opened a can labelled "beet tops," you would be treated to canned venison, as, for some reason it was illegal to can deer meat. So, Aunty May's cans of venison were labelled beet tops just in case a government inspector came around.

Through it all, May raised three children, Suzie, Jacqui and Dick Junior. In 1950 or so, Suzie was May Queen at Gibsons where the children journeyed each weekday for schooling. Before Dick Junior was born in 1953, Dick Senior promised May a fur coat if the new baby was a boy, and he kept his promise. But where could she wear an elegant fur coat on Gambier Island? She solved that by wearing the coat along with gumboots while driving her tractor on cold winter days. And in a way, that said who she was.

May Lund Atchison was petite and pretty even in blue jeans and gumboots. Her looks were often compared to the Norwegian figure skater Sonja Henie, or American actress Grace Kelly. When she dressed up to go to "town" she was an absolute knockout. May had a sparkling personality and a ready sense of humour. It followed that she was a favourite dance partner at the Hall.

The Army, Navy and Air Force Veterans Hall at Gambier Harbour was the heart of the communities. The executive members at the Hall took their responsibilities very seriously, and were inclined to go precisely by the book. There was an old juke box for dance music, most of long out of date. The Scotch Waltz was a favourite. Big Joe Mitchell and his family used to travel all the way from Long Bay on his fish boat, *Zariffa.* Joe had hands the size of dinner plates; he was a large man but light on his feet.

Members of the ladies auxiliary took turns baking their best cake to be raffled off each
Saturday night. To encourage the sale
of raffle tickets, Harold Wood from
New Brighton, a former vaudevillian,
would do a soft-shoe dance or perform
one of the risqué pantomime skits in
his repertoire.

Once on a New Year's Eve in the
early 1950s, the executive insisted that
we had to be out of the Hall by
midnight—because it said so in the bylaws. Some of us convinced them that
the by-law said we had to leave the
premises, but didn't say we couldn't go
back in. So what we did was, we left just
before midnight and stood outside and
on the stroke of the hour we sang "Auld
Lang Syne." I remember that so clearly
because just then it started to snow
heavily. It was a touching and poignant
moment. Then we all trouped back
indoors and danced into the wee hours.

After Margaret Lund passed
away, Gus's retired nephew Vic Pearson
came out from Edmonton to live with
him. Vic had worked with Gus logging
on the B.C. coast before the war, and
then served in the Canadian army for
the duration of the war. Vic soon

*1948 Joe and Margaret Mitchell dance at the Army, Navy
and Air Force Veterans Hall. Courtesy: Mitchell family.*

became a popular fixture at the Hall. One of the most decent and kindest men I ever met, Vic
had a certain way of peering at you inquisitively over his reading classes. He wore a soft-
leather slouch hat that visitors to the Hall used to try to buy, sometimes for a considerable
sum when they were in their cups. But he always said to them, "If I sell you my hat, then what
will I do for a hat?

Gambier Island is a scenic and tranquil place of the heart, the mind, and the soul that
folks visit on weekends and vacations, and cling to while trying to eke out a living, or retire to
until they grow too old and infirm for the island lifestyle. And in this life, times continue to

change dramatically, and unexpected tragedies happen to some. Still, there were not often births or deaths on Gambier.

Eventually Gus Lund moved to an old folks' home at White Rock and ended his days there. May Lund Atchison's cabin burned to the ground, and her canning machine and all her family photos and keepsakes went up in flames. Her health went downhill from there, and I have always felt that the fire took something out of her. She passed away before her time at New Westminster. Dick Atchison Sr. ended

Right: Victor Pearson.
Left: 1942 Jeanette Lund Benson - Gus Lund's eldest daughter - Don Benson's mother. and Don's brother Bobby Benson. Courtesy: Janet Benson Stewart.

his days at North Vancouver, and I still shake my head that an experienced woodsman like Vic Pearson was killed on Gambier by a renegade alder tree he was falling.

They tell me there has been a lot of development and change on Gambier Island over recent decades, but I haven't been over there to see it. I suppose that's because when I look across to Gambier from Keats Island where I live, I can "hear" Dick Atchison Senior's ready laugh, and I can hear the strains of the Scotch Waltz drifting from the old Hall, and "see" Vic Pearson in his old slouch hat serving up a beer. I can see my Grandpa Gus trudging past my Auntie May's place with his wheelbarrow of hand-tools, and see her looking up from picking raspberries in her garden and waving to him as he smiles and nods, and for now I'd just as soon leave things that way, because, like the man said, you can't go home again.

Memories at Druid Bay

Chris Wootten

Lawrence and Edith Killam came to Gambier Island in June 1929 and purchased Louis Dalamere's property for $50 an acre. Over the years, they built a number of small buildings, which still remain, including the cook house; a Cape Cod style house for Lawrence and Edith; a house for their four boys, Bill, Lol, Ralph and David; and another for their daughters Kim &, Ruth. There is a photo of the family in Miramar I.

Meanwhile, Bill Killam became enamoured with Kay Hebb, who summered nearby at the time at Grantham's Landing. Bill was often seen canoeing over to visit her. Kay was one of five daughters of Thomas Carlyle Hebb, who founded the Physics Department at U.B.C. and

Edith and Lawrence Killam property. New wharf under construction. Courtesy: Bunker Killam.

for whom the Hebb Building at U.B.C. is named. In the course of these visits, in 1932, Bill Killam persuaded Dr. Hebb to purchase 12 acres on Gambier Island adjoining the Killam

Property, running from Avalon Bay to Druid Bay, across from Grace/Twin Islands. The Hebb's built a cabin on the SW point of Gambier, overlooking what is now Langdale, along with a sleeping house overlooking Grace/Twin Islands.

David Allison Killam D.S.C Lieut., R.C.V.R. enlisted Naval Officer missing at sea off Letarre, July 1943. Mt. Killam was named in his honour. Courtesy: Bunker Killam.

Not only did Bill Killam subsequently marry Kay in 1933, but two of his brothers, Lol and David also married two of Kay's sisters, Evelyn and Elizabeth. Three Killam boys married three Hebb sisters! David, an enlisted naval officer, married Elizabeth in 1943, and received the Distinguished Service Cross for a sustained and highly dangerous attempt to rescue stranded British officers under fire on a French beach and destroying German installations. He was however killed in action in the English Channel in 1943 while under command of a torpedo boat. Subsequently, Mt. Killam, the highest mountain on Gambier Island was named in his honour.

The original Hebb cabin burned down in the early 1950's, igniting a small forest fire. Two weeks after the fire was extinguished, a smouldering fire was discovered more than 100 feet away, having travelled underground via buried roots.

Two Hebb sisters built on the Hebb property. Kay and Bill Killam built their own cabin in 1949-50 on Druid Bay and also purchased the adjacent Shaw-Laird property in 1948.

In 1959-60, Evelyn Hebb Killam and her husband Lol built on Druid Bay just south of Avalon Bay. Both cabins remain in the family.

Above: 1946 –48 Framing Bill and Kay Killam's house at Druid Bay. Courtesy: Bunker Killam. Below: Tom, Dave Killam, Gus Lund and Fred Stoddard building Bill and Kay Killam camp at Druid Bay Courtesy: Bunker Killam.

"Camp is a Magic Place"

Maud Killam

For several years before 1928, the family, Lawrence and Edith Killam and their six children rented a cottage in Granthams Landing and camped around Howe Sound. In 1928, Ralph was sent over to Gambier to stay with the post-mistress to do some reconnoitring of available land. He was first shown some land on the west coast, around from Avalon Bay but decided there was not enough sun, so then he was shown our bay and after another visit with his parents and brother Lol, the family bought the property for fifty dollars an acre! They completed the first one room, board and baton cabin and the adventures began...

Right: Ruthie Massey's house overlooks the garden. Courtesy: Maud Killam.

Boats were always a part of their lives, often being rescued and renovated or built from scratch. Edith Killam (nee Humphrey) spent much of her time, developing her beautiful gardens and painting her wonderful paintings.

Bill, Lol, Dave were dating three Hebb sisters and Bill convinced Doctor and Mrs. Hebb to buy the adjoining property, across from Grace/Twin Islands and around into Avalon Bay –Druids Bay. Bill and Kay, and Lol and Rose took over the Hebb property. Sadly, Dave was killed in World War II in 1944, at age 26. One of Gambier's two mountains is named in his memory.

The camps today are not too different from those of earlier days, still without electricity, relying on wood stoves for heat and kerosene lamps and candles for light. The trails in the woods are much the same as those trod by our parents and grandparents. "Camp" is a magic place filled with our history and treasured by us all.

Edith Killam's Journal of February 1937:

These trips in early spring or winter are the most thrilling of all—it is so much more of an adventure. Everyone is shocked at our foolishness. "Won't you be cold? BRRR! I'd much rather have my home comforts, thank you."

We order a few trees to plant and the food from Spencers and feel we must go in spite of various duties which always crop up.

The boat finally reaches Grace Harbour – we greet all the old friends – Fred, Mrs. Lett, sometimes Captain Larsen, Arthur, and the last two years, Mr. McNuety. Arthur loads our various bundles on his boat. Fred takes the lunch basket and we walk slowly over the trail to camp. The first feeling is... Did you ever smell such air? Walk on such soft springy earth?

The ferns are still green, though flatter and not so beautiful as summer. The fallen leaves from the tall Maples and alder trees are a glowing yellow and brown—giving an entirely different color effect from the dainty twinkling green of spring or the heavier, less airy green of summer. The mosses are at their best—tender yellow green—rich gold and green— bronze, and each beautiful shape is worth study.

Lawrence walks with his long stride while the farmer picks her way with a cane to sound the depth of puzzles and wet boggy parts of the trail.

The old trail past Fred Stoddards—the alder trail so grey and cool and filled with interest. The farmer keeps an eye on each huge upturned root, fern clad and so beautifully arranged one sighs and wishes for Mother Nature's skill.

Edith Killam passed away in 1962 at which time their property was left to my father, Ralph.

Ruthie Massey's children/Edith's grandchildren (order unknown)Raymond, Binty and Nathaniel help their granny, Edith Killam plant a tree in front of the "Boys" house. Courtesy: Maud Killam.

1913 Charles Lett petitioned the Federal Government to build the first dock at Grace Harbour; it was constructed from a series of logs with planking for the deck. Courtesy: Leiani Anthony.

Grace/Gambier Harbour

The Old Days at Grace Harbour

Mollie Alemany (nee) Larsen

We came to Gambier on the Union Steamships but knew little of West Bay or New Brighton except that they were part of the island. The core of the house, which Nora now owns, was built by my grandfather as a wedding present for my brother Pat in 1937 -38.

      The main events at that time were the arrival of the Union Steamships, picking up the mail and shopping at the Gambier Store. There was no electricity on the island so the store only carried non-perishables. Each household ordered meat from the Vancouver department stores, usually Woodwards and the orders came to the island on the steamships. Fridays were the most exciting of those lazy days as they were big freight days and many fathers arrived after a week of working on the mainland. Sometimes we would go to Hopkins or Gibsons Landing for our groceries, but as our boats at the time were smaller than those of today, there was usually only room for one or two adults.

      The days on Gambier can be summed up in a few words: sunshine meant going to the beach and swimming – rain meant board games, cards and beading. We always had something to do and we were NEVER BORED.

      We spent many summers at Gambier Harbour or Grace Harbour as Leiani Anthony (nee Brimacombe) still calls it.

1955 All in swimming Grace/Gambier Harbour. Courtesy: Dulcie Baxter.

The Old Days at Grace Harbour- Mollie Alemany (nee) Larsen

Friends, Family and Getting to the Island

Ted Smyth

Many people have asked about past history of Gambier Island and especially of Grace Harbour and what it really was like in the old days. I, being the oldest living property owner and

grandson of the first original settlers, Mr. and Mrs Charles Arthur Lett, will relate the story of Grace/Gambier Harbour on the south west corner of the island.

1912 Charles Arthur Lett and daughter Dulcie, mother of Ted Smyth. Courtesy: Leiani Anthony.

Being of the adventurous type, the Letts began to search for a retirement location away from the city. At first, when exploring in Howe Sound, they took a liking to Soames Point but it was on the mainland and might eventually get too populated. So eventually, they settled in a small bay on Gambier Island named Grace Harbour. Imagine if you can Mr. Charles Lett, arriving with his wife in the year 1912, on a rocky beach alongside a high bank densely covered with large fir, hemlock and cedar trees, and sparsely dotted with maple and alders. They would have to be of a hardy type and have some imagination to visualize the future possibilities of homesteading: think of the clearing, the getting supplies, obtaining a parcel of land and finding a spot to build.

My grandmother, Mrs. Lett was an amazing person. Being brought up in Brandon Manitoba, she was prepared for what was ahead. Such as hauling and carrying water from a hand dug well, collecting firewood for the cooking stove, and fireplace and as there was no electricity or telephone in those days obtaining coal oil for light and heat. The supplies such as groceries, etc, were ordered from Woodwards at Main and Carrall Street in Vancouver. She would send in a mail order and ten days later the supplies would arrive by freight boat or mostly by steamship. My grandmother would go and climb up the fruit trees and pick the fruit even in her seventies.

In the old days, it was difficult to get supplies to build a house. Even today with all the modern conveniences, shipping supplies is still not easy as we all know. Today we have barges, cranes, fast boats, trucks, cars, wharfs to dock our boats and machines of all sorts, and above all electricity.

1912 Arthur Lett, son of pioneer Charles Arthur Lett. They lived in tents while they cleared the land. Courtesy: Leiani Anthony.

In 1890, when the Union Company was just starting, thousands of settlers between Howe Sound and Prince Rupert were dependent on the Union Steamship service and were very thankful for it. "Boat Day" became a part of coastal life after the "*Comox*" made its first run in 1892. At that time, coastal residents were so thankful for a regular link to civilization they considered the Union Boats a great blessing. The three ships most used on the West Howe Sound run were the *SS Britannia* (the oldest of the three), the *SS Capilano*, and the *Lady Evelyn*. The skipper most often on the bridge was Captain W.L. (Billy) Yates who mastered over seven vessels at different times.

Before the 1920s, the Union Company updating was necessary and they with confidence got rid of some of the older steamships. The departure of these early boats from the Union Fleet marked the company's change into the busiest period of its history.

In the later twenties, the inboard gas engine appeared. It was mostly the Briggs and Stratton and they replaced the tedious rowing. It was much less work and they were very reliable, similar to the old Easthope engine. They would chug along forever; the only disadvantage was that the engine took up room in the center of the boat with a hot exhaust pipe sticking outside of the boat. One had to be very careful not to touch this hot pipe.

These boats were propelled and steered by a propeller/rudder out the stern. One problem was that when beaching a boat care had to be taken that the propeller did not strike the beach or rocks and be damaged. Later, smaller outboards came along.

I had a three horsepower Elto, which attached to the stern of the boat with clamps. It could be tilted out of the water and was safe to beach. With care, this engine lasted for twenty years. It fell off at least once and went to the bottom of the sea only to be recovered, cleaned out with fresh water and away it would go again. It was a good engine and would travel about as fast as a Briggs and Stratton but was perhaps not quite so reliable. The advantage was that it was light and could be stopped and pulled out of the water when beaching; protecting the propeller from harm.

There were plenty of fish in the 1920s. Our favourite fishing was rowing between "Burns Rock" now owned by Mr. and Mrs. Charles McNeight and Rose Island opposite of Ralph Killams property. We would troll with a silver Tom Mick spoon and catch as many as six to ten

Grilse (small salmon) in an hour; they were delicious eating. "Twin Island" now named "Grace" was the favourite spot for salmon. Mr. Graham, then the owner of Twin Islands would watch for herring, and if they were around, he would always get a salmon. Later came the more powerful engines that we have today. They can get us to the fishing grounds quickly, if there are any fish around.

Waiting for the Union Steamships for hours on the wharf on a

Early 1920s Lett's house at Grace/Gambier Harbour. To the right we can see two chimney stacks remain after the 1923 fire burned down the Lett's main house. Courtesy: Larsen family.

hot summer day could get a bit tedious as often the boats would have unexpected delays. One of the principle discussions about the Union ships was how they could possibly be so late. This did not happen so much on the west Howe Sound but it was a very familiar occurrence up-coast. They seemed to wander in at all times with no relation to bad weather, tides or months of the year. People wondered about the unscheduled jaunts the Union crews must be taking. By comparison, CPR ships seemed to be able to stick to a schedule. Why couldn't Union ships to the same. For the most part CPR ships served main ports such as the Vancouver to Nanaimo route and Vancouver to Victoria with not only a day-boat but also a night-boat with sleeping accommodation, and with proper unloading on dock facilities with scheduled times for leaving an arriving. Union ships, on the other hand served approximately 150 ports-of-call, often loading at rickety floats or even into rowboats in open waters. There were some places the ships wouldn't dock because either a bay was too shallow or it became too difficult to get into. The inevitable results were unexpected delays that put them behind schedule.

1933 Peggy Madlock, Mary Smyth - age 18, Robin Johnson at New Brighton dock. Courtesy: Leiani Anthony.

The *Lady Cecelia* and the *Lady Cynthia* were small chasers in the Great War and both were fairly fast. Occasionally, the *Lady Cynthia* would travel the West Howe Sound route, which consisted of leaving the Union dock in Vancouver Harbour at 9:00 a.m. to go through the First Narrows, past Point Atkinson and Passage Island north of Hood Point on Bowen Island to its first port-of-call which often was Camp Artaban at the head of Long Bay especially when there was a change of campers. From there, if necessary, a stop at the West Bay float and then on to Grace Harbour from there to Gibsons, the main port-of-call on the West Howe Sound route. Sometimes it would go to New Brighton, after Grace Harbour then on to Williamson Landing, YMCA camp, Port Mellon then to Hopkins Landing, Granthams and on to Gibsons where it would stay at least a couple of hours unloading and loading before returning to Vancouver.

In the event the ship would go to Gibsons after leaving Grace Harbour which it did most often then it would have its two hour stay before proceeding north to Granthams,

Hopkins, YMCA, Port Mellon, McNab Creek, New Brighton. If there were any passengers going back from Grace Harbour, it would call in and then head for Vancouver. This was the only means of boat transportation to town that there was.

One could very often tell who was skipper on the bridge of the incoming boat long before it reached the wharf by the way it docked. Some captains would make a perfect landing, others not so perfect, conditions such as tide and wind had a great deal to do with the ship's landing.

1946 Helen Negroponte and Elizabeth Beck. Ted Negroponte untying the ship lines. Courtesy: Helen Negroponte.

In the late twenties, very often, Pat Larsen and I would be on the wharf as the ship approached to receive the light bow and stern lines. Attached to the light line was a heavy main rope strong enough to hold the boat close to the wharf after being attached to the metal cleat. Depending on the tide, the ramp from the dock to the wharf would either be level or at a steep angle making one feel as though they were climbing a steep cliff.

The mail would be carried off first and handed to the postmistress, in those days it was Mrs. Lett, who in turn handed it out to those recipients on Gambier wharf. Then came the passengers and guests followed by the freight which could consist of many different things such as replacement of broken parts, flour, sugar, yeast, cloth and mending material.

Mr. Thorleif Larsen built an attractive house across the bay from the wharf in 1921, which due to ground conditions deteriorated to the extent of having to be torn down. The

Larsens had three sons: Jack, Pat, Ned, and one daughter, Mollie Alemany. Mollie at present is living on the island. Jack and Ned had since passed away.

Owen Houston, another popular name on Gambier, still spends his summer with his wife Eileen in the original home that his grandparents, Mr. Alfred and Louila Houston built in 1923. Owen and Eileen have three sons, Greg, Brad, and Guy. The Houston house still stands, as do four others on the waterfront just east of Gambier wharf.

1930s Larsen House, Grace/Gambier Harbour. Courtesy: Larsen family.

The first was built by Mr. Radwell and is now owned by the Cromptons.

Mrs. Enid Stoddard was a very famous portrait painter who painted many notables. Mr. George and Mrs. Mary Cambie built in Gambier Harbour. Mrs. Cambie (nee) Stoddard was also an artist and specialized in painting animals.

In those old days, there was little or no pollution, as we know of it today. Especially from the automobile and even now except for a few boats, cars, trucks, and motorcycles we have very little compared to the cities. City folk—providing they can afford it—like the peacefulness and tranquility of the island. A lot of water has passed under the bridge in that time. Many situations have come and gone, and many have been solved. We have a desirable location with amenities such as swimming, boating, fishing, fresh open air, walking, hiking and plenty of sunshine. Yet Grace, now Gambier Harbour, is not that far away from the big city of Vancouver and the probably coming casinos.

Mrs Eva Drage and Mr. Bradbury

Leiani Anthony interview – January 1981

Mr. Bradbury:
I came to Gambier in 1938 and shacked up in a log cabin part way to New Brighton, before Lunds owned it. It was only half the shack, I just moved in and shacked up. There were no windows, no doors, and only half a floor. I stayed in there one winter; it had a cast iron stove, I don't know where that came from. Lund came in 1945 but the government owned it up until then. They had ten acres in that one lot, Lot 20 and ten acres in Lot 19. I could have bought it for six dollars an acre. Cartwright, a school teacher from the Cariboo, built the log cabin in 1935 or '36. He also built Miss Stoddard's house down in Gambier Harbour with logs. He built

them because he figured on moving down here. He built one, and then Miss. Stoddard wanted one built and she gave him Lot 4. He took it over but he let it go for taxes so she grabbed it again.

Mrs. Eva Drage:
Cartwright was a very nice fellow, he and his wife were going to split up, they'd come from Barbados or something. When he'd come up, he preceded to tell Brad and Frances all his troubles. We used to feel sorry for him.

Mr. Bradbury:
In 1938, McNulty was the road foreman. I don't know where he come from but he lived in Adkins old house. He had a little white house then, made of planks off the wharf. Foreman, three days a month, just going around and scythe the trails and his foreman was a general foreman for the Public Works Department. It wasn't Highways, it was Public Works.

Miss Eva Hazlitt (married name – Drage) on left, her sister, Miss Hazlitt on right. Courtesy: Brian Smith.

Grant got the Foreman job and I was supposed to work with him three days a month and he was supposed to get five days. But he couldn't live on five; he had a family and two kids so he quit and went to Port Mellon. Then in 1942, they asked me to take it over. So I had it from 1942 to 1963 when I retired. I'm eighty-two.

I bought Lot 40 up here in 1939, from Mr. and Mrs. Drage, the one that Hjorthoy had up here, in New Brighton. I built the house on it, the first little twelve foot by eighteen foot next to Burton's, and I sold it to Hjorthoy for four hundred dollars. That was ten acres. It went from me to Hjorthoy to Mark Derrick.

Mrs. Eva Drage:
I was 81 in July 1980. It's wonderful how fast time goes. When you get older you never get bored up here because things are slow. I remember after Christmas, time would drag on and drag on. Well, I don't know where the time goes now.

In 1937, we were in Vancouver and we had the little house up here, and there was nothing doing in Vancouver. We could live up here quite comfortably. At that time, Fran got the post office and through buying the property, she got quite friendly with Leiani's great uncle, Arthur Lett.

I bought the property I live on now in 1936 and had the house built by Arthur and Bill Bailey before I came up in 1937. I bought the land from Arthur Lett—my goodness; he owned everything around here back then.

It's so long ago I can hardly remember, and what we used to buy. We used to go all up the road and down that way. All we could think of was getting it [property] for firewood. That's all we ever thought of.

Bill Bailey, he built the original house on this place, The House in the Woods. It was the old store, which was down by Leiani's mother's.

Mr. Bradbury:
Al Kingston from New Brighton moved it up here with that one horse. He put it on skids and used block and tackle to move it up here, for Ormie Cambie. He owned it, but all the kids used to tease him and get him to come outside so they could steal his candy. They had a wonderful time getting him out then he wanted ice, he didn't have no fridge, you see, so he had to have an ice box to keep milk and everything in. He ordered the ice from Vancouver. It came up on the freighter—two blocks of 100 pounds each. Well, he couldn't handle that. Arthur wanted to

buy one, but oh no, Ormie was going to save them. He left that ice at the side of the road, just on the hump.

Leiani Anthony:
I remember going to Mrs. Cambie's for tea as a child with my Nana Smyth, and I remember Ormie quite well. I was afraid of him, to tell you the honest truth, because I was only a child you see and he was a bit strange.

1912 Dulcie Smyth.
Courtesy: Leiani Anthony.

Mr. Bradbury:
Poor Ormie, he was an awful man. He is in a home somewhere in Vancouver.

When I was road foreman, we just kept the brush cut down with a scythe and the ditches cleaned. I worked alone and then in the summertime, with Mr. Paul. He lived in The Barn. I don't know how they ever managed to live in that barn—five dollars a month!

Then the war came on and we all joined the P.C.M.R., the Pacific Coast Militia Rangers, Francis Drage was the Captain; Hjorthoy, Joe Mitchell, George and I were all Lieutenants. Oh, we had a good time until 1945 when we had a stand down. During the war, I was only getting four days a month. I was going to go to Port Mellon to be the Security Officer up there for a hundred thirty a month, board and room. So the engineer in town, Mr. Stowe, asked if I would stay on Gambier. They made me a permanent foreman so I could get my time in for my pension and that's the way it was.

Mr. Hugo Hjorthoy and Anna Dahlen came to the island in the early 1900s, long before me. Mother and Father Hjorthoy started off farming on the island; he was a judge in Norway. They had a place named, Bowenview, between Long Bay and Halkett Bay, along the south shore. They had two houses and a big orchard with about twelve hundred trees. They used to take apples all the way to Horseshoe Bay in a boat and take them in a team of horses from there into town. Hugo Laurentius, their son, got married and later got a job as a caretaker in Camp Fircom. Hugo Jr. and Sonja had two girls and a boy.

Then of course, they separated, she went to work on the ferries from Horseshoe Bay to Nanaimo and he went up to Twin Creek. Then he left Twin Creek and they gave him a job running the small ferry, Dogwood Princess I, there and to Gambier Island. Hugo Jr. and Art, from Pender Harbour, he ran his own ferry at Pender Harbour and he sold out and came down to Gibson and got a job there. Hugo was really good.

Mid 40s Joe and Gord Mitchell. Courtesy: Mitchell family.

The Hjorthoys bought a piece of property up on the corner here in the early fifties. They got that before they moved away from down there—Long Bay. They didn't sell that property for years and years and years, then a longshoreman from New Westminster bought that block of land in there. They subdivided. When they subdivided into acre lots they had no trouble selling all the waterfront. They had three or four easements going down, six feet wide, so the people at the back could always get down to the water. After they got that cleared, I used to have to go down and looked after that road, all them young alders and maples growing up. I looked after Camp Artaban to Brigade Bay; the trail there had to be kept open.

Mrs. Eva Drage and Mr. Bradbury – Leiani Anthony Interview, 1981

Hugo's mother moved into the house in Gambier Harbour. She was there for quite a little time.

Leiani Anthony:
I remember going there for tea with my Grandmother. Hugo was her son.

Mr. Bradbury:
And then she moved to Gibsons. Hugo had that land for many years before he sold it and moved to North Van, where he died years later.

Leiani Anthony:
The Burton's have since discovered that the Hjorthoy's house was in fact on their piece of property. Anyway, they took it all down, because it was falling down.

Mrs. Drage:
There was quite a good well on that property. One thing I was horrified when Pat was talking about it I said, for heaven's sakes there used to be a good well, whether it was a top on it now or not I don't know. She said Brad told her there used to be a good well.

Mr. Bradbury:
We were building Andys Bay Road when Reginald Godfrey came over and talked to Frances about bringing a ferry over, passenger ferry. That was in 47-48. We started building these roads in 1947, not so much the one out front here, we did Gambier to New Brighton one year, then Austin Trail and part of West Bay the next year, it was several years before we did the Grove Road in West Bay in '48. Then in 1954, we got to the Andys Bay Road. The road system hasn't

1935 Entrance to Camp Fircom. Left to right: Ruth Roddan, Jenny McNeill, Isabell Clark. Courtesy: Diane Clark.

changed much, it went backwards. We had Andys Bay Road going right up to Andys Bay camp. It's all blocked off now, you can't get in there.

There is still a camp at the booming grounds. They take the logs in by water and they're stacked over there. The boss lives right there.

I went to Keats Island and looked after the roads there, and then I looked after the roads from Hopkins to Twin Creek, Camp Artaban and Camp Fircom. I'd go over to Keats Island to the Baptist camp on the west side, pick up three old men and walk to wherever the job was and work until half past two, three o'clock and then walk home. By the time I got home it was pretty near five. I'd leave from Avalon Bay. Not much has changed not in building, or improving anything, no.

Arthur Lett owned a lot, and then Ted Lett put up a log cabin before he got married. Arthur Lett lived down below on the waterfront. When Eva sold the property to Reynolds, they tore it down and built the present one.

Mrs. Eva Drage:
At the time I sold the property to the Reynolds, I thought it was a good idea because I could see this island was going downhill so fast. Everybody was either dying or moving away and I thought, well, I'm going to be alone here, whereas I knew the Reynolds were going to stay. She can be quite kind when she wants to be. She helped me find my little dog one time when he got out, yes, and that was before we had any trouble. I say, 'Hi, Bet' and she says, 'Hi,' and that's the end of that. When you hear of them, worse than that happened down East, we were very lucky, I think.

Mr. Bradbury:
Getting back to Bill Bailey, he was single and helped Arthur build Eva's house, and then he built Nel's house, (the little house by the beach stairs, the little house that burned to the ground about 1968) and then he built Johansson's, now Ralph Killams. He left the island because there was no work and went to Port Mellon to work. I couldn't say if he was still alive, last time I heard he was up the valley somewhere cutting cordwood. Imagine cutting cordwood with a crosscut saw!

Leiani Anthony:
I remember doing that with grandfather quite well. On the end of the crosscut saw, it took awhile. It seemed poor granddad spent his life cutting wood, to keep warm. Nowadays it's zap zap zap.

Mr. Bradbury:

You take Dick Atchison senior up there, my God, he can cut all that wood in two days. Not eight hours, only about three hours a day and he got all them trees cut and he splits with a maul, he don't split with an axe.

This kind of life is really for younger people. It's all right to have a summer home but not to live here permanently for a young fellow, no way.

Mrs. Drage:

It's no place for young person and it's no place for an old person. Not good this isolation, just in between.

Leiani Anthony:

Arthur was a cantankerous old thing.

Mr. Bradbury:

I didn't always get along with Arthur Lett. Not always, no. I threatened to split his skull open with a shovel one day, the way he talked, he was difficult but if you told him to do something, he'd do it. Teddy Lett looks like him and acts like Arthur Lett. Leiani Anthony: Mother claims it was because Uncle Arthur was spoiled as a child. Mom says he was very badly spoiled and his father spoiled him and the reason why he wasn't left any of the property was because his mother, who owned it all saw

1948 Mary and Barbara Brimacombe, Wendy and Charles Smyth – Mary's dad. Penny is in his lap. Leiani Brimacombe sits on the sand. Courtesy: Dulcie Brimacombe.

what he'd done with all the rest of the property. He kept selling it and selling it and if he needed to pay off debts, he'd sell off some more and she didn't want her property frittered away, she wanted it kept. Arthur had been given all the property he needed; I gather he'd had the waterfront.

Mrs. Drage:
We bought all our property from Arthur Lett. He was difficult and yet a lot of people that knew him just thought the world of him. He kept his friends.

Mr. Bradbury:
He'd go out in that row boat and go way down Long Bay. He'd go down to Mitchells to give him three cents, take him all day. The Mitchells would be thrilled to see him. He'd spend the day with them and have dinner with them, and come home in the dark. He'd have a coal oil lantern sitting on the bow of his flat-bottom boat and that's the way he rode home.

Leiani Anthony:
Uncle Teddy is a bit like that, he doesn't like to owe anybody anything, he'd give you the shirt off his back and he's very kind but he's also quite ornery, can be. Auntie Betty's a saint. Uncle Teddy's daughters would never let him get away with that kind of behaviour, not anymore

Mr. Bradbury:
The Bournes lived on the island and they all died, Grandpa died, Gramma died, the mother died, Sylvia got married and Bertie got married, Bertie was her boy and Sylvia was theirs.

Leiani Anthony:
I understand they lived here before the war. When he came out, he was going to be a big chicken farmer, so he got his gratuity and got George Frost and Gus Lund to build that house for him and he never made out. He wanted the boy to do all the work. He was supposed to have a disability cough, lung trouble. As I recall, she gave him an adrenalin shot and she phoned and got in touch with me and asked me to take him down, they'd phone for a plane to take him into Shaughnessy and she had a bottle with adrenaline. He sticks his arm out and she gives it to him and she runs out of adrenaline so I took her home to give her another bottle, just got her back, and she gave him another shot, got on the plane, the plane came in and rushed him into Shaughnessy. Unfortunately, he was dead in less than one hour after he got in there.

Mrs. Drage:
Florence phoned the house, I gave them our telephone number.

Mrs. Eva Drage and Mr. Bradbury – Leiani Anthony Interview, 1981

Mr. Bradbury:
They were living in Ebby's property.

They sold it to the Smiths, to a logger for a thousand dollars and he took over two thousand worth of logs off it and then he sold it to the Japanese for five thousand—waterfront and a good well. The Americans own it now. They had it up for sale for $50,000 and nobody bought it and I don't know why. There's three acres of it sold to Caravan.

Mrs. Eva Drage:
Mrs. Bourne didn't last long after she left here, she had an awful accident, she slipped on a log and the point of the log went right in her, she sat on it and I think that started cancer. She was a sweet woman. And I'll tell you another person who's a sweet woman and that's little Winkie, but oh that miserable creature, she's expecting next month and do you see the packs she carries? It's dreadful. She falls down and he just looks around and laughs at her, he don't help her get up.

1945 Mildred Ridley and Frank Heay at Ridley property.
Courtesy: Betty Ridley.

Mr. Bradbury:
Frank Heay lived here before and after he got married. She came to the island as a bride. They didn't have a family; all they had was a cow and some chickens. They had a lovely garden. Mrs. Heay lived on the island a long time before she sold her property and moved to Gibsons

1930s Mrs. Eva Drage's mother and her sister. In background – left – Arthur Lett's house, Hazlitt's place. Courtesy: Betty Forbes.

Mrs. Drage told me she'd never split wood in her life. You ought to see Margaret Terfry split wood with an eight-pound hammer. She gets the big long handles and cuts them off. She puts the wedge in a little bit and she swings. If a man did that with a short handle like that it would jar his head off but it don't bother her.

Mrs. Drage:
Margaret's a lovely cook you know, and she does a lot of sewing, so that helps her out with her time.

Mr. Black was a road foreman for a while, but he only looked after his trail from his home out to Mountainview Trail. Black's Beach is halfway up on the west side of West Bay. Mr. Black left the CNR and came up to Gambier in the summer. He was a CNR policeman. That beach has little pebbles and lots of oysters.

Leiani Anthony:
The people over there sponsor a Polar Bear swim every New Year's Day, Lisa Alemany got a medal for this year's swim. Johnson's are very friendly with the West Bay people.

Mrs. Drage:
Linfoot Lake is right between the mountains, a girl brought some friends from the East to see the lake and she said Mrs. Drage, we couldn't get out of there fast enough. She said litter, garbage, no toilet facilities, but it didn't worry them one bit, it was so pretty up there. It was named after Linfoot.

Mr. Bradbury:

Bill Bailey lived over at Killam's. He was here when I come to the island. He gave me my second job. He built a log house for Miss Hazlitt, Eva's sister, the one that burned down at the top of the Gambier Harbour dock. He was supposed to be a builder, he took a contract, anyway, he asked me if I would hew the logs and I said, "Sure." I went down that morning with a broad axe and bent over to hew, and God, I couldn't straighten up!

Leiani Anthony interview with Mrs. Eva Drage and her friend, Mr. Bradbury on Saturday, January 3, 1981, at Gambier Harbour.

1941 Grace Harbour. Mrs. Dulcibella C.E.G. Smyth, Mrs. Mary Stewart Lett, Mrs. Mary E. D. Brimacombe. Courtesy: Leiani Anthony.

Delightful Times on Gambier Island

Dulcie Baxter (nee) Brimacombe

Gambier! The very name conjures up summers of fun where shoes come off and we go barefoot for two glorious months.

There were the usual groups of kids at Gambier Harbour in the 50s who played

together according to their age. My pals included my cousins and the Larsens. Penny Smyth, my first cousin, was my closest friend. We did everything together.

Wendy Smyth and Nora Larsen were of the same age and allowed Penny

and me, a few years younger, in on their games. The best game of all was one called, "Boys." The main props

Above: 1949 Dulcie Brimacombe and Penny Smyth.
Below: Mary and Barbara Brimacombe, Penny and Charles Smyth, Dulcie Brimacombe, Wendy Smyth on the grass.
Courtesy: Dulcie Baxter.

were made from small flat pieces of wood we found on the beach. This made-up game, played by the four of us occupied the hours from after breakfast until lunch time, when our respective whistles blew calling us home. Ours was one blast, summoning us Brimacombe girls home from wherever we might be, two caught the Larsen children's attention and three blows on the whistle called home the Smyth children.

Now, back to our game of "Boys," the flat sticks of wood, about 6 in. long and 3 in. wide were our children. We would crayon faces on sticks and give each child a name, and funnily enough they were only and always "girls" names in spite of the overall game being called "Boys." We would play this game on the beach at the far left or east side as you are facing down the wharf. Our "houses" consisted of natural cave-like formations created by old gnarled driftwood stumps and the long sturdy roots of the trees bending over the bank from above. Our bowers were unique; we carved out little spaces for our individual "homes" amongst these bleached driftwood logs at the back of the beach.

By the hour we would play house,

Above left: 1953 Dulcie Brimacombe at Gambier Harbour.
Above: Dulcie Brimacombe and Penny Smyth – cousins. Courtesy: Dulcie Baxter.

spanking our children when they were naughty, and taking them for controlled swims when they were good. We would throw them in the sea and fetch them in from floating too far away by using a long thin curved "hooky stick." You could see us standing on some stationary log or stone shrieking at our girls if they floated too far away. We would feed them from Pepsi bottle caps placed right over their crayoned mouths, and then we'd put them to bed in rows on shelves made amongst the tree roots. We played this game daily never tiring of it. We jabbered away, all four of us pre-teenage girls; playing out life with our children. What fun!

1954 Gambier Harbour. Back row: Livia Bourne, Jimmy, Barb Brimacombe, Wendy Smyth, Leiani Brimacombe, Lora, Evelyn. Front row: Ewing, Dulcie Brimacombe, Linda, Betty Welbourn. Courtesy: Dulcie Baxter.

As we grew up, we put away childish things and concentrated on two-legged boys. Our favourite past time was rolling barrels on the wooden wharf. These were the empty oil barrels, which the freight boats would leave. Wendy and Norah were the most skilled.

The boys who would tease us were Robbie Forbes, Donnie Crompton, Kenny Crompton, Grevel Larsen, and sometimes a Killam boy who would speed over in his boat from the point. They were forever "jabbing" at us verbally and poking fun, or else giving our barrel a push.

Another past time was lying in the sun, sun tanning. The brownest person at the end of the summer would win, and was considered the most beautiful! Norah was usually the winner.

Delightful Times on Gambier Island – Dulcie Baxter (nee) Brimacombe

When we got too unbearably hot, we would dive into the water and cool off. Ah, those were the days, when there wasn't a care in the world and the sun shone all day long every day at the end of the 1950s.

One incident, I shall never forget. Teens usually get up to some mischief and our gang at Gambier Harbour was no different. My Great Uncle Arthur was an elderly man or at least he seemed so to us. He was also a bit of a grouch, and almost never smiled. He delivered the mail to Gambier Harbour Post Office in those days, and he took his job seriously. His small, old wooden boat with its inboard motor would be moored at the end of the float. It was a most strategic spot and "reserved" for the mail carrier.

Well, as young teenagers are want to do, we all decided to play a prank on him. We untied his precious boat and retied it at another spot on the float. I think too, some of the more naughty ones than I, may have put some salt water in his gas tank. Be that as it may, he was infuriated and it caused him no end of grief. We watched him fussing and fuming from the cracks in the shed where we were hiding.

When word got to my mother, who was his niece, what the young ones had done, she went to work and baked a blackberry pie. All of us had to march down to his little hut on the rocks and apologize. One by one, we had to knock and say, "Sorry." That was my mother for you: a champion of righteousness. I had never seen old Uncle Arthur smile but I did that day. It did the trick, he forgave us, and we never ever touched his blessed boat again! It was a powerful lesson to all of us.

One summer, I remember my older sisters "sneaking" out after they had been summoned home to bed at 9:00 p.m. That hour was our bedtime and one shrill blast on the whistle had

1912 Dulcie Smyth. Courtesy: Dulcie Baxter.

summoned Leiani and Barbara home. I, being younger, was already in bed. I was 'little sister'. I remember to this day them tip-toeing over the floorboards careful to miss that loose one with the awful "squeeeeeek." Mother slept in the back room, Dad was usually in Vancouver with his work. I was in the front living room bed under the window. Tommy and Eugene Killam were usually the two older Killam boys who would frequent our field after hours, waiting to meet the older girls.

One night, Mum called their bluff. She dressed up as a witch in her dark dressing gown and her long hair flowing down. Flashlight in hand, she tip-toed to the front porch and opened the screen door. Well, Tommy must have seen her, this black figure with long flowing hair. He screamed out, *"Great balls of fire!"* in sheer fright, and that saying has been remembered down through the annals of Gambier History. The girls, needless to say, slunk back in with Mother on their heels. "Mrs. B." as Mum was so fondly called by the Killam tribe, made her memorable mark on us that night.

On a dark stormy night in November when Mum and I were living up at Gambier alone (I was 10 years old) there was a sharp knock on the back door. As there was no electricity in those days one would light the coal oil lamps when it got dark. We both went timidly to the door. Two tall men greeted us. One was Ray Crompton, the other Doug Forbes. These strangers were looking for the Hall. They also asked Mother if there was any land for sale around here. She hospitably told them the directions to the Hall, and then said that old Mrs. Shearer might possibly sell them the big flat rocky bluff at the right of the wharf as you are coming up. We used to rent this fabulous waterfront place but the house was quite old. Indeed, when they inquired of this property, a deal was made and the Cromptons and Forbes came to Gambier Harbour to live in 1957, thanks to Mum and me! Their offspring are there to this day.

These vignettes are but glimpses into the delightful times we experienced on Gambier Island.

Memories of Gambier

Jillian Smyth

My earliest and happiest memories of my childhood were of loading up my dad's old wooden boat and heading up to Gambier Harbour for the summer. As the years passed, I always managed to get to Gambier during the summer no matter where I was living during the winter. Even when I was living in New Zealand with my sister, we managed to come all the way across the world to have some summertime at Gambier.

My great-grandparents were some of the first settlers in Gambier Harbour. At the turn of the last century, my great-grandfather, Charles Lett, cleared the land and built a home on what is now known as The Field. Unfortunately, in February 1922, his home burned to the ground and he died as a result of smoke inhalation. His wife, Mary Stewart Lett, lived on for another twenty-two years in a small cottage, that was built for her, and which our family still uses today. Their

Fall 1989 The Barn. Courtesy: Leiani Anthony.

chicken coop/barn was converted into another family cabin and is also still part of a cabin used today and known fondly as The Barn.

When I was 10 years old, my father, Ted Smyth, bought the old Burn's home on the point, which became known as The Rock. We had many happy years there and my dad's bonfires for the children and "Happy Hours" for the adults became legendary. The Rock was later sold, but luckily was re-bought back into the family and now belongs to my cousins, Robin Carver and his daughter, Pamela Thomas.

I was part of a group of children who were younger than the Gang my older sisters and cousins were part of. I tagged along as much as I was allowed and watched in awe the wild activities between the At night, they would all sneak out to Lover's Rock which was the bluff across from the Johnson's place in Gambier Harbour. I would crawl along behind hiding in the

1949 Adults: Mary Brimacombe and Betty Smyth. Children left to right: Leiani, Dulcie, Barbara Brimacombe, Wendy and Penny Smyth. Courtesy: Dulcie Baxter.

long grass to observe. My older sisters, Wendy and Penny Smyth, and my cousins Leiani, Barbie, & Dulcie Brimacombe, as well as Nora and Linda Larsen attracted the boys from far and wide. Many summer romances took place over the years in Gambier Harbour. The girls even perfected their own type of whistle to call one another and spoke in Pig-Latin. What they didn't know was that I became fluent in their Pig-Latin and could understand everything they were trying for me not to hear!

My own group of friends included the Cromptons, Pratts, Lees, and Forbes who arrived on Gambier Island when I was very young. This was the beginning of the "great divide" between the left and right sides of the wharf at Gambier Harbour. Those on the right side supported the "Hall" (as the Anavet's Hall was called) and those on the left side hated the noise and commotion that took place every Saturday night. As we became teenagers, it was not unknown for some of the members of the left side family's off-spring to sneak into the Hall at the peril of being disowned by their families if discovered.

As children, Saturday night was the highlight of the week. We would all gather at the bench on the end of the wharf and watch the numerous boats come in and tie up to the various floats that were there at that time. When all the boaters had headed up to the Hall sometimes the boys would sabotage their boats. When the boaters came back down the wharf (usually quite inebriated), we would watch with amusement as they tried to figure out why their engines would not start or the ropes were all mixed up.

In the summer, all the children would head out after morning chores and not return until dinnertime. After dinner, we would then head down to the wharf. Each family had their own whistle to blow for their children to come home. The Smyth whistle was three blows. Much to my dismay, my whistle always blew the first at night and I always seemed to be the first to have to go home.

The boys in the harbour all had homemade wooden boats, so our summers were spent on the water. We all fished and the annual Fishing Derby was the big event of the summer. One year, my cousin, Dulcie and myself, headed out in our rowboat at dawn to fish for hours ending up at the New Brighton wharf just in time for the weigh-in. All I had was a one-pound red snapper and Dulcie had a quarter pound flounder. Fish were scarce that year and I won first place and Dulcie fourth. We were overjoyed!

The Killam boys had fast boats and mischievous behaviour. It was exciting to see their boats roar around the point and head to the harbour. We always knew some excitement would ensue. One time, they poured gasoline in the ocean off the wharf and threw in a lit match. Flames shot up in the sky and the ocean appeared to be on fire as they roared away in their boats heading back home.

Maud Killam at Gambier Harbour. One summer night in 1968, Jillian Smyth and Maud Killam snuck out to paint this Love Not War and peace sign. Courtesy: Maud Killam.

Maud Killam, Ron Pratt, Greg Crompton and I were the last of our generation left in the summer. Maud and I each had a twelve-foot aluminum boat. We had a great time those last couple of idyllic summers. One night, Maud and I snuck down to the wharf and painted the old shed with a peace sign and the words, Love not War, on the front. I took a picture of

Maud in front of the shed the next day. This was the beginning of the "hippie era" and several draft dodgers made Gambier their home for a few years.

As children, we spent our days swimming, hiking, fishing, boating, and playing card games. Betty Forbes always arranged wonderful card and games parties for us. Our biggest sin was playing Strip Poker in the cave around the corner from the harbour.

On Sundays for several years, Mrs. Crompton senior would hold church services in a little cleared chapel area in the woods up behind the Burton's home. All the children would march up to the woods on Sunday mornings and Mrs. Crompton would sing and her voice would echo through the woods. We would all get candies as we left.

Ned Larsen, who was the headmaster of Shawnigan Lake Boy's School, held school classes in the mornings for his own three children for a couple of summers. My brother and I would attend and my marks soared in school after one summer of this. Ned and his brother, Jack, once dressed up in old swimming costumes and a crowd gathered as the two of them cut down a huge dead maple tree in the middle of The Field.

Over the years, the children of Gambier Harbour became like extended family. It was a place to run free and have numerous summer adventures. Many of us still return to Gambier in the summers now with our own children and grandchildren. Certain legacies have been passed on, such as "Swimming the Distance." Children are not allowed to go down the wharf in Gambier Harbour without a life-jacket until they can swim the distance. This means they have to swim the distance from the beach to the wharf at high tide. Great cheers are still heard around the harbour in the summer when another child has made this rite of passage. After that, comes the jumping off the pier.

Our ties to Gambier lie deep within our souls. My great-grandfather arrived at Gambier Harbour, which was then a remote spot, a hundred years ago and he gave his family and future generations of his family this wonderful legacy for which we are very grateful.

Memories of Summer Time at Grace Harbour

Leiani Anthony

There weren't very many families at Grace Harbour in the late 1940s and fifties; the Brimacombes and Smyths, the Larsens, Killams, and the Houstons were offspring of the earliest pioneers. "Gambier" was primitive, water hauled by bucket from wells, coal-oil lanterns and wood stoves were the norm. We children, fresh from school, were very keen to renew our old acquaintances from the previous summer. As soon as we arrived by Water Taxi from Horseshoe Bay, we took off our city shoes and went barefoot until the day we returned to the city, which was Labour Day.

There were quite a few of us "kids" who hung out together; we ranged in age from about 9 years to 15. We had none of the toys available to youngsters today but we did all have a rowboat of varying size and shape and a few of the boys even had engines for their boats; old six h.p. Johnsons which sputtered and made a terrible noise as the boys did wheelies around the bay. The Killam boys build their own plywood "K" sleek speedboats always painted with a black hull with red and yellow stripes. They would roar around the point and the fun on the dock would begin as everyone tried to outdo each other careening off the top of the wharf. Nothing has changed in that regard as today's teenagers still congregate to while away the summer afternoons.

The game of "Boys" was that unique and somewhat strange name of the game made up by three of us. It consisted of flat pieces of wood, which my sister, Barbie, Linda Larsen and I coloured with crayons. A girl's face on one side, the name and age on the reverse. The name "Boys" was a misnomer as all the coloured pieces

1912 Charles Arthur Lett and Dulcie Smyth. Notice the wood in the tent and the bucket in her hand. Courtesy: Leiani Anthony.

Left: 1954 Leiani Brimacombe, Johnny, Barbara Brimacombe, Ewing Larsen. Notice the metal drum on the right. Drum rolling was a regular pastime for the young people.
Below: 1954 Ed Houston and Leiani Brimacombe. Courtesy: Dulcie Baxter.

of wood were girls! We would fling our bundle of "Boys" into the sea and, perched on a rock at the edge of the beach with long stick in hand, we would precede to scream and yell at our "children" as they floated out to sea and out of reach. If any boy was extremely wayward, it got soundly thrashed with a stick while we, the parents, screamed at them. I don't think it was a reflection of our own upbringing as none of our parents behaved the way we did with our "offspring." The noise was terrible and I pitied our parents and grandparents as they must have heard the din emanating from the beach up to their cottages. The game of "Boys" caught

on, and three of the younger girls established their territory for the game at the other side of the beach. It kept us yelling and screaming for hours and continued for several summers until we finally outgrew it.

Eager to keep us out of mischief, my mother, Mary Brimacombe, encouraged us to pick the little, elusive blackberries that hid amongst the grass. It kept us busy for ages with the promise that Mom would make pies. She baked them in her wood oven and we would set up a little pie stand and sell them. People eagerly awaited the arrival of these home-cooked pies and they sold out instantly at 30¢ each. That would buy us three Cream Sodas at the little Gambier store at the top of the dock. I wonder how many mothers today would go to that extent to keep their children out of mischief.

Looking back, I'm sure all of us would agree that we spent idyllic summers on Gambier. It was a paradise for us children and we forged lifelong relationships with those whom we played with and shared many an adventure with all summer long.

Above: 1957 Bill Hardy. Leiani Brimacombe at 17-years-old. Right: 1954 Ewing Larsen, Leiani Brimacombe, Johnny. Courtesy: Dulcie Baxter.

Those Early Days Shaped Our Lives

Betty Forbes (nee) Crompton

The closing days of 1999, we probably are reflecting on past wonderful memories of our favourite places visited and possibly lived for some time such as the case with me and I would like to share some of them with few.

Mr. Alexander (Frank Lee's father), came to Gambier in the early forties. Frank Lee married Jean, Alexander's daughter. Alexander owned Caravan property and retired here in 1953. Frank told Ray 10 acres were for sale. In early July, Ray Crompton, Mary and Barb Brimacombe came to look at the property. We didn't want a large property but then we saw Mrs. Shearer's property, St. Neots.

The rocks remain at St. Neots. Courtesy: Betty Forbes.

Marg and Ray went up May 24, 1955, cleaned up the old shack, and decided to rent for the summer. We loved Gambier so much that in the fall of 1956 we, the families of Betty and Doug Forbes, Madeleine and Frank Crompton—Ray's dad, Ray and Margaret Crompton, purchased "St. Neots" in Gambier Harbour from Mrs. Shearer. Gus Lund witched the property for a well. It was at that time in rather run down shape and we proceeded to spruce it up and make it liveable and when we were satisfied with the result's my father, Frank, who at that time worked with the Vancouver Parks Board, had the carver of Stanley Park produce a beautiful sign. At the "Christening" ceremony when we were all present, the sign came out of hiding. Imagine our surprise when father hung a sign, which was carved "The Holies." Madeline was the most horrified as the cottage was to be named after her home in England "The Hollies"…The slight error in spelling was soon rectified. So now, when you visit the house on the rocks at the right of the Harbour, take time to look up and remember this old tale.

Our children, Frank and Madeline's grandchildren, were a source of delight—Ken, Barbie, Don Crompton and, Rob and Rick Forbes. In those days, the kids spent the whole summer in bare feet, thongs not having been introduced. They kept busy, as camp kids do, all summer, almost from the day school finished for the summer to Labour Day.

Super Service was developed in the 1960. The older boys, Ken, Rob and Don, went into business, gathering grocery orders from the neighbours each week. They then took the orders in their putt putt boat over to Hopkins landing, filled the orders and on return, deliver them and charged 10% for their efforts. The 10% was just enough to cover the cost of the gas and their candy so the next year they upped it to 15%. This proved a little too difficult for them to figure out so they went back to 10% but the increase their business by picking up laundry on Wednesday to be washed in Gibsons. Super service was passed on to the next age group, Rick Forbes and Wayne Pratt. By this time, they had a motorboat so things were better and they could handle 15%!

Not to be outdone, Barbara Crompton also became an entrepreneur, selling lemonade to the passersby on the wharf. Mr. Graham made root beer for the boys so they cut into her business with their root beer scheme, making it by the dozen, this became a money maker but in retrospect, they drank most of it, making just enough money to buy the ingredients for another batch.

Margaret and I also kept busy because at that time. There was no electricity on the island; we had to pump our own water so we had some pretty interesting days from Monday to Friday when the

1960 Betty Forbes and Frank Lee – Miss GNE.
Courtesy: Dulcie Baxter

daddies arrived to help take over. Imagine the excitement when B.C. Electric decided to modernize Gambier and put electricity into our community. The rain was pelting down when the big event arrived. We decided to have another "Christening" to proclaim the arrival of lights, etc. To do this we commandeered old utensils used for making toast, and countless other objects, and we strung them on a rope and hung them from wall to wall. Then we invited the B.C. Electric man in charge of the project, to come into our cottage and at the signal, cut the rope. To this day, we wonder what those fellows were thinking as they did this chore. The kids thought it was superb!

In order to keep the kids from wanting to go back to the big city for the P.N.E. we came across another idea, and that was to hold our own exhibition, namely the G.N.E. or The Gambier Island Follies. We organized a parade going down to the float, with Grandfather Frank leading it, the participants all in costume, the best of which was Mary Brimacombe, who marched down dressed as Aunt Jemima, mixing a batch of pancake batter in a huge bowl. What a sport! She went the complete distance of the wharf, and when she reached the end, jumped in the water, costume, pancake batter and all. We held a beauty contest for "Miss Gambier Harbour," swimming contests, contests to see who could make the best cake or the best fudge. These Gambier National Exhibitions became a "must" and continued for several

Mid 50s front row - Joley, unknown, Barb, Bobbi. Back row: unknown, Donna Pearson, unknown, Leah Pearson, Diane Robinson. Courtesy: Donna Pearson.

years 'til the teenagers pulled the plug and decided they wanted to see our real exhibition. Probably every Gambier family has funny stories tucked away in their memories. Take the time when we actually put a man on the moon. The only Gambier Harbour resident at that time to own a TV was Mr. Houston who generously offered to bring his TV to the Hollies for us all to watch; another thrilling memory.

We mustn't forget other fun days on Gambier like Mermaid Contest or Greek Day, when women feed grapes to the men, and then there was the dancing. "Friends, Romans, Countryman lend me your wives." Betty, Doug Forbes were roman goddesses riding on the *Madeleine C* (Ray's dad's boat).

In the late fifties, Church in the Woods at the back of Burton's property, was also an inspiration to our youth. We decided that Sunday's should be special, even though we couldn't participate in church services, so we cleared an area in the woods (all the boys in the family helped in this project) arranged logs for a seating. I remember the big cedar with the cross on it. We held Sunday Services, mostly spearheaded by Margaret Crompton who

brought in local talent, including "Nana" Crompton who was the chief soloist. Doug and Betty Forbes gave the sermon. We sang hymns, read from the scriptures, included all family pets, even had a few dogfights, and perhaps the highlight of these regular Sundays was at the end when Nana would hand out candies to all the children and Margaret's mother, Grace Graham, invited the adults to tea and scones. Most of the time, on average, there were 30 people and mostly from Gambier Harbour. Donations would be made and given to the children's fund.

If you happened to be present at three in the afternoon, you might be lucky enough to join the tea party held in Mary Brimacombe's front yard.

Church in the Woods. Sketch by Eliza Killam.

A few quick notes on some of the folks and events I remember:

- Peggy Pratt came in 1959. She moved into Burton's house (Big Tom). In 1960, Ray and Marg Crompton bought this property. Madeleine and Frank moved into Leiani's house (green gables). Frank Rodgers bought the place in the early seventies.
- The house over the dock burned down in 1963.
- On Saturday, the kids would speak out and throw rocks at the drunks coming from the

- Hall. I remember Vi played music at the Hall and she had a diamond in her belly button.
- The fishing in those days was wonderful. Rick and Grev caught lingcod in 5 minutes after dropping a line at the cod hole, in front of Rick's house.
- At the house on the beach, Barbara, Jill Smyth and Anita Lee built miniature houses on the beach and floated our dolls in the water.
- Frank Lee bought Arthur Lett's property (Moxon property) for $500 in 1950.
- The four matrons, Marg and Maureen Crompton, Peggy Pratt and myself, Betty Forbes purchased the seven acres from Major Heath. It became the "Four M" property. Major Heath lives in Bruce McGregor's house.
- May Atchison was beautiful; all the guys loved her.
- Mr. McKinley retired at Gambier.
- Miss Margaret Terfry is Louise Potter's aunt.
- Ray and Doug built a 12-foot speedboat for the kids with an 18 h.p. outboard. They then put a 35 h.p. outboard on and flipped the boat when taking some kids water skiing.
- Pete the horse loved apples.

Elizabeth 10-years-old. Mr. Breacher and Old Pete.
Courtesy: Dulcie Baxter.

I could go on and on but suffice it to say it was a wonderful life. You might wonder what happened to the characters mentioned above... I am proud to tell you, each one of them turned out to be entrepreneurs and now their offspring are doing the same. Hard to say if it was Super Service or the Lemonade Lady that had a hand in this way of life... Whatever, I shall be eternally grateful for the time spent at Gambier Harbour.

Those Early Days Shaped our Lives – Betty Forbes (nee) Crompton.

Gambier Harbour: Our Time Spent There

Betty Forbes (nee) Crompton

My husband and I visited with Bill Errico Jr. at Horseshoe Bay about a year ago, on November 17, 2009. We discussed—mostly—the history of Gambier Harbour and our time spent there. This is a follow-up on that discussion.

We are Rick and Laura's parents, Doug and Betty Forbes, and we spent many years with family in The Hollies, at Gambier. A rather strange thing happened recently—

Doug and I were on a tour bus in the summer and met a lady who turned out to be very interested in Gambier. During the conversation, she told us about her time as a young lady–teenager—holidaying with her Grandmother who owned a cottage in Gambier Harbour, the name of which was "St. Neots." St. Neots, as it turns out, was the cottage our family bought in 1955 from a Mrs. Grace Shearer.

Imagine our surprise and the animated conversation we had. She, Joan Duncan, who now lives in Vancouver, recalls many of the names of people she played with i.e. Smyths, Brimacombe, Larsens, etc, also, she recalled, Mr. Lett, Mrs. Drage…. And the names went on and on! As a result of this meeting we have become friends and Joan has sent us a number of snaps which I have duplicated for you.

Mrs. Shearer sits on the rock in front of St. Neots with a guest. Courtesy: Betty Forbes.

Here is some info regarding Gambier Harbour:

Joan tells us that her grandmother, Mrs. Grace Shearer, purchased St. Neots in 1931 and she paid $950.00… $500.00 in cash and a $450.00 mortgage. That is where we, the families of Forbes and Cromptons came into the picture! My parents, Frank and Madeline Crompton, along with my brother Ray and his wife, Margaret, and with Doug and myself purchased St. Neots from Mrs. Shearer and re-named it, "The Hollies," that was in 1955. The Hollies, is still in the Crompton family, Barbara Crompton and her husband, Garry Peters, are the landlords.

The property that was owned by Major Heath was purchased by four Gambier matrons,

myself, Peggy Pratt, Margaret Crompton, and Maureen Crompton. Because our Christian names all began with the letter "M" we named the seven waterfront acres the "Four M" property, which it is legally named. This property was divided into four and each of the above ladies owns and have built on their section, the latest one being Maureen Crompton. Peggy has Lot #1, Marg has Lot #2 and the third lot is now occupied by Rick and Laura, the fourth and last is Maureen's.

As for the recent history of Gambier Harbour... Our son, Rob and his wife Elaine, bought the home that once belonged to Capt. Larsen, and had it demolished and have rebuilt. History lives on, doesn't it? Who would have thought that in 1955 all this would have become a reality?

Mrs. Shearer with her daughter and son. Courtesy: Betty Forbes. Below: Gambier Harbour. Courtesy: Harper family.

Gambier Island: Our Time Spent There – Betty Forbes (nee) Crompton

Recollections of Grace/Gambier Harbour, Gambier Island

Pat Larsen Interview with Leiani Anthony August 1985

My parents, Thorleif and Irene, came here in 1921. They came over from Bowen Island when I was a very small child, before I can remember. I have seen pictures of my brother and myself, when I was barely walking, at Mount Gardner where we rented a cottage. Of course, they went there because the Eastman's went there. Mac Eastman was a professor at the University and the professors knew one another. I suppose by word of mouth they talked of Mount Gardner and my parents apparently went there. I've heard they would come up on the Union Steamship to Snug Cove and he would have a box of groceries on his shoulder and he would walk to Mount Gardner with the week's groceries.

1913 Gambier Harbour's original dock. Charles Arthur Lett's tent is above the dock. Courtesy: Leiani Anthony.

My mother, in those days, had a bit of money and she thought it would be nice to have a place of their own, so she made a bid on Grafton Bay; she made a bid to buy the whole bay. When she was trying to close this deal, I think the sellers were being slow, so Mother and Father decided to get a rowboat and row over to that island - over there. They rowed across from Mount Gardner and ended up at Grace Harbour, on Gambier Island and of course, even then there was a wharf here because Mr. Charles Lett had seen to it that he had a wharf.

There was a WWI veteran who lived in a small house down there. His name was Mr. Beasley. There were many WWI wrecks. They'd had a pretty bad time and I guess all they wanted was a quiet place where they could bury themselves. Mr. Beasley was probably penniless and he must have been asked if he wanted to sell that place because Mother bought it from him. It was Lot 5. Arthur Lett owned pretty well all the land right around and up the back and everywhere, and presumably, he had sold Beasley the lot and the house, say in 1919. Arthur had been given all that property right to the point, and really, it was select property too. So, Mother bought Lot 5, for not more than two hundred dollars an acre in those days.

There was just the small original house there at the very beginning, and my parents brought some carpenters up here to build the big room on at the side of the house and the big living room. There were two bedrooms at the back and a big veranda across the front and then the sleeping houses were built out of poles for framework and then shakes. Of course, there was the woodshed and the pump house.

I remember one morning, I guess it must have been about 1922-23 or somewhere in there, we woke up to hear people chopping in the next lot, Lot 4. It is Grevel's lot now, a big corner lot. Mother was very upset and said, "What on earth is going on!"

It turned out that Johannsens had purchased Lot 4 from Arthur, presumably, a completely normal transaction, nothing wrong with it, but Mother just wasn't going to have someone building right next to her like that. Good heavens, this was just too much, so they had to do something about that and went over there and started to talk to these people. They said as far as they were concerned one place was as good as another, and she said, "Well, I will buy it." Mother bought all that land, a huge chunk. Anyway, she bought it, and exchanged it for Lot 4 because she didn't want people encroaching on her privacy.

So the Johannsens said, fine, as they got a good deal out of it. They got waterfront and huge lots, beautiful land and that's why they moved over there. They were the old Johannsens, and they had I think three children, two sons and a daughter. They were in their twenties and thirties. In 1923, I was only eight years old so to me, they were adults. They had it cleared and wells dug. They built quite a small house over there, nothing much to it really and it never came to anything. I think the old people either passed away or lost interest in the place. The Johannsens became very successful in the lumber business. They were always very busy, and didn't really have time to develop this land.

Mom now had Lot 4 and 5 and the shock of almost having someone right beside them, living in her lap got her going. She bought all the nine lots at the back block behind her and she probably got that for a hundred an acre but she was buying all the land that bordered hers as insulation. She also bought Lots 6 and 7 and then there were Ted's Lots 8 and 9. Mother wanted to buy the whole thing; she wanted to buy right out to the point. She attempted to buy that from Arthur but he wouldn't sell it. For reasons that I don't know, he wanted to keep those last two lots.

There was another incident that occurred which was typical of the stress that existed amongst various people in those days. There was a very tall fir tree right behind Tolo's house. Now, there was another very similar tree, back in the early days, that was just a little further along, a huge thing, and after we had bought a lot of the property, apparently, Arthur went over there and he felled that huge tree, and you can see some of the remains of it lying on the line. He felled that tree because he wanted to stress where he considered the property line to be. He felled that enormous tree right beside that rock. It crashed down there and he said, "There, now that's it." It wasn't exactly on the line, it was quite away from it, subsequently, I think Arthur sold those two lots to the Burns. Burns and my dad were quite friendly so they made a little deal. They decided that they would move the line over this end and move it the other way at the top end, just take the line and make their rock complete. When the Burns sold to Ted, he gave Ted a letter stating that this arrangement was just a gentleman's agreement, that it had no authority in law or anything like that and the surveyed line had not been changed. That line was subsequently surveyed and put back where was it supposed to be. In my parents declining years they didn't come up anymore so they gave their place to Ned and they gave those two lots to Mollie, where she is now.

The purchase of Raggett's place goes way back. They purchased it from Arthur because that was Arthur's house originally, and I think his father built it for Arthur and his bride, this was when he came back from overseas and that house was sold to my grandfather in 1925.

My grandfather was born in 1856 and that would have made him 69. He retired then, the old age pension started at seventy in those days. He was a seafaring captain and he had been quite successful in business. He originally settled in New Westminster, when my dad was two years of age in 1890. My grandparents where interested in coming up here because in 1925, it was well developed, and their son, my dad, had his place going and it was getting quite nicely established.

Mother still had a little bit of money and she could have people come in and do a lot of things like drains put in as there were just a bunch of skunk cabbages in the back there. This work was all done by the Hjorthoys, they came over from Hope Point. There were a number of sons who came, and they dug these ditches which of course drained the whole property and made it very nice. They dug the wells and I think they built the woodshed and probably the shake buildings that we had as sleeping houses. Dad wasn't a carpenter or anything like that.

So, the grandparents came in 1925 and they spent a good deal of time here because they had a boat which they anchored in Avalon Bay. It was a thirty-six foot built in Steveston. It was a Norwegian name, *Urd*, a very strange name. They could live on it as it was fully equipped. In the wintertime, they would take it into town and tie-up to docks in Coal Harbour and they would live on the boat.

A little later, there was a building in Avalon Bay built by a fellow by the name of Mackenzie; he had a boat called the *May Mac*. He was a bachelor and he built that house. One of his hobbies was to pick up cedar logs, bring them in, and make shakes out of them, so that huge building was made out of shakes. He didn't have anything else to do and I think he did a bit of fishing and odd jobbing around. I think that would have been in the thirties.

Top left: 1925 Ed Houston.
Top right: Late 1940s Avalon Bay Ed Houston.
Bottom: 1920s Dorothy and her brother Ed Houston in one of the first boats in Grace Harbour. Courtesy: Houston family.

Recollections of Grace/Gambier Harbour, Gambier Island – Pat Larsen Interview with Leiani Anthony, 1985

It was quite normal for us to walk over to Avalon. We had a dinghy there and we would row out to the boat and this fellow who owned the property was quite happy with people coming across there because there certainly weren't many people around in those days. It was just a very little trail, these roads were always that way, the way they are now, just grass roads. They were put in originally when this place was surveyed in 1911 and that was all part of Leiani Anthony's great-grandfather's efforts. He saw to it that these roads were put in, and all the right-of-ways and so on; all the roads were in when we first came. There were very lovely roads that weren't messed up with gravel and trucks and that sort of stuff. They were just nice trails. I don't remember anybody doing anything with them particularly.

There was an old character who came out of New Brighton. He was the road man and he was deaf. He used to have squabbles with Arthur all the time and you could hear him screaming and yelling at the top of his voice at Arthur out on the trail. We kids used to think this was great fun to hear this guy screaming and yelling. When you're young, everybody's old and he struck me as being an old man, I don't know whether he was. I remember one time Arthur went so far as to build a fence across the road and this fellow came over and just raised heck about this. Maybe Arthur said the road was on his property, but it was one of those pointless arguments that seemed to come up—one of the crazy things that went on.

I remember when Bill Bailey came. He had a rather colourful past because he was a kind of a colourful person. In the early years of the war, I was on a train going to an army camp in Vernon, I ran into a chap on the train and we started to talk. I don't know how the name, Bill Bailey came up, but this man knew Bailey and he said Bill had quite a life.

When Bill arrived here; he was pretty much a broken man. He'd just survived a hunting accident; one of his heels was shot off. The fellow walking behind him had been careless, the gun had fired, wounding him very badly and really messed up his foot. He was in the hospital for a long time resulting in the loss of his job, his wife, *and* his business—he was a salesman in the coffee business. When he was here, he used to do odd jobs. He limped quite badly and was in a lot of pain.

He had quite a large piece of property behind Johannsen's which was loosely called, "The Bailey Property." He built a small house out of shakes and moved in one of those large kitchen ranges, and made himself very comfortable. He had great plans for the future there, he planted holly trees, which were going to be at the entrance to the big home he was going to build, but it never materialized. The trees grew and they are still there. He was a bit sad in a way, and broken. After he left here, I ran into him in Vancouver on the bus and he told me he was in the flooring business. He lived in Tahsis on the west coast, was married again, and for short time, he and his wife ran some sort of an establishment over there but I understand he got into some sort of difficulty with the town. Small towns are pretty critical about anybody who is unusual and I think the last I heard was they were no longer in Tahsis and I suspect that he's been dead long since. the house that Bill Bailey built that was of any

Top: 1940s Avalon Bay Marie Houston, Nadia Waring, Evelyn.
Right:1925ish Peggy Heay and Dorothy Houston.
Bottom: late 1930s Donald Glass on the steps of the cottage, Maggie, Gramma Houston in front of Helen behind Fred and Edgar. Courtesy: Owen Houston.

Recollections of Grace/Gambier Harbour, Gambier Island – Pat Larsen Interview with Leiani Anthony, 1985

consequence was the one down near the wharf, the Hazlitt's cottage. I'm not sure who he built it for but I was under the impression that he built it for Ormie. Well, Ormie had a store; he had that log place down there as the store originally. When he was on Gambier, he used to do odd jobs and had a singular dislike for Drage, couldn't stand the sight of him.

Francis Drage was another character in his own way, too. Drage was the sort of fellow who wanted to know everything about everybody, and he generally succeeded in finding something on you, and would hold that as a sort of weapon. There was no love lost between those two.

I remember when they arrived, too. I remember quite distinctly, the scow arriving with all kinds of building material and here was this rather portly guy, obviously over-fed. He was not dressed for Gambier life at all. He wore a white shirt and a tie and he looked terribly out of place. All the contents of the scow were unloaded on the wharf and of course, this was the house they were going to build. They built it at its present site (Janet Morgan's now).

He was bankrupt. That was during the later years of the Depression, around 1937. He had been in the real estate business and had got into some difficulty on a real estate deal which had turned out to be a swamp or something like that. He was ruined. He had absolutely nothing, and of course, during the Depression companies and suppliers were always very sensitive about giving credit, you either had cash on the barrel head or you didn't succeed in doing any business. I suspect the property was in Mrs. Drage's name because Mr. Drage would have had it taken from him. He quickly sized this place up after he arrived and of course, he teamed up with Arthur Lett. Arthur, I guess, was sort of a country-boy accosted by the city-man. Arthur did things I don't think he would otherwise have done, such as getting involved in the store and business, generally speaking. So they got going and he bossed his wife around, she never said, boo, anytime. She couldn't really do anything without being domineered by him.

Drage was an opportunist and he played on whatever weaknesses he could find in others, and of course, the "Captain" Drage nonsense that he kept up was an offshoot of the First World War, in which he was a captain. Well of course, Major Heath was another one of the same type, they were so alike and it was strange that they should have both ended up here, and their wives were very meek and mild. I'm sure they must have been very nice women before they were brow-beaten into a sort of submission.

He gave us a lot of trouble.

There was a logging camp here. A man named Jackson had a logging camp at the Killam's present property. It was a full-fledged logging show, with steam donkeys, big machinery and the whole bit. I remember the logging camp very well. You can see some of the trees with the marks around them where they had the cables. They would drag the logs out of there with the steam donkeys but the thing that used to terrify me was the enormous trees they were falling. They had trees there that, I swear, must have been six feet in diameter or maybe even more and they were the original trees. These trees used to crash down and I don't think the people in charge over there wanted a kid running around. That must have been right at the very beginning so I would say that would be in the year 1922 –23, somewhere right in there when they were just cleaning out the logs and they'd come right as far in as the Bailey property. They were taking timber from there and I would say they were probably there for a couple of years, that's about it. I guess there had been some timber left behind, because this was originally logged around the turn of the century and they probably came in there to clean up and take out a lot of the stuff that was left. I can remember there were some shacks but I don't really know for sure.

I would estimate the Killam family came around 1927 –28, somewhere in that period because I remember being on the wharf and these two fellows got off the Union Steamship boat and they turned out to be Lol and Ralph. I didn't know them at the time but these two fellows got off the boat and they asked me if anyone around could take them to some property that was near Snake Island and I said, "Sure, I can take you there." So I took them through the trail to the property that was near Snake Island because my brother, Jack and I used to spend our lives on Snake Island and Twin Island and all along that property. It was funny about the Killams because I took them over and showed them their property. I suppose I'd have been about ten or twelve. They were delighted. The boys had come up to look at the property that had been purchased by their dad, Lawrence Killam, the Manager of the BC Pulp and Paper Co. and the next thing we knew, there was a big barge full of lumber and there was a tow boat called, the *A-1*. I remember it because the *A-1* is running to this day out of Woodfibre, pushing logs around and so on and evidently, the Killams got the *A-1* to pull this barge load of lumber and pulled it into the bay there. There was a gang of men, I don't know how many men there were but there was a real crowd of them and they built the original place there probably in a weekend, soup kitchen setup and the whole bit. There are a number of little houses around there now, including the rather substantial big house, which is occupied by Ralph. The first summer that the Killam family spent here was presumably the summer that this house was being built. The whole Killam family camped at Avalon Bay in tents in that grassy meadow place that's just off the road there. Old Mrs. Killam had a camp kitchen there, and they pitched tents there and they had all the six kids and they spent the summer in Avalon Bay. Kim Killam, a girl was the eldest, then Bill, Lol, Ralph, David and Ruth. Kim died as a result of a heart attack or something like that.

This is where we were because the Shaw property was there at that time. I'm not sure when they came but they certainly were there about the same time as we came here. Magistrate Shaw was a bit of a character and all his family and his in-laws were there. I think the Shaw's owned the property in the forties. There was a family retainer, a Miss Laird, she was a nurse and governess to the children of the family. She had been with them ever since the Shaws were children. They grew up under her care and Miss Laird, and I think her sister used to be with her. There were two of them but I'm not sure whether they were sisters or not. The Shaw's didn't come up very often but the Lairds did and it became known as "Laird's Property" but it didn't belong to them. Ian Shaw owned the property, he was the son of the Magistrate, and it was Ian who sold the property to Bill Killam, much to the annoyance to the rest of the Shaw Clan. A number of them hoped that at sometime in the future, they could come and build a cottage there because the house that was there was falling down. You see in those days people were just too busy working and trying to make a living, the thirties were devastating, they didn't have the money and everything went to rack and ruin.

In the Hebb family, a boy, Malcolm, the eldest was a brilliant scientist, then came Kay,

1920 The Shaw family on Captain Larsen's boat, the URD. *Courtesy: Houston family.*

Rose, Elizabeth, Dorothy and Marian. Booty died of cancer. Elizabeth died tragically of bone cancer.

My whole family has been wiped out by cancer, both my brothers and my dad. I think cancer was the factor that really finished Dad off, in his intestine, he reacted very badly to the operations that he had and he had brain damage as a result. He just disintegrated and died at seventy-two years. Ned died at fifty-eight, Jack died at fifty-three and Ewing at thirty-nine, so that was a bad scene all the way through.

I suspect people decided to come up here because they were looking for summer places. I can remember hiking along Whytecliffe and Fishermen's Cove and all along that waterway there; you could walk all along there and never see a house.

David Killam was my friend. We were of an age and for many, many summers after that I used to practically live at the Killam's. I sort of grew up with them and got to know them very well and in later years, the Killam and Hebb children became interested in each other. Their parents knew each other for many years because they were at U.B.C. Professor Dr. Hebb was Professor of Physics, subsequently Head of the Department of Physics, and Lawrence Killam was originally a Professor of Mechanical Engineering at U.B.C. before he became President of BC Pulp and Paper, and Leiani Anthony's dad was Professor of English. The Faculty people communicated with each other a good deal. 1933 was the lowest ebb of the Depression, absolute bottom, my dad had a job. The fact is that we had food to eat and we lived

Evelyn/Rose and Lol Killam camp under construction around 1959 at Avalon Bay. Courtesy: Bunker Killam.

at home, which we owned, because Mother purchased before the Depression started. Like so many others, she speculated in the stock market during the Roaring Twenties and in October, 1929, the crash occurred and all the money was gone, just like that, overnight. She lost the whole ball of wax. Even though that happened, we as children didn't notice anything special.

The Hebbs had a cottage at Granthams, which they rented each summer. Bill, of course would go tearing off to Granthams every night, they had outboards that were very noisy and they'd go tearing off across the Sound and visit Kay and then come back very late at night, making a lot of noise. I don't think he was terribly popular at Granthams with all the noise he made. These kids got to know each other a little better as time went by. The Hebbs lived on

12th avenue in town and that took them to King Edward High School. Of course all the Killam's were on Laurier and they went to Prince of Wales so they hadn't known each other particularly well until this summer situation came along. I think Evelyn/Rose sort of set her cap for Lol and that eventually developed into more than just a casual acquaintance, although it was a very rocky sort of friendship over a great number of years. In the university years, Bill went to U.B.C. as did Kay and Rose. Kay graduated from U.B.C. and Bill, I think took his degree from McGill. They were subsequently married and moved to New Brunswick, a pulp mill town where Bill took a job there to learn the pulp mill business from the ground up. Lol went to U.B.C. but didn't complete his degree. Evelyn/Rose went to U.B.C. until her final year but didn't graduate because she was more interested in getting married. She wasn't going to go out into the world and make a living, that wasn't the idea. Most of the women didn't go there in order to get a job, that wasn't the lifestyle that was expected of them. Lol learned the pulp mill business at Woodfibre, he worked in every department and learned it thoroughly. He was very successful in sales with the BC Pulp and Paper Company. In subsequent years when the company was sold they left the company and under very favourable terms and were able to start businesses of their own.

1939 Marie, Owen and Edgar Houston. Courtesy: Houston family.

The Houston family were part of the early group. On the other side of the wharf, a

Top: 1950 Ed Houston. The Sea Wolf makes its way into Gambier Harbour.
Bottom:1956 The Gambier Clan. Courtesy: Owen Houston.

Recollections of Grace/Gambier Harbour, Gambier Island – Pat Larsen Interview with Leiani Anthony, 1985

family called Radwell built the first cottage. They built the home and they were the ones who called it after a place in England. St. Neots was its original name, now it's, "The Hollies." Our place was called, "Little Paxton." It was named after Paxton Hall in Britain, I don't really know what it even refers to, I have a sort of recollection that it had something to do with my mother's birthplace, but I'm not absolutely certain. My grandfather's place was called, "Cross Hall Lodge" which is now the Raggett's. I don't know the origins of that name either but it's also from England.

My dad had a way of naming everything, he liked to draw the letters on a piece of paper, colour them black, cut them out and then paste them on a board and put varnish on them. That's how he made his signs. We had everything named. Another thing he did was put the date on it in roman numerals. So I was introduced very early in the game to Roman numerals, he didn't use MCM for 1900, he used MD and 4C for 1900 and then of course the Xs, Vs and Is for the other part, and for instance he even built a wooden box for wood that we'd brought up from the beach. It was open-sided with a little roof over just to keep the rain off it. The wood was to burn in the fireplace and he had all the letters written out. He used to paint everything in brown and the letters were in black, which was one of the oddities of the place. I mean the little cottage that Jack and I slept in was called, "The Coop" and the other sleeping house where our visitors used to sleep was called, "The Pastures," obviously related in some way to a place in England. The woodshed was called, "Jiggs" after the comic strip "Maggie and Jiggs." It was a very famous comic strip; a satire of American life, each unit a story unto itself.

To get back to the houses on that side, the first one was St. Neots, the second was built and occupied by the original owners by the name of Carwardin, the third was occupied by the Hoylands, and then came the Houstons. Old Mr. and Mrs. Houston were the father and mother of Edgar Houston and Dorothy Houston; we used to go over there before Arthur built that home along there. On the shore, they have some large slabs of rock and they were great for bonfires. I can remember as a child going over there all the time for the big bonfires that they had and the marshmallows and wieners and all the goodies that went with that, it holds fond memories, and the Houstons were very hospitable. Dorothy was a particularly fine person, I don't know whether she's still alive or not, but she married a fellow by the name of McLaren, his brother-in-law was Don McLaren, a well-known flyer who tragically drowned on the Bow River. I would say that the Houston house was built in the early twenties. Dorothy was secretary to the owner and manager of Spencer's Stores, she prevailed upon her boss to hire Edgar (her brother) who was not too well-gifted, and he was given a floating job, security man, well-dressed, and helped people who needed information. When Spencer's was sold to Eaton's they tried to fit him into a job that would suit him.

All those houses along there were built roughly at the same time and all about the same age. The other homes that are over there like Lee's (now Moxon's), Cameron's (now McNeight's) are really all come-lately people. I remember when the Cromptons arrived. There was Mrs. Castle and Miss Eva, they were sisters, and they took over the second cottage, (Armstrong's) they were quite a pair these two, widow and the maiden and they didn't look alike or anything, my were they busy, they were interfering into everything.

The store was at the head of the wharf, a very convenient spot, Arthur Lett and Drage put the store together. They ran the store and it was very successful. It was patronized and they had things that people needed. Things like if if if that could work in those days, people were more satisfied with just a few dollars a month, they seemed to be able to get by all right and I think the post office gave them ten dollars a month, but it was Mrs. Castle and Miss Evans who put an end to that. They informed everybody that that lot was a park and that the property map showed it as a reserve. They got lawyers and they made such a fuss over this thing that they had to move the store, lock, stock and barrel up to the other side of the road at the top of the wharf. I suspect it would have been mid 1940s. Anyway, they moved it and the whole uproar ceased and that little piece of land has remained vacant ever since. They accomplished absolutely nothing but created this fuss over some technicality. Anyway, these things seem to have a way of happening.

Of course, there was the Smith place that burnt about 1968, formally Miss Hazlitt's, Mrs. Drage's mother's maiden sister.

I don't think at anytime was it a hardship for anyone with a septic field going down over the bank.

1959 The Group leaving Camp Fircom after a long hike up Mt. Artaban. Back row: left to right – Nora Larsen, Wendy Smyth, Dulcie Brimacombe, Penny Smyth. Front row: left to right – Johnny Lee, Rick Forbes, Grev Larsen. Courtesy: Dulcie Brimacombe.

Mollie Larsen Shares Her Memories

Mollie Larsen Interview with Dodie Errico April 23, 2006

I remember when Mr. Arthur Lett felled a tree, right at the rock along the side of their land. That was how he marked the property line between Ted Smyth's old place and our land. He scared me a little. The Johannsens were past Maisie's on the left hand side; an opened area with a small house and lots of trees. Further down the road toward Killams on the right hand side was the entrance to Mrs. Killam's garden. Mr. Bailey lived in a little hut. He was the gardener for Mrs. Killam. Bill Bailey probably arrived during the depression. He did work for Mrs. Killam. The Burton's house was Ormie's mother's house, and I always knew it as the "Haunted House."

Mr. Larsen, my dad, loved to come to "Camp" in the spring. The first thing he did was cut the grass. First with a scythe, then rake it and then with a push mower. He built trails, put up cedar fencing to protect fruit trees and fenced all around the yard. He kept a cleared area along the fence so the deer could walk around. I remember him tarring a roof on a hot summer day.

Mom spent her time sewing covers for cushions. Their cooling system was crocks sunk in the shaded cool areas. Their weekly menu consisted of:

Friday night – pork sausages
Saturday – roast beef
Sunday – pancakes or something simple

Above left: The day the Larsen kids snuck out of bed at 6:30 a.m. – Tommy, 5, Brenda, 3, Cindy, 2.
Above: 1951 Mary Larsen.
Next page: Left - 1933 Mary Smyth with Beata.
Right – Mrs Larsen with Reata. Courtesy: Dulcie Brimacombe.

Monday – hash

Tuesday – canned everything for the rest of the week until Dad came in on Friday.

Life was about getting up, having breakfast, waiting 1 hour, going to the beach, getting called for lunch, and waiting for another hour before heading back to the beach. I still had to "save" time to listen to radio soap operas.

Just off the property, Dad used to landmark the trees to get his bearings so he could remember where to drop the anchor for the boat. He had a little Briggs and Stratton "engine boat." I learned to row in it.

In 1938 -39, when my brother, Pat married Sheila, their wedding present was the house where Nora's is. It was built by my grandfather and Clem.

Ned Larsen, my older brother, used to torment Mr. Drage by putting a toothpick in the doorbell—the crank kind—so Mr. Drage would come running down to see who it was.

Mr. Burns and his son Conrad lived next door to us. Conrad was home schooled and they raised pigeons. Mr. Burns wrote a couple of children's books. Mr. Burns had one arm. He built the fence with Ned, and Ned was fascinated by Mr. Burns. I remember Mr. Henry Moxon and his children, Elizabeth, Dave and P.J. as well as Henry's sister, Mary Wyness. I went to Hopkins with Mary to celebrate VJ Day.

All part of our carefree days on Gambier Island.

Pacific Coast Militia Rangers Unit 276

W.W. Errico past President PCMR Unit 276

During the Second World War Captain Francis Drage (retired) conceived the idea of forming a Pacific Coast Militia Ranger Unit on Gambier Island. The total population at that time was about fifty. The group that formed the Unit, consisted of men who were either too old or unfit for military service.

They got together to make up a home guard of sorts, to protect Gambier Island from possible Japanese attack. Their duties included military drills, using wooden rifles and airplane spotting. Their numbers were small, but their enthusiasm was substantial. It was from this group of veterans that A.N.A.F. Unit 276 was formed.

A hall was built at Gambier Harbour, by voluntary labour, with lumber supplied by the local sawmill owned by the Anderson brothers, Ed and Jack, on property which had been donated by a local resident.

Owen Houston Certificate of Discharge from the Pacific Coast Militia Rangers, December 31, 1945.
Courtesy: Owen Houston.

The Hall was inappropriately known as the Legion while officially it was the Veterans' Memorial Hall.

Before any event, we had to get the furnace going to heat the place up, and make sure the water was running. Sometimes if we lost the siphon, it would take us about an hour to get it going again. We would have to carry buckets of water to fill the line just to get it going, and we always made sure we put extra water in it.

Captain Drage was the first president. The Unit, with due ceremony, received its charter in 1943 with the first constitution and bylaws adopted in 1948.

Numerous volunteers held the Unit together throughout the years. They looked after the maintenance of the hall, organized Saturday Night dances, pool and billiard games, cribbage and bridge tournaments and of course, the refreshments. Mac McKinley, the perpetual secretary, could always be found sitting in the office working on the books. His claim to fame was being a Veteran of the First World War. He was probably the oldest secretary in the A.N.A.F. organization at that time.

Later, the Unit became more involved in community work by holding the Annual

Children's Christmas Party, and a New Year's Party, which was attended by all on the island. It also hosted such things as the Easter Egg Hunts, annual craft fairs, and acted as a polling station during elections. Probably the highlight of the Unit's career was when it hosted the Provincial Command's Quarterly meeting. I am not sure of the dates, but from all reports, they were a big success, having been catered by the local women and attended by over one hundred delegates.

P.C.M.R. 276 was not big, nor was it rich, but it served the community well. It was a focal point for local social intercourse and gave many a sense of belonging. Please forgive me if the above is not absolutely accurate, as all our records were lost in a disastrous fire, which destroyed the Hall early Easter Sunday morning in 1987. This was after a rip-roaring Saturday Night party, which featured our first live band.

The fire seemed to have taken the wind from our sails as we have not been active since that time. That, and the fact there are only three active members left on the island. To those of us that are still here, we hold those memories dear and we wouldn't have missed those times for any price.

Written in the early 2000s.

1987 Easter morning the Hall burns to the ground. Courtesy: Richard Potter who lives across the road from the Hall.

West Bay

Orville Becker of West Bay

*Right: Orville Becker displays his catch
as the West Bay wharf. Courtesy:
Bryan Becker.
Below: Janet, Bryan, Denise Becker at
Orville Becker's Aunt Helga Kselby's
place. Courtesy: Bryan Becker.*

The Hibberd Family of West Bay

Hibberd Family

In 1941, we bought property on Gambier Island, and it was the "lucky dip" of our lives. Mr. Pearson, a Vancouver neighbour, called our attention to an ad in the paper which read, "For Sale –Gambier Island, waterfront lots of about 1 ½ acres each, $50.00 per lot."

On Easter Monday (Cyril had to work), the children and I went with Mr. & Mrs. Pearson to see this property. We went by Union Steamship to Gambier Harbour – about 2 ½ miles from West Bay where the lots were located. We asked an old timer of the area, Mr. Heay, to show us around. He was less than encouraging. In fact, he insisted that we would never get water on these lots. We couldn't find any property stakes and we were soaked through, for it had rained

1954 West Bay Left to right – Gladys Hibberd with grandson, Rick. Edna Fitchett, a family friend. Joy, Dick's wife. Nora Day and Karen. Cyril Hibberd in back. Jack and Marge, Jack's wife. Courtesy: Hibberd family.

all day. Finally, we sloshed back to Gambier Harbour and caught the boat home; discouraged and miserable.

Cyril listened to our tale of misery with a noticeable lack of sympathy. He was warm, dry and well-fed, and he had an entirely different outlook on the venture. "Now look," he said, "I have been thinking—just what can we lose at that price?" It was the remark that changed the course of history for the Hibberd family. We bought Lot 8 and 9, and embarked on the ever-challenging projects of developing our Gambier property.

Boat days were popular in the community. Throughout the summer, the Union Steamships arrived on Mondays and Thursdays with groceries, supplies, mail and lumber. People gathered at the dock to catch up on the local news and for the kids to swim with their friends. All in all it was exciting summer living. It wasn't all fun and easy going though, for the first well had to be dug, the bush cleared, and the Pearson cabin completed.

The Pearson family cabin on Lot 5 was built first by the two families and we all lived on Lot 9 under tents and tarps for both sleeping and cooking. A daily chore was carrying water up from Whispering Creek near the West Bay wharf. Frank Heay carried our new cook stove on his back from the West Bay dock to our tent location.

1962 Cyril Hibberd, Janet Poore, Gladys Hibberd.
Courtesy: Hibberd family.

We went to Gambier whenever our work allowed, and began to dream of building a home there. In the meantime, the little cabin we built in 1941 served us for wonderful holidays. The cabin just had a tarpaper-over-shiplap roof and, of course, let the rain in to drip into catch-pails making a weird melody of discordant sounds. We even had friends to share the joys and comforts of our little cabin: mice, bats, grouse, bugs and wasps all felt quite at home there.

Myrtle Rae, a pal of mine, brought her three children up. It rained every day throughout that whole week. We played games and talked—all to the accompaniment of the *ping, pang, pong, ping* of the drips. One day we built a log raft on the drips. One day we built a log raft on the beach in the pouring rain. I'm not quite sure why, but it was all fun. Myrtle said she never enjoyed a holiday more.

The children brought their friends often. There were as many as 14 bodies in that 16 by 16 foot cabin sometimes. Dick even brought his scout patrol up one week to practice their cooking. He made rice for them one day, putting two pounds of rice in the pot, and then spent the rest of the day scooping overflow rice into every available pot and pail.

1967 In front of Hibberd house with family and friends. Cyril and Gladys in front.
Courtesy: Hibberd family.

Frank and Peggy Heay lived just up the hill. Frank was a booming man and his property along with ours was a big sorting ground. Log booms were brought by tug from other areas of B. C. West Bay is one of the places on Gambier where they would sort the logs before they were towed to the mills. Sometimes the mills would come to the sorting grounds to choose the logs for their mill depending on whether they were shake, plywood, framing wood—2 by 4's or post and beams, etc. Cat dozers could go right to the beach from our property.

A decision was made in 1949 to build our West Bay home. Mr. Wade and his son helped Dad build the house and it was essentially completed by 1953. Water was a concern until it was discovered that there was a spring under the back corner of the house. Cyril spent many hours chiselling rock to enlarge the flow. The water was hand pumped to the attic to provide gravity feed.

This reminds me of the biggest salvage operation of all; the children and I were swimming and playing down in the bay when we spotted a beautiful cedar log lying above the tide line on the beach. It was four to five feet thick and in perfect condition for roof shakes. So we went home for the crosscut saw and lots of rope. Back at the beach, we proceeded to cut it into twenty-seven inch lengths. Then we rolled these together and rowed that lovely roofing to our beach (we had not yet bought our engine-boat). The last trip was a bit hectic, for the wind came up and our load slewed all over. I remember Jack and I jumping into the water when we reached our beach and shoving and tugging our precious cargo onto the shore. Then by levering and pushing, we rolled them up the beach to the house level. We could hardly wait to tell Daddy when he came about our find. Cyril and I spent an entire summer cutting shakes for the roof.

Lumber, gyproc and bricks were all delivered to the Gambier wharf and ferried around to our beach in West Bay by our little cedar rowboat. To get the lumber we started at the crack of dawn and it took all day to get the lumber to our lot, and that was just one load.

Joy, Dick, Cyril and I tackled the chore of bringing 3,000 bricks (for fireplaces and chimneys) around. Joy was putting the bricks at the edge of the wharf; I was rowing them to our landing; Cyril did the unloading by putting four at a time in a hoist bucket and Dick hoisted them up to the house. All went well until the last load. I had overloaded the boat and found I had less than an inch of free board. The water slopped over the top and I pulled like mad to get to shore and save our precious bricks. Cyril said afterward, "I wasn't worried about my wife, she could swim but the bricks couldn't."

Another time, Cyril had made a raft of the rough lumber, and when we pulled it into our cove, the raft broke up. Cyril and I jumped in and rescued each board and 2 x4; swimming and pushing lumber all over the bay. Thankfully, all the knotty pine and gyproc had to be carried round by the road and up the hill; the boys did much of this heavy carrying.

One day we heard that Port Mellon was dismantling all the old town site, much of which had almost new lumber in it. Since all this material was to be burned in September, we took our little boat with the Briggs & Stratton engine, the seven miles up to salvage some good lumber. The steps in the living room were made of this salvaged lumber. We had also salvaged the big front door from the old Capilano Hotel that, after 40 years, was being torn down to build the parkland around Cleveland Dam.

Rick, our oldest grandson, was born in 1953. Cyril and I worked like Trojans to finish the living room at Gambier so that our little grandson—and his mummy and daddy—could have adequate room. Rick's little footprint is still decipherable in the patio cement. Jack, too, had his initials in the cement of the patio—and well deserved—for he worked very hard on that patio job. The initials were in a corner and eventually had to be covered with new cement as the drains ran under the house there. The boys worked at the hardest jobs at Gambier. Dick did a lot of the landscaping, Jack cut down the big dangerous trees, and Jim put up the clothes pole. All together, we were making it the beautiful place it eventually became.

When we next went to Gambier, we bought a TV and refrigerator (kerosene). Dick had located a lighting plant for us. Also a second well was dug by Jim, Shirley's husband, at the back of the property.

In 1955, Shirl and Jim were there and Jim helped the electrician to wire the house. Jack paid for this installation, fifteen hundred dollars! So, with electric light, fridge and TV, life was more pleasant. We broke up our heavy working days to socialize on the island. The results of our efforts had reached a stage where we could have guests come to stay overnight and for weekends.

Around the beginning of October 1959, Cyril had a heart attack, a coronary. Pains in chest and arms were suspicious, so I ran for Bob Bryan. He, in turn, ran for Dr. Ridley – a dentist who lived nearby. We had no phone but Dr. Ridley managed to flag down a passing tug, and so ordered an ambulance at Horseshoe Bay. Four men carried Cyril on a makeshift stretcher to the Doctor's boat and then to the ambulance, and hospital. He rallied well, but they kept him in hospital for a month. Mildred and Charlie Ridley insisted on my staying with them. They were kindness itself and I shall always be grateful for their consideration. Shirley and Dick found a little house for us in Powell River to rent for three months so that Cyril could convalesce after his illness. We went home to Gambier in March of 1960.

In 1963, the power and the telephone came to the island. Then we were able to get an electric stove, frig, stereo, TV, etc. and get rid of the old lighting plant which hadn't been very satisfactory.

We had fun and adventures, and shared them with many friends. We felt a sense of community at Gambier and built friendships with people around the Bay. These included the Pearsons, Bryans, Becker, Wades, Hancocks, Ridleys, Charlesworths, Hilda Smith, Frank and Peggy Heay, Steeles, Richardsons, Poores, Raglan, Grais', Vic Morris, Twyla and John Graeme, and Earl Butcher.

Each year, it became more and more our beloved home in the wilderness – and our "belonging place."

From "Mother –Her Story" written by Gladys Hibberd and from additional notes supplied by Dick and Joy Hibberd and Shirley Koleszar (nee Hibberd)

Hibberd property – West Bay.
Courtesy: Hibberd family.

The Hibberd Family of West Bay

The Wrigleys Find West Bay

By Bill Wrigley

Above: August 1942 Wilma and Edith Russell.
Top right: 1950 At camp, Bill Wrigley Doing Chores.
Bottom left: 1947 Agnes at camp.
Courtesy: Wrigley family.

Bottom right: 1947 Jean, Betty, Annie, Kay, Bill, Fred.

Mrs. Russell, my mother-in-law, visited friends on Gambier in the 1930s. In 1940, in response to an advertisement, she bought a lot for $50.00. Later she told her neighbour, Wilda Dawson about West Bay. Wilda became interested, spent a summer at New Brighton, and subsequently bought a house and an acre in West Bay.

Mrs. and Mr. Russell tented while they built a small cabin, 8 feet by 10 feet. In 1948, Mr. Russell added another front section.

Bill Wrigley met Wilma in Vancouver and saw Gambier in 1953. He traveled on the *Black Ball* to Gibsons then "Nantons Lane" to New Brighton. The ferry that came in after the *Black Ball*, called the *Langdale Queen* was built in 1903. She was a warship before replacing the *Black Ball*.

Top left: 1952 Wilma Russell and June waiting for "Mac" the Tymac launch from Vancouver.

Top right: 1953 July, West Bay Darrel, Vic, Marie, Wilma, Wilda, Donna, Gwen, Heather, Richie, Bonnie.
Bottom left: 1957 Wilma putting on new roof.
Courtesy: Wrigley family.

Wildlife

Dorothy Poore

Intelligence seems to vary in the avian world. Many grouse used to inhabit our environment, but gradually disappeared. A mother grouse and her chicks would roll around in the dirt in the vegetable garden and waddle across the lawn often in front of the lawn mower.

Robins, on the other hand, would watch while we dug dirt, and hop down to find the worms in the tilled soil. The Robins sang a distinctive song each year as they saluted the human digger. One time its cadence was, "Won't you come and dig me worms?"

In the early forties, a crippled raven hopped from tree to tree along the trail, accompanying us, and trying to take part in the conversations of the humans.

Herkimer, a seagull, adopted my father, Charlie Poore in the 1950s. Charlie and a young cousin had been fishing in West Bay. They pulled their dinghy up on the rocks, leaving their baited hooks in the boat while

A lone Grouse drops by for a visit.
Right: Herkimer perches in the Douglas fir tree, watching for Charlie to come home. (At the point of the arrow.) Courtesy: Dorothy Poore.

they came in for lunch. On returning to the boat, they found one of the lines had been pulled out to sea. Herkimer had swallowed the bait, hook and all! Charlie gently reeled the line in and cut the leader to release Herkimer, hoping that Herkimer's digestive juices would dissolve the hook and leader—apparently, they did.

From that time on, Herkimer would wait at the West Bay wharf every Friday night to welcome Charlie home, and would perch on the

Douglas fir tree in front of the house on Saturday mornings to wait for Charlie to go fishing. Herkimer would keep a discreet 20 feet behind the boat as Charlie rowed back and forth along the West Bay shore.

Charlie Poore fishing at West Bay. Courtesy: Dorothy Poore.

As the years went by, Herkimer took the great interest in our family, prompting us to buy a yellow plastic dog-dish in which we put food scraps, and then place it out on the rock slope beside our dining room window. Herkimer would respond to our call of, "Here, Herk!" He would land with a thud on our neighbour's roof before hopping down to his dinner. We watched him from our dining room, which was only fair, as he sat in the fir tree watching us at every meal in our dining room.

When we built a rumpus room behind the rock slope next to the house, Herkimer did a remarkable double take when he saw another seagull in the top window. Then he strutted down the slope to discover another gull in the lower window and dramatically repeated his performance!

Herkimer's mate, Matilda, did not join in the fishing expeditions, but would sit on a pole and watch the proceedings. After a while, their

1956 Charlie and Netta Poore, Janet. Courtesy: Dorothy Poore.

son, Murgatroyd, would emulate his dad as much as possible, and follow the fishermen about 20 feet behind. Charlie with Herkimer and Murgatroyd would travel back and forth from the wharf to the point beyond Black's Beach. Murgatroyd's mate, Eloise, emulated Matilda as an offshoot shore watcher.

After some years, Herkimer developed arthritis in his left leg. He would stand on his right leg in his tree, and in response to, "Poor Herky," he would shake his sore foot.

In later years we were plagued by Canada geese who made the front slope hazardous and unpleasant with their droppings, and who were very territorial around their nesting places.

A few years later, a large doe was charmed by my mother's violin. This delicate animal would recline, with their legs tucked under her, facing the dining room window where Mother was practicing. One day, Mother glanced out to see the doe nudging her two young off-spring towards the

1960s West Bay. Charlie, Dorothy's father splitting up the tree in pieces for firewood to get it off the roof of the house. Courtesy: Dorothy Poore.

house, seeming to say, "See here's the lady I was telling you about." The deer twins loved to circle our fence. They would respond to human conversation.

As they grew older, the female, Doey, was more skittish that her brother, Bucky. When I was working outside the fence at the back one day, the two deer were munching close by. A sound made Doey jump and move away, that Bucky remained by my side, lifting his head to watch the meter-reader come through the back gate. I said to Bucky, "It's okay, it's only the meter-man." The facial expression on the meter-reader's face was priceless!

The squirrels were amusing, and annoying. One, named Alvin, used to hang around our neighbourhood, Herb Smith, who kept peanuts in a shirt pocket. Alvin would wait for him to sit down, and then run up his leg, and across his shoulders to help himself to peanuts out of Herb's pocket.

Above: 1960s Dorothy Poore help clean up after the tree come down in a windstorm.
Right: Duncan and Mary Notman, Dorothy Poore in New Brighton. Courtesy: Dorothy Poore.

Either Alvin or one of his relatives enjoyed our Greengage plum tree, running up to sit on a branch to spit out the fruit and hold the seed in his cheeks until his face puffed out. Then he would depart to deposit his seeds in a safe place, and then come back for more. This prompted Dad to plant two hazelnut trees for the squirrels.

In the early days, skinny-dipping at night was a favourite pastime. Sometimes, a passing tug boat with flash a search light in our direction, causing a lot of splashing. On a couple of occasions, we were amazed to find a seal swimming with us.

In more recent years, a young friend was staying with us, and decided to swim across the mouth of West Bay towards Carmelo Point. I was upset because I didn't think he realized that many boats came in and out of the bay. However, he was not hit by a boat, but was thoroughly frightened by a seal popping up beside him!

Another time, we had a visitor from Australia who was fascinated by the huge log barges that came in the bay to dump their logs. We were sitting on the bluff, being attacked by mosquitoes, as the barge began to tip. I suggested that she go up to the house to

watch the dump while I stayed down front to take a picture. I was very fortunate to snap the shutter, (1) as it tipped, and (two) as it bounced back, and (3) just in front of me, a seal popped up, looked around, and seemed to say, "What was that?"

Dorothy Poore left Gambier Island in 2001.

Mrs. Mildred Ridley (nee) Thomson

From an interview with Leiani Anthony, June 11, 1986

When I first came up to Gambier Island, it was 1903, and I was four years old. I'm 87 now.

We rode to the island in a little steamboat and we'd stop and pick up bark and bits of wood to get the steam going. It took us a long time to get to Gambier from Vancouver. We went right to the very end of Long Bay where we met an old man by the name of Mr. Arthur R. Davies. He had the most beautiful farm I had ever seen in my life. He had every kind of fruit, every kind of vegetable, everything you could ever imagine and in the summertime, he

would row to Vancouver with his produce; if you can imagine that.

My dad, Charlie Thomson was a great friend of Mr. Massey. The two of them dealt with old Mr. Davies for the following year. He let us tent on part of his property, which is where Camp Artaban is now. Mr. Davies had a big, big farm and he had a big family. His son bought property in Snug Cove on Bowen Island and had the store there for many years, right where the ferry docks.

Approximately 1915 The Thomson's whitewashed cabin at Massey Point. Courtesy: Betty Ridley.

The next year we came up, we just camped there for two months. By this time Mr. Massey had, instead of the steam boat, got a boat with a little gasoline engine and the name of the boat was *The Swiftsure*. Every year we went up to the island. At first, we left from Coal Harbour and then later on from the Rowing Club.

Both Mr. Massey and my dad were great on the outdoor life. They came to Vancouver in about 1885 or 86 from Toronto.

I don't know how we ever got started going up there. The first year we were in tents, the next year we went up, there was an old boathouse right up on the beach, so they fixed that up and we used that as a camp. Dad and Mr. Massey used to go fishing all over and to all the different spots. And oh, we used to have the grandest time as children because this old Mr. Davies had cows and sheep, and he had everything, it was terrific.

1910 Massey Property. Mildred's mother – Hannah Thomson - on the right and below is Grandmother. Courtesy: Betty Ridley.

In 1909, Mr. Massey, who had a lot more money than my dad, bought what they now call, Massey Cove, that's between Centre Bay and West Bay, it's one hundred and sixty acres. He bought it from an old fellow who was going to have a farm there. There were all kinds of trees, fruit trees and everything else. It's where the Winrams are now. They bought it from Masseys. They built a house, a cabin in the orchard; you have to go up a little hill to get to it. The loggers had been in there before the Masseys and they had left a great big old bunkhouse. Dad was going to put up a tent and my mother said, 'Well, why can't we use this old bunkhouse?' So we took the bunkhouse. It was a great big long building with great high ceilings and they whitewashed it inside and out. My dad put a rustic veranda on it, and then added a lean-to kitchen. We divided this great big space off by using sheets strung on wires. Part of it was the bedrooms; we had four because there were four kids, my grandmother, and my mother and father. The rest was living room and the lean-to kitchen. Oh, it was just so lovely. We just thought it was the only place in the world. I didn't want to ever go anywhere else and you know the day school was out, we were up there. We'd have a great big ham and a slab of bacon hanging behind the stove. We stayed up there and Dad would come up every Friday.

At that time, at the very beginning, there were people coming up in their boats and Dad would come up with them. Later on, there was a boat called, *The Bebe*. It would come from Vancouver. Dad brought everything we needed. The second year we were up there Mr. Massey bought a boat called, *The Limit*, which was the fastest boat in Vancouver; he bought it from Alfie LePage who made boats. Alfie LePage built this boat and won the race to Alaska and back. We used to pass every boat going up. We did that until 1915, when my mother took sick and we went up that year but the next year she couldn't go. She died in 1917. Dad loved it up there, but when we didn't go up Mr. and Mrs. Massey didn't go up either. My dad, my sister and I would go up there for a couple of weeks.

Mrs. Ridley (nee) Thomson – Interview with Leiani Anthony 1986

Above: Mid 1920s Massey family launch. Courtesy: Betty Ridley.
Below: 1935 PNEUMA owned by John Howard Everett Murray. Courtesy: Murray family.

In those days, Mr. and Mrs. Heay lived at the top of the hill. Mr. Heay and his mother, Mrs. Heay was mother's help. Then there was Mrs. Angus and her two sons. Next door to the Angus' were the Rosses, they had the Neen's place, then next to them, there was the Blacks and then next to Blacks was old Joe Mitchell, he was a character, they were all characters.

Joe Mitchell's mother died and he and his brother, Redge and his sister, Billie lived with their father in West Bay; how they got there, I don't know. They said Joe Mitchell's father was part Maori. Joe Mitchell was born on the island and his sister died on the island. When Joe and Redge were little kids, they used to row over from their place into Massey's.

We had a bonfire every night, and we'd walk on the coals. We had great big empty gasoline tins with the tops taken off and a handle put through them. We'd fill one of these tins with clams and put it on the fire. Everyone had cups of butter and they'd dip the clams in the butter. We'd do that every single night.

Later on, the Angus', I think they rented to Judge Harper, the Angus' were in West Bay first and then they bought the place over in New Brighton. If you come down into Long Bay, the first people you'd meet were people by the name of Fawcett, they were in Centre Bay and they had a very nice place there. We used to row over and get our eggs. Across the Bay were the Murrays, they were in the plumbing business and one of the boys was a great hockey player. They had a big, big family and lived there for years, all year round. I think it's the Yacht Club now. The Murrays and the Fawcetts were there in 1910 and there was an old fellow called Olaffson, he lived on Alexander Island - the little island in Centre Bay. Massey's property went right into Centre Bay, about half way down, the Winrams own it now.

When you come out of Massey Cove and go across to go in to Centre Bay, away up the side hill, there are the diggings of a copper mine. They did that long before 1910 because it was there when we arrived. When we were at Massey's, Dad and Mr. Massey dug a well, of course they didn't know anything about digging wells and they lined it with cedar. I'm telling you, there was this great big well, we had to wash our dishes in the water, but we couldn't drink it. I can still smell it. So every day we had to go with our great big gasoline tins with handles and we'd have to row from Massey Cove into West Bay. Just about across from where Hibberds are, there's another mine and of course it was abandoned, but it was full of the most beautiful water. We'd go every single day, with about ten of these gasoline tins and get our drinking water.

I think all of these properties were pre-empted. I know the Heays pre-empted theirs and so did Mr. Davies. They'd get it from the Crown for nothing.

Arthur Lett used to come down when we were in West Bay. He'd row down and he'd get our grocery order and then he'd come back, and oh, we just used to look forward to his coming down, he was always so nice. Some other people were Hope and Farmer, now, they must have pre-empted a big spot because they had the park, and they had where Grais' are. They made a sub-division. That's Mrs. Ellis's father. We'd been up at Massey's about two years, which was

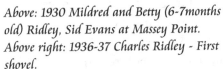

Above: 1930 Mildred and Betty (6-7months old) Ridley, Sid Evans at Massey Point.
Above right: 1936-37 Charles Ridley - First shovel.
Below: 1937 House under construction.
Courtesy: Betty Ridley.

1910, about two years later we were up for the summer and right there on Grais' Point a sign read "Gambier Island Park." It was going to be a park. They subdivided and sold those places cheap, thirty five to forty five dollars.

I remember that awful night at Bert King's mother and father's place halfway up the road in 1915. My mother had gone into town with my dad because she had been operated on for cancer, and she'd gone in to see the doctor, that's why I know it was 1915. We were all sitting around and old Mr. Heay came around in his boat to get Mr. Massey, he wanted him to come over to West Bay because there was trouble. He hitched up the boat and left. So Harold Massey, one of the boys, said to me, 'How about taking the canoe?'

It was a beautiful night and we headed over and just as we got to *The Limit*, which was right near our house is now in the bay, I heard Mr. Massey say, "My God, my God!" Bert King's mother and two schoolteachers were in swimming, and Bert and his sister were just tiny little kids and Mr. Heay came down and found these two little kids wandering around and they said they were looking for their mother. Instead of him coming right away for help, and going to Joe Mitchell because he was one of the ones who was up there at that time, he started looking in the woods for them and couldn't find them. So he came over to get Mr. Massey to see if they had been in swimming. Bert's mother was pregnant at the time.

When the tide would go out there used to be quite a little gulley and then there would be a patch of sand, and apparently, she, Mrs. King, got up on this sand and she couldn't swim and the tide came in, the two girls could swim but the whole three died.

They just lay the bodies on top of *The Limit* and in the morning, they went to the mainland, and as they were going into town, my dad and mother were coming out on the *Bebe.* Mother said, "If *The Limit* is coming into town, there's something wrong." Bert's father, Mr. King raised him, but Bert didn't come up to the island for a long, long time.

Then years later, there was Orville Becker. Orville Becker's wife, it was a cabin away up in the bush somewhere, but anyway this old girl had bought this cabin I remember she came down and she said, "There something's wrong. There's been a murder." Charlie and Mr. Heay went up and someone had shot a deer and had dismantled it.

Then there was Judge Clements, he built a beautiful log cabin right in West Bay about 1911-12. I remember Mrs. Massey and my mother going over to call on Mrs. Clement and they had white gauze on, if you can imagine how long ago that was. Every single log in that cabin was the same size. It was a beautiful cabin.

After I got married to Charles Ridley, we bought our property right in West Bay but we didn't do anything with it, we just bought it because Charlie wanted a place here. He bought it from Mr. Hope. It was supposed to be the park but tough times were coming along, and Mr. Farmer was away in England and Mr. Hope was a patient of my husband's and Charlie was saying he wanted some property and I guess Mr. Hope must have been hard up or something, because he sold a piece of property to Charlie. We bought that corner, a little over an acre, and

Above: 1937 Head of West Bay. Stayed in this cabin while they were building their own cabin. It was one was on tug property.
Left: 1935-37 Mildred Ridley in centre, rowing.
Right: 1935-37 Mildred Ridley at right , Jack Ridley in center of boat. Courtesy: Betty Ridley.

then later on we bought the one up above, and the one on the creek and there was always the most awful trouble with stakes. People were always moving stakes, moving them just where they wanted them and some of them are still not right. There was so much feuding up there, the Heays and the Mitchells would have nothing to do with one another, and then the Heays and the Blacks would have nothing to do with each other.

I can remember when everyone came, I remember when the Hibberds and the Pearsons came, it was the most terrible rainy day you ever saw in all your life and they all walked over from New Brighton and they were like drowned rats so, we brought them in.

When we were in Long Bay there was logging; a fellow by the name of Hudson. We used to ride up with the horses and get pink lemonade at the cookhouse, that would be before 1910 and they were logging it all by hand, using horses, and skidding it down to the water.

One year, Charlie and I went up to Gambier for two weeks with our children, Betty and Jack, and we discovered that people had torn down our old place to use for firewood in the fireplace at Massey's place. When we were told they were going to re-log that property and the "show" was coming right down past the house, Charlie said, "We'll go over and get a place in West Bay."

So Old Mr. Heay said, "Why don't you try and get the log cabin, they were just using it for the booming grounds down there." So, Charlie contacted the people at Straits Towing Co. They said, sure we could have it but they wouldn't rent it to us because if they did they'd have to give us access to the beach. We moved everything over: stove and beds, and everything from our place at Masseys and we were there for about four years. This is the log cabin at the head of West Bay that the Clements built. One year, when we were cleaning it up for the summer, a man came to the door, he was one of the head men in Straits Towing and he had decided he was going to have it.

Charlie said, "To Hell with it, we'll build a place of our own." We got old Mitchell to come over and cut down the beautiful little trees that were around and build the house as close to the wharf as we could because it was convenient and of course, in those days, the old *Lady Rose* used to come up, and she brought all our lumber up. It was the 1st of July 1938, and we had packed all day. Once we got started building that house, we added on and tore down, and oh my goodness. It's the little green cottage at the head of the West Bay wharf.

That wharf was put in so many different times. In the first place there used to be a floating wharf between Grais' and Hibberd's, in that little cove. We'd go up that road and down here and if the tide was in, we'd have to go in the row boat to get out to the wharf. We had a floating wharf in West Bay for a long time, too.

I remember my husband, he used to bring people up, he had one of the first Turner boats, and then some of the taxis in Horseshoe Bay got them because our little boat was so sturdy and good in the water.

Mrs. Ridley (nee) Thomson – Interview with Leiani Anthony 1986

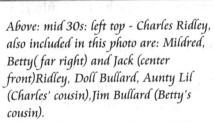

Above: mid 30s: left top - Charles Ridley, also included in this photo are: Mildred, Betty(far right) and Jack (center front)Ridley, Doll Bullard, Aunty Lil (Charles' cousin),Jim Bullard (Betty's cousin).
Above right: 1937 Friend, Betty Ridley.
Lower right: 1940 Mildred and the kids.
Courtesy: Betty Ridley.

Leiani Anthony:
Did you know my grandmother, Dulcie Smyth?

Mrs. Ridley:
Yes, sure and Charlie Smyth. My kids used to go down to visit Dulcie and Charlie Smyth, and one time he sent me a bouquet of hydrangeas. When they wilted, I took one and stuck it in the ground and I bet if I got one, I got ten or fifteen from that one cutting. I also grew some of the most beautiful red roses from a bush Mrs. Drage gave me.

Leiani Anthony:
My grandparents used to have a well outside the house and I remember the bushes of hydrangeas were all around the well. Years ago, the well got filled in, and I don't know what ever happened to the hydrangeas but I remember them as a child.

Mrs. Ridley:
We used to pick berries when we walked over to the store; it was a treat. Arthur Lett had the store in the first place and then Mrs. Drage, and then Bradbury.

Mr. Bradbury first came up to Gambier in a rowboat. He camped on Massey Point but Mr. Massey put him off because he was just a soldier, so he went over there to Grace Harbour and got in with the Drages, and he's been there ever since. He was the kindest man.

When we were at Massey's there used to be a trail right through from our house to the very end of West Bay. Years and years ago, in the 1900s, there used to be a hotel there. This is before we ever went over to West Bay. There are also remains of the old mill; at least

1945 Charles Ridley and his good old fishing. Courtesy: Betty Ridley.

Mrs. Ridley (nee) Thomson – Interview with Leiani Anthony 1986

Top left: 1941 Betty Ridley's cousin Beverly dressed for a costume party.
Bottom left: 1941 Frank Heay dressed up for a costume party.
Above: 1945 the Gopher sailboat belonged to Betty and Jack Ridley.
Courtesy: Betty Ridley.

some of the posts are still there.

They logged over on our side and we'd see the logs coming down into the water. When we were over in Massey's, the Japanese logged and they brought their logs right down past where we are now and they had their tables and everything there, and as a matter of fact when we built our house, the old shed had been a stable or something. We used to sleep in it while we built our house. All down our property, along the back, there are all kinds of cascara trees which the Japanese planted. We found all kinds of little Saki bottles and opium bottles, different things like that. The Japanese had come from the lower mainland. They left after they finished their logging operations. Over the years, there have been many loggers.

The Bartells were here for quite a long time too, and then the Poores.

The fishing used to be much better. My dad, Charlie would fish right out in front of our place and down past Poore's. I used to get up every morning with Charlie at about 4:30p.m. and we'd go out. The logs in West Bay were covered with seals. He'd go fishing every day and there were all kinds of fish and then later on Charlie would go to Lasqueti Island and we'd have a whole great big washtub full of fish. Everybody could take all they wanted and Mrs. Heay used to can them for everybody. She was awfully good to us. Those days are gone now I guess, but the crab, we never used to have crabs here years ago.

I remember, only one time when we were over at Massey's, a great big whale came in, it must have been sixty feet long, it was as long as *The Limit*, which was a sixty foot boat and we were afraid it was going to do something to the boat. Then one night when Charlie and I were looking out from our place, the whales came right into the bay in there. I used to keep track of the fish and every year they'd come up the creek within two days of the last year's date.

Life was not always perfect. Mrs. Heay planted daffodils right from her gate to New Brighton and somebody dug them all out, and she planted all the daffodils down on our point. The fellow that owned the subdivision planted all kinds of trees, he went to town and came back, and all his trees were gone. They were over in Joe Mitchell's, Black's, and Massey's, so he gave up. One of those trees was right out on the point, it was a plum tree and every year it would produce beautiful big yellow plums. Mrs. Heay would go down and pick the plums but often somebody had picked the plums first and she was always trying to catch who it was as she'd go and fertilize the tree. One day she went down to pick the plums and they were all picked so she was so mad she went up and got an axe and cut the tree down! Now the poor old tree comes up and blossoms every year but there are never any plums on it. At one time, she had every kind of fruit tree you could ever imagine and she used to have a cow, too.

Everything was lovely in those days. We had better service then than we do now; the boat came in every week. First of all, it was the *Britannia*, then the *Lady Rose*, and then the *Tymac* used to come in on Friday night. We had such good service, and Mr. Heay was the postman. Everybody had to be on the dock, the mail bag would go to Mr. Heay, and he'd yell

Above: 1947 Bill Wright and Jack Ridley. This house was hauled to the Ridley property in West Bay and taken up on the beach.
Below: 1947 The building on the left appears to be the same house as in the above photo. Courtesy: Betty Ridley.

out your name and pass you your mail, I think it was after 1938.

Leiani Anthony:
You'll be glad to know that the Newton-Masons who bought the Heay's place love it up there and they're good stewards of their little piece. They're there most of the time year round. Ella has been going around with the Grais boy now for two years.

Mrs. Ridley:
I remember the church group that came into West Bay. I don't remember the name of it, no church, it was a cult. When they first came up there, the man, he called himself, Pope John, would bring all these people who were just out of jail and people on dope. They built the camp with all the people he brought up. They were just terrible, they were so bad and we were always afraid they'd set a fire and Charlie wouldn't let them go up on the point, and we got a sign up.

It was after our kids were married, I think it was the early sixties and he could give you a degree for anything. Charlie had a patient who was a reporter for *The Vancouver Sun* and Charlie exposed this guy because he was dreadful. He had this old boat and he had all these poor people and he was just getting all their money, they'd sell their souls to give it to this "church" and they had a big monastery out in Burnaby. He used to bring these people up in this old boat and it was the worst old tub, it had cement in the bottom. Anyway, this one day it was absolutely crowded, and it was a terribly stormy day, and he took off with all these people and he finally had to put down into Long Bay for shelter.

His wife, she was an artist and eventually divorced him. Apparently, they were married up in Kamloops on top of the mountain.

The Higgins boy owns this now and the Cocos are next door. There was a fellow who came up and he said to Charlie, "Did you hear the commotion? Were your ears burning?" This "pope" used to come down with a big cross on with two aides on each side, he had a sort of robe on and apparently somebody had moved this "pope's" float and he went swearing about.

Charlie said, "Does that cross mean anything to you? Because you're not using it very well with the language that I hear you're using, it's not very good." Charlie was so fed up and at one time that he offered to sell all our property, the dock and the point for sixteen thousand dollars and the boat thrown in with it.

But, anyway, the "pope" said, "I have quite all I need, the Lord will provide."

We had a fire and of course I had no way of knowing, because Betty and I were in the living room sitting by the fireplace and Charlie and Jack were out on the veranda. When all of a sudden our lights went out, just like that, so Charlie went out to the shed where we had a machine to make our own light. There wasn't a breath of wind and I'm telling you I was just petrified because the shed was so close to our house and as a matter of fact, it shocked Mrs.

Left 1948 The Barge Bill Docksteder, Marge Bullard, Bev Charlesworth, Jack Ridley, Don Climley, Betty Ridley, Bill Wright, Evan Boston, Al Jordon. Below left: Fireplace at Doc Ridley's cabin at West Bay.

Right: 1947 Auntie Peg Charlesworth (Mildred' sister), Betty Ridley, Aunt Doley Bullard (Charlie's sister), Marge Bullard (Doll's daughter/Betty's cousin). Photos courtesy: Betty Ridley.

Heay so much when she saw the blaze, and thought it was our house, she got shingles and I think she had shingles for years. She was covered with them. I thought if that fire starts burning up the hill all the people down in West Bay will be caught. So the first thing I did was I ran up that road to tell everybody that there was a fire and then of course Mr. Heay started a bucket brigade, and there was a can of gasoline in the shed and a machine, I don't know how we ever got it out. It was an absolute miracle.

Mrs. Mildred Ridley was born Mildred Rhonda Thomson in 1899 to Charlie and Hannah Thomson. She later married Doctor Charles Hubert Ridley.

Above: 1948 Frank Heay waiting on the dock to be picked up by the tug boat.
Left: Mildred, friend, Charles Ridley.
Courtesy: Betty Ridley.

Mrs. Ridley (nee) Thomson – Interview with Leiani Anthony 1986

Charlie and Mildred Ridley, West Bay, Gambier Island

Betty Bestwick (nee) Ridley 2010

Charlie and Mildred Ridley bought their first property in West Bay from British Columbia in the late 1920s, a few years after they were married. This property was located beside the creek bridge, directly across the road from where the current West Bay wharf ends.

1925 Charles and Mildred Ridley. Courtesy: Betty Ridley.

Charlie and Mildred were drawn to Gambier as a result of Mildred's family connection to West Bay which dated back to the early 1900s. As a child, Mildred had come to West Bay to picnic and camp staying on property owned by the Massey family, a large tract of property that extended from Centre Bay to West Bay. Today this property is still together, and is now owned by the Sauder family. Mildred's family, the Thomsons, was close friends of the Masseys, and they had their own cabin on the property. This was a simple whitewashed shelter with fabric partitions for walls. For the winter, the structure was emptied and items such as dishes were buried so they would not be vandalized. A copper mine was located close to the property.

Although they owned property, Charlie and Mildred initially stayed on the Massey property with their two young children, Betty and Jack. Subsequently, they also stayed in a log cabin that belonged to Straits Towing situated on a point further down into West Bay from 1933-1936. When the cabin was reclaimed for Straits Towing, the Ridleys started to build on their own property. The main cabin and out buildings exist today in much of their original form. A fire in the woodshed threatened the main building but was brought under control with a neighbourhood bucket brigade.

From early on, Mildred and the children stayed at Gambier for long stretches in the warmer months. Charlie commuted every weekend in his own boat, and later added a midweek one-night commute in the summer. He started off with an old fish boat and finished with a well-loved and seaworthy clinker-built Turner Sea Skiff. Charlie and his boat were called on to help people stuck in rough waters that no one else wanted to tackle.

I fondly remember the early years at Gambier in the 1930s and 40s. Early "neighbours" to the Ridleys in West Bay were the Black, Heay and Bryan families, who were all permanent residents. The Black family owned a large strip of waterfront from Gambier Harbour towards West Bay. Mr. Bryan was around the point further down into West Bay. The Heays were very good friends and lived just up the hill on the road towards New Brighton. Their property included an apple orchard with the best yellow transparent apples for Mildred's applesauce and countless apple pies, and a beautiful flower garden. Frank Heay managed the

Above: 1937 Charles Ridley.
Right: 1945 Ned Larsen, Owen Houston, Jack Ridley,
Jack Hibberd, Betty, Marge, Margaret Savage.
Courtesy: Betty Ridley.

log booms, which were a constant fixture in West Bay. At any time of day or night when the tugboats were approaching and sounded their whistle, Mr. Heay would run to be picked-up to direct the drop-off or pick-up of log booms.

Mr. Heay also had the pleasure of officially handing out the mail in the years when the Union Steamship boat made a stop to drop off mail, grocery orders, other supplies and passengers. Most everyone gathered on the West Bay Government dock for this weekly ritual. Fairly soon after acquiring their first piece of property, the Ridleys purchased additional lots adjoining their property. The waterfront point property was purchased from Mr. Heay and eventually a small cottage was built on the upper point. This was damaged shortly after in "Hurricane Frieda" in 1962. It was then rebuilt on the main camp lot as a

Charlie and Mildred Ridley, West Bay, Gambier Island – Betty Bestwick (nee) Ridley

guest cottage. In the 1970s, a second family cabin was built on the lower point lot, close to where a boathouse had once been located.

Long lazy summers include memories of lots of people always being around. There were many families with children around West Bay, and Charlie and Mildred welcomed an endless stream of extended family and friends to stay with them. For the children, there was a sense of simple freedom: wandering barefoot all summer, roaming on land and sea and testing one's physical limits. Activities included: sailing, rowing, kite flying, fishing, swimming, and walking to the store. There were few rules, a great sense of community and a festive atmosphere that included countless picnics, nightly beach bonfires with sing-a-longs, fishing derbies, and moonlit dances at the end of the West Bay wharf with music provided by a wind-up gramophone.

While most groceries were delivered by the weekly Union Steamship boat, small orders were filled by two stores in Gambier Harbour. Mr. Lett had the oldest store located close to the water. After placing an order with him, he would sometimes row from Gambier

Above left: 1945 Ned Larsen.
Above: Margaret Savage from Avalon Bay, Owen Houston, Marge Bullard, Ned Larsen, Betty Ridley, Jack Ridley, unknown – front- unknown. Courtesy: Betty Ridley.

Harbour to West Bay to deliver the goods and then pick up any pop bottle empties. During the war, Mr. Lett is also remembered for saving chocolate bars from the winter supply to be available as summer-time treats. Mr. Drage owned the other store in Gambier Harbour. In the early days, the store in New Brighton was located close to the Government wharf.

Fishing was a big part of the Ridley's Gambier life, both for food and recreation. Countless photographs show evidence of the bountiful Coho and Spring salmon that were caught. There was also an abundance of cod. A fishing trip never came back empty-handed and Charlie shared his catch with neighbours in the Bay. Experiences with catching crab and shrimp came much later.

Mid 30s Charles Ridley in his boat Placebo. *Courtesy: Betty Ridley.*

Charlie was also interested in the Chum salmon in the creek beside his cabin. The Department of Fisheries consulted with him on the size of the runs and referred to the creek as Ridley Creek, which is also known as Whispering Creek. Mildred maintained a book, recording the date when the first fish "was seen" in the creek for many years.

In the city, Charlie had a dental practice. On Gambier, this training and the related medical knowledge led to him being called on to attend to all kinds of medical problems. He removed many fishhooks, administered various forms of emergency care including stitches, and he often taxied sick or injured people to Gibsons or Horseshoe Bay. This special attention to the Islanders earned him the honorable name of, Doc Ridley.

Some might have found Charlie an intimidating man. He demanded respect, however, he usually had a twinkle in his eye and he could always be counted on to lend a helping hand. His tool shed was well known to have one of everything, and if he didn't have it he'd figure out a way to make do. He also

Charlie and Mildred Ridley, West Bay, Gambier Island – Betty Bestwick (nee) Ridley

owned the first small tractor in the area and it was used to save many back muscles in the transporting of supplies down the long West Bay wharf for neighbours and friends.

Mildred had a warm and generous heart that made everyone feel welcome. She always had a cup of coffee or tea and some fresh baked goodies ready for anyone who dropped by. The Camp garden was beautifully kept, and with a well-maintained fence to keep out the deer,

it gave her huge pleasure. She had many rhododendrons, wisteria, roses, wild sweet peas, hydrangea, and pink poppies which are now largely a memory. Every spring there is still a large display of daffodils on the Point property that were planted by Mildred and Mrs. Heay.

After retirement, from 1960 to 1982, Mildred and Charlie lived on Gambier full-time between April and November of each year. Their last visit to Gambier was in 1984 and they have now both passed away. The property continues to be owned by the family with six generations having enjoyed special times at West Bay, Gambier Island.

Looking at the cabin from the water. Courtesy: Betty Ridley.

War Bonds for a Down Payment

E. Butcher

In West Bay in the 1930s, one couple, Mr. and Mrs. Frank Heay lived up the hill from the current Government wharf and, it was said, he actually had something to do with getting the wharf where it is now, in West Bay, for the steamships to dock. Frank had a few sheds at the end of the ramp and the new wharf down by the creek where he kept tools, supplies, rowboats, etc.

The steam tugs working in the bay would blow their whistles, when coming in with a tow and Frank would run down, jump into his boat and then row out to the tug while standing up. I was always fascinated with the sound of the steam tugs working in the bay, some as large as 75 footers and up. While visiting the Jester Lodge when I was four years old, I could hear them at night when I was in bed.

In 1943, I bought a war bond and later used it for a down payment on 66 acres in West Bay, Lot 1576. It was around this time, the Sir Thomas J. Lipton was beached in the head of the bay to keep the logs off the beach at low tide. I asked Frank Heay if I could have some planks that were floating in the bilge, two decks down, and he replied, "Yes, but only the ones floating." These same planks are the current floor boards in our original cabin, which is still in use. The old ship had been used as a barge in its last days with bunkers about 150 feet by 12 feet made of 4 by 12 foot planks. People later came from all over to strip it to the deck when no one was around.

1935 WOLVERENE owned by John Everett Murray. Courtesy: Murray family.

Carmelo Point

Thoughts on Carmelo Point

Pat Winram

Mills and Lois Winram purchased Lot 878 in 1953. As far as we know we were the third land title holders. The homestead family had been the Johnsons. The property was then owned by the Massey family. Old Dr. Ridley's wife was a Massey and it was her family who held the lot. She told me that the property was also called Seven Beaches. The Johnson family built the old home (around 1890) with a wrap-around porch whitewashed and by the time the Winrams inhabited it, it was mouse infested. There were three bedrooms in the house, kitchen and living/dining room. There was an outhouse placed strategically over the stream so the contents washed away. Close to this main building was an outbuilding that I was told was a crew shed for the

The landing at Seven Beaches and old cabin at Carmelo Point. Courtesy: Pat Winram.

Chinese or Japanese labourers. There is more than one historic midden of broken glass and pottery shards that include parts of rice bowl sort of containers.

There was an apple orchard and many of these trees have fallen down now or were swallowed by the forest. Some continued to produce quite a crop, ready for harvest around Thanksgiving. There is evidence of a house garden. Some ornamental grass is all that remains, along with the piled up rock marking the flower-beds.

Original house built by the Johnsons in 1890s. Courtesy: Pat Winram.

Original house overlooks the beach. On the right is the crew shack of a whitewashed board and batten construction. Photos courtesy: Pat Winram.

Not far from this home was a log cabin with one window facing the sea. This was not a very large building probably 14x16 feet. WE don't know when it was built, but there were four large fir trees, one at each corner of the cabin and by the 1970's these trees were starting to crush the cabin. Very little evidence remains of this building.

There was a large landing at the beach, which in the 50's was mostly rotting and dangerous to walk on, but at one time it had been a large staging platform for arrival and departure, no doubt small boats could have been stored here.

We could never figure out why the site had been selected, because it was not a good harbour. It seems that the year-round stream and large level area to the north of the building site would have been the incentive. We found remnants of a dynamo in the stream, so at one time there must have been an attempt to produce electricity.

In the mid 50s, Mills & Lois decided to build a place close to the sheltered harbour, just east of the original homestead. Jack Goodie was hired to clear a meadow. He pulled out many of the stumps but to make the field more level Mills and Lois dragged a log across the ground. Grass was planted and a small storage shed was built.

In 1958, a new summer home was built. This took 4 or 5 men all summer to build. They did all the work by hand with no power tools.

During the late fall of 1962 or '63 the original 1890's house was burnt down because it was a haven for mice, and parts of the building were rotting and dangerous and no longer a safe place for people. Courtesy: Pat Winram.

Centre Bay

Centre Bay

Paul Cosulich

I came to know Gambier as a result of my family's acquisition of real estate through the merging of two tugboat companies, Straits Towing and Rivtow. Straits had extensive holdings on Gambier. Four southern bays acted like a warehouse for the raw product required by the Vancouver area sawmills. As a way to secure towing, the tugboat firms would offer storage services. Complimentary to this were the related log sorting and booming operations, both on Gambier and on the mainland on the western side of Howe Sound.

I acquired company-owned property at the head of Centre Bay that was once the home of Pacific Coyle Navigation's booming ground. In fact, my old cabin was the boom shack originally delivered to the property in the forties. I was also responsible for the Rivtow lands at that time.

Much more recently, I purchased an adjacent property, the "Old Farm," originally a homestead from the beginning of the century.

Left: 1947 Bill Warn, Hope Point. Right: 1947 Mary and daughter, Fran Warn at the head of Long Bay. Courtesy: Mitchell family.

Daisy/East Bay

Harold and Carrie Warn

Leiani Anthony

Harold Warn came to Canada in 1913 to see his brother in Saskatchewan near Battleford. He did not like the farming life in Saskatchewan so he joined the Royal Mounted Police. He did active service in S. E. Saskatchewan until 1916 when he joined the Canadian Army militia. In 1917, he married his girlfriend in England and they had their first son, Jack.

In 1919, when the war ended, Harold Warn came back to Canada. He was discharged on July 1, 1919, in Quebec and came straight to Vancouver. His first job was driving a touring car for the Northwood franchise around Stanley Park.

Harold worked at Lee Motors on Kingsway in 1924, selling gas and spare parts. He bought the Red and White store on Royal Oak in Burnaby in 1927. Harold returned to England and setup and operated a bakery from 1932 until 1938. In 1938, he sold out the bakery business and came back to British Columbia where he bought that Glen Olbee Farm because Jack was now interested in farming, and Harold wanted to operate a resort. Their son, Bill (William)was 18. The name Glen Olbee was derived from the names of McLennan's three daughters, Glen, Olive and Beatrice.

The farm was purchased with all the machinery, livestock, and all the other improvements. It is reputed that McLennan spent $110,000 from 1915 to 1920 building the Glen Olbee Farm. That is equivalent to three million dollars in today's money. To clear the fields, McLennan hired 50 Chinese labourers. They used oxen to clear the huge cedar stumps left by the loggers of the previous generation. After McLennan's death in 1927, the livestock was eventually sold and the fields/pasture that were so labouriously created were allowed to deteriorate and alder quickly took over.

Harold and family operated the farm as a summer resort from 1939 to 1944 and had as many as thirty-two guests at one time. In conjunction with this, he operated a dairy farm and supplied milk to the pulp mill at Port Mellon. They also sold apples from the orchard to the Empress Jam Company in Vancouver for $1.00 per No. 38 box.

In 1948, they sold 10 acres at the south end of the bay on the east side (D.L. 3201) to Ken Clark who built the summer house which he used for seven years then resold to Warn in 1956. Clark house was used as a cook house for the men that operated the booming grounds.

Harold Warn lived in the Clark house until 1966 when he will moved to Gibsons where he now resides.

Long Bay

Maureen Zueff (nee) Mitchell

Leiani Anthony

Maureen's dad (Joe) was born at Camp Artaban in 1892. Her grandfather was William Gandy Mitchell who bought 40 acres in West Bay. He ran a sawmill at Camp Artaban. Her

grandmother was Emily Jefferys. The family story is, she died in childbirth, when Joe was 12. Joe was sent to school in North Vancouver (Saint Thomas Aquinas). He left school when he was 16 and came back to live with his dad in West Bay. Joe's sister, Susan Mitchell, died of TB at age 12. Grandfather Mitchell (Joe's dad) died in Long Bay in 1940.

Joe Mitchell and his wife lived in Long Bay for 52 years. He learned boat building (dinghies) and boat engine mechanics. According to Maureen, he was pretty much self-taught. Maureen remembers how her dad would copper paint the bottom of boats and then take the paint brush and clean it by writing the name of the boat on his workshop wall.

Joe Mitchell looked after the booming grounds for Fraser Mills. He also looked after Camp Artaban for the church. There is a cairn erected at Camp

1942 Margaret and Joe Mitchell in the orchard. Courtesy: Mitchell family.

Artaban thanking Maureen's dad for all his years of service to the camp.

Joe Mitchell's third house burnt down in 1960. Apparently, it was a hot summer and sparks from the woodstove landed on the shake roof. Maureen and Al remember seeing smoke from Gibsons, but didn't think a lot about it.

Joe Mitchell died at age 94, in 1986. The only time he left Gambier was to go overseas during World War One, where he was gassed. According to Maureen, there were no long-term effects of the gassing on his health. Her mom, Margaret Davies, died at age 88. She was from West Vancouver originally. Maureen tells the story that her Grandfather Mitchell forced her dad, Joe, to take this group of hikers from West Vancouver up Mount Artaban. Apparently, Margaret Davies was the only one of the group to make it up to the top with Joe.

Joe used to charge $7.00 to pull out boats onto his ways, but he allowed boats to tie up indefinitely to his float for free. There was a Russian captain who jumped ship in Vancouver and became a fisherman. He tied up to Joe Mitchell's wharf and stayed forever.

In the Mitchell's later years, they moved in to Gibsons, where they died.

Note: Gord Mitchell writes [see Errata] - Gordie was born and lived in Long Bay for 6 years and went to school in West Van. He came back to Gambier at age 15 and looked after the booming grounds in Long Bay for five years - Cliff Towing Steam Tugs.

Left: 1942 Alex Znotin came to Gambier in 1930 to get his boat overhauled by Joe Mitchell and ended up living on it and becoming part of the family.
Below: 1960 Jack Goode at his property in Daisy Bay. Doug and his father, Gordon Mitchell. Courtesy: Mitchell family.

Maureen Zueff (nee) Mitchell - Leiani Anthony

Early History of Joe Mitchell and Margaret Mitchell (nee) Davies

An Interview with Leiani Anthony January 4, 1981

Joe Mitchell was born at Point Graves, on July 17, 1892 at what is now Camp Artaban. There is a cairn commemorating his birth at the top of the wharf. The family originally lived in West Bay on Gambier Island. His father was a New Zealander and his mother, part native Indian. Joe's dad worked in the Watkins logging camp at Twin Creeks and was the leader of the Dukhorn and Johnson Shingle Mill in West Bay. In those early days, West Bay had a lumber mill, a hotel, a licensed premises and a boarding house on the right hand side of the bay just as you go in. They were torn down to build Judge Clement's house; two log cabins.

Joe Mitchell's birthplace in 1892. Courtesy: Mitchell family.

The hand loggers would take down the logs, shove them down into the water and row them across the bay to the mill where they would get paid right then and there. Then they would go straight over to the hotel and get drunk. The Mitchell family moved over to Long Bay on November 1, 1922.

Margaret met her future husband, Joe, through two sisters, Ida and Jean MacLaren. She recalls being invited up to Gambier Island by her girlfriends when they rode to the island in Joe's boat. They would go over to the Burns & Jackson logging camp.

Mrs. Mitchell:

"The loggers would stand at the top of the hill, very, very steep you know, and there would be an engine there and we'd sit on this carrier. For fun they'd reverse the engine at the top, and then I jumped off into the little gully there."

When they were courting, Joe would walk along a trail from West Bay to the Post Office at New Brighton for his weekly letter from Margaret, who grew up in West Vancouver.

After they were married in 1925, they moved right up to Long Bay. Mrs. Mitchell was 23 years old. Joe purchased two houses and property from Bert Kennedy for $1000. Mrs. Mitchell washed everything in tubs by hand; they had a big cooler with the screen. They would pickle corned beef and pork. They had a cow, a few cats and goats. The Mitchells lived there for 52 years.

From 1922 to 1970, Joe ran the booming grounds for: Canadian Western Lumber, Canadian Tug Boat Company, M.R. Cliff Towing Company, Young & Gore, and Rivtow. The Mitchells had three children and Mrs. Mitchell taught two of them. One of their sons died at 36 of a brain tumour.

Two of the Mitchell's homes burned down, they felt it was sparks from the chimney falling onto the wooden shake roofs. They had to completely start from scratch. The home they have now came down by barge from Echo Bay in the early sixties. With a winch and a couple of Cats, it was pulled up on nine boom sticks with nothing broken. The house was built by a logger, put on a float and moved around from camp to camp. Even with all those moves all the windows and doors of the home were intact.

Joe was the official "passenger and freight boat" to Camp Artaban, bringing all the children to camp from the time it started, under the guidance of Rev. Jackson in 1921. Joe built his boat, the *Zariffa* and launched it in 1944. He also did many runs to the Lower Mainland and into Horseshoe Bay to pick up ministers, and whomever else needed to get to the camp.

1935 Mrs. Singleton Gates, and Joe, Margaret Mitchell, Liz Fawcett, with Maureen and Gordon Mitchell at lower left. Courtesy: Mitchell family.

Camp Artaban was originally further out towards Hope Point.

Where it is now, there used to be four homes, one owned by Davidson and another by Magistrate Alexander. Artaban took them all over in 1924 with the exception of the Alexander's.

Joe Recalls the Weather in the Sound:

"We used to have a cribwork when we were in West Bay and when the south-east winds blew we used to walk on it and it would shake. Tons and tons of rocks inside this cribwork and it would still shake when we walked on it."

The weather patterns in the Sound seem to always be changing, the north-east winds, known as "The Squamish" used to be so strong you couldn't face them. On one occasion,

the back window of the boat was knocked out in a westerly going towards Horseshoe Bay. Joe then put two and half tonnes of rock ballast in the *Zariffa*, and that kept her about four inches lower in the water, and kept her even. Fishermen called coming around

Above: 1925 Long Bay shop after fire. At left: 1958 left 1959. Courtesy: Mitchell family

Hood Point, "The Cape Horn of the Howe Sound." It could be dirty in those days. Joe lost the anchor right off the bow of the boat and in the early 1920s, when the family lived in West Bay there was snow, three feet deep, right down to the waterfront.

On Fishing:

> "When we lived in West Bay, before 1922, I used to go out in front of the house and catch a salmon. It was nothing to catch half a dozen Spring Salmon, big ones, six to ten pounds. We used to pickle them for the winter. I had one spoon which was a dandy, and hooks and that's all I had."

Entertainment: Joe recalls building the Memorial Hall at Grace Harbour. It was built with volunteer labour. Gus Lund and others put the foundations of logs in, and Joe put the flooring in on long weekends. It was dedicated on September 21, 1947.

XARIFFA put in the water in 1944. Courtesy: Mitchell family.

Mrs. Mitchell:

> "We had grand times over there, it was wonderful. What we used to do was, we'd wait until a full moon, and that was once a month, we had sandwiches and cake, we had a PA system, and we would persuade friends to come up for the weekend for the "Big Do" as we used to call it. It was up at Warn's at the end of the Bay, well that was McLennan's in the lodge part, and it was such a big house. One night we had forty people there. This was in the summer, square dancing, schottische, oh, we had a great time and every Thursday afternoon, Joe would pick up women who were there in Centre Bay and Long Bay, and take them to the different houses. We'd alternate homes and have afternoon tea and a chin wag and then he'd take them home again. It was really nice."

Early History of Joe Mitchell and Margaret Mitchell (nee) Zueff - Leiani Anthony - 1981

Every so often, Arthur Lett would row over to Long Bay with groceries or money owed the Mitchells. He'd stay for a visit and dinner and row back in his flat-bottom boat, with a coal oil lantern sitting in the bow.

People mostly got along well in those early days as they' lived so far apart.

Above: Mitchell boat XARIFFA copper painted at Potts Point.
Right: Mid 50s Joe and Margaret Mitchell.
Left: Late 50s winter wood supply.
Courtesy: Mitchell family.

1960 left to right: Don and Margaret Mitchell, Alex Znotin, Joe Mitchell and Gord Mitchell working on new house.
Below: 1960 New house being pulled out of the water and up to new location.

Early History of Joe Mitchell and Margaret Mitchell (nee) Zueff - Leiani Anthony - 1981

Left: 1960 New house in place.
Below: Mitchell home in Long Bay
and machine shop. House burned
down in 1960.
Courtesy: Mitchell family.

Maureen Zueff (nee) Mitchell's Story

Maureen Mitchell from an interview with Dodie Errico Jan. 13, 2006

Born in 1930, Maureen Mitchell was home schooled in Long Bay. At the age of 13, she moved to West Vancouver to live with her aunt and go to school. Every weekend, her dad picked her up in Horseshoe Bay in his boat, The XARIFFA. It took him 12 years to build this boat and he launched it in 1944. Apparently, her mother wanted a good solid commuter boat for the job.

Maureen remembers being brought up on goats milk, and her older brother was brought up on cow's milk. The cow would wander down to the beach and sometimes even went out on the log booms. Eventually, the cow drowned.

As her father, Joe Mitchell, was president of the ANAVETS 276 for nine years, she was allowed into the hall at age 14 or 15 because her parents didn't want to leave her and her brother alone in Long Bay on Saturday nights. Her brother would stay in the front room (pool room) and she would sneak into the back room to get chips and pop for herself and her brother.

The ladies of the island gave Maureen and Al Zueff a bridal shower at the ANAVETS when they got married. Maureen and Al lived in Long Bay after their marriage and the birth of their twin boys. They lived in a small two-room cabin on her parent's property. Al Zueff bought a two room house in Coal Harbour and towed it to Long Bay. Jack and Ed Anderson (the Anderson brothers) helped Al and Maureen join the two houses together.

1948 Maureen, Joe and Margaret Mitchell at ANAVETS Hall. Courtesy: Mitchell family.

Maureen and Al moved out of Long Bay and to Gibsons in 1959, so their children could go to school. Maureen was trained as a teacher but didn't want to home-school her own children.

She remembers the Union Steamship coming into Daisy Bay every Thursday. It carried the mail groceries and building supplies.

Maureen also knew Morse code. When her parents wanted to invite Mr. Farrell over for dinner and a game of whist, she would send him a Morse code message.

Mitchell's Neighbours in Long Bay

Mr. Farrell:
He was a one-armed violin player who played during square dances held at Warns' barn at the head of Long Bay. These were held the Friday closest to the full moon so that people could see to get there.

Joan and Jack Warn:
Joan Warn came to Long Bay as a counsellor at Camp Artaban, which is where she met Jack. They were married in the outdoor chapel at the camp and the ladies of the bay cooked for the wedding reception.

Mary and Sam Ward:
Mary Ward thought she was a see-er. Apparently, she could "see" Maureen's brother's death by falling down a well. Maureen's brother is still alive and well at this writing.

1946 -47 Fran Warn, Margaret, Maureen, Gord, Don, and Joe Mitchell. Courtesy: Mitchell family.

At the Head of Long Bay

The Alexanders lived on the left-hand side, Camp Artaban was in the middle, and the Warrens were on the right-hand side. She remembers being picked up by boat to go and babysit the Alexander children: Anne, Dick, Hal, Keith, and Helen Alexander.

Ken Alexander was disabled, but an avid birder. He used to catch seagulls and band them so he could keep track of them. He would lecture at the school in Gibsons about birds. He was also the self-appointed mail sorter when the Union Ships came into Daisy/East Bay on Thursdays.

Fircom Bay/Halkett Bay/Camp Fircom

Camp Fircom was built by Alexander Browning in 1935.
It is at Fircom Bay in Halkett Bay on the south side of Gambier Island.

Above left: 1935 Ruth and Sam Roddan, Isabell Clark.
Above right:1935 Camp Fircom Alex Browning.
Right: 1934 Isabell Clark at Camp Fircom Hospital
Courtesy: Diane Clark.

Camp Fircom

Above left: 1960s Jubilee Hall Alex and Isabell Browning. Above right: Isabell and Alex Browning at look out built by Alex Browning at Camp Fircom. Below: 1935 Opening of Jubilee Hall at Camp Fircom.

North/Brigade Bay

<u>Charles W. Wiegand</u>

Charles W. Wiegand, purchased land on the north-east side of the island at what is now, Brigade Bay. This land was originally pre-empted in 1888 by John Simpson, and then with the adjacent lot, was pre-empted by Frederick and Thomas Keeling and John Thomas Sisson in 1891. Wiegand, a wealthy Vancouver merchant, purchased the land in 1907.

Upon his retirement, he had a comfortable home built; and landscaped with a lovely garden and artificial lake. Mr. Wiegand raised pheasants, canaries and Belgian hares and kept deer in an enclosure close by. He enjoyed growing violets and lilies-of-the-valley. North Bay, according to Wiegand, was named Brigade Bay in 1946, for the Boys' Brigade that had a summer camp close the Wiegand boundary line. North/Brigade Bay was a sheltered little bay, which gave easy access for mooring his boat.

Charles W. Wiegand died in 1950

This is an account from the Provincial Archives, July 4, 1968, for Gambier Island, Howe Sound, B.C. collected by Leiani Anthony. For more information, see "Early Vancouver, vol. 7, p. 438 and p. 440." Also, see the 1919 directory.

Gambier Invitation, Gambier Initiation

Barbara Blewett writes about Elsa Weigand of Brigade Bay

Christmas 1964, was my first visit to Vancouver. As an Easterner, I had a very vague knowledge of Canada West. First off, I went down to Spanish Banks to touch and taste the Pacific Ocean. Proudly, my future husband pointed to a rather foggy outline of land in the distance. He declared it was Japan I was seeing. "Really," I said, "I never dreamed it was so close! No wonder you were all so nervous during the war." He never let me forget it. I now believe that outline was Gambier Island with Bowen in front of it.

Such was my introduction to the West Coast. Although I was only here for a week,.I did meet one of my most interesting lifetime friends, Elsa Weigand. She was a great champion of my intended and it was she who first mentioned the name of Gambier Island to me. She was living in a place called Brigade Bay. In the early twenties, she often had my husband visit her there when he was as a young boy. She was emphatic that I come here to visit her on her "magical island."

At that time, I had no concept of what those words meant. I didn't know how much a part of my future life, this island would become. It would be another three years before I would move to Vancouver. Even though Elsa could not come to our wedding in Ontario in 1965, she did send masses of Lilly of the Valley from Gambier Island for my bouquet. The aroma was incredible and very much a part of that day. I shall never forget that gesture and the presence it had for me during the ceremony.

Elsa was a nature lover, bar none. Sadly, before I came out, she had been forced to sell her island land. She was now in her early eighties and the difficulties of island life became too much for her. However, together, we did lots of exploring of the nature 'round and about Vancouver that was accessible by car. When my daughter Kristy was born, I asked Elsa to be her Godmother.

Elsa had been a schoolteacher. She loved children, however, she never married. Along with many, many men of that time, her brother Carl was killed in the First World War. She had worked in Lillooet as well as spending many years at Strathcona in East Vancouver. She was famous for her production every year of the play of Peter Pan.

I understand that Charles Weigand, Elsa's father, came to Vancouver from Germany in 1885, when he was 25. He had a furniture store on Westminster Avenue opposite the old City Hall in Vancouver and was there for many years. He was a member of the Pioneers Association and was well known and well regarded. Many pioneers bought their home furniture from him. He retired to Gambier Island shortly after the First World War. Elsa joined him, I suppose, after she retired. They built a beautiful Japanese Garden with a man-made pond with an arch bridge over it. They gathered and sold salal and sword fern to the florists in Vancouver.

I was there two years ago and I could still see the remnants of the pond and old house; lots of Lilly of the Valley, too.

I was sad that I never did see Elsa's beloved Brigade Bay with her. She did, however, talk constantly about it until the day she died.

Much later, after she had gone, my husband and I acquired a sailboat. We would often revisit his childhood haunt and he would reminisce about what he and Elsa would get up to. I still have a letter he wrote as an 11 year old to his mother from Gambier Island. My understanding is that there was a post office on Anvil Island and that Mr. Weigand would row across from Brigade Bay to get the mail. However, the copy of the following letter was sent via a family called Pickards, who I presume lived in Port Graves.

> Port Graves,
> Via Horseshoe Bay,
> April 4, 1953

Dear Mother,

Thank you so much for the meat and biscuits. They were delectable and because of Elsa's cooking, the meat was very tender (she forced me to say this).

I got up here at seven on Thursday night and was met by Charlie.

Before I forget, I was in such a hurry while down at the bus depot that I mislaid my $1.20 return ticket to Horseshoe Bay so that I had to buy another.

On Friday, Charlie and I took Cropie and the stone boat over to the Pickards and brought back the luggage we left and two bales of hay. Cropie was fine taking the empty stone boat over the trail but coming back was a different story. She stopped every ten yards. After we put her in her pasture she broke out and trampled all over Elsa's best [flower] bed.

Rufus the Red, alias Old Topps has still got his fighting spirit. He attacks Charlie when he is feeding him.

His mode of offense is different now. He fakes a rush below Charlie's shield (copper bucket in which Charlie puts the feed) and suddenly leaps up over the bucket and digs his spurs into his flesh.

Elsa and I are going over the trail tomorrow (Sunday) and

give this letter to the Pickards to deliver.
Give my love to the family.
Peter
P.S: just before I left for Pickards I fired a shotgun shell at a crow on the island in the middle of the bay. Every sharp shooter misses sometimes.

I was with her when she died in 1972. She had decided to take a night course to refinish her lovely furniture and the fumes destroyed her fragile lungs. It happened the day before Christmas Eve and I had taken her a live Christmas tree. Shortly before, she was softly singing "Oh Tannenbaum" in German.

Many years later, 1989, I came to stay on Gambier at West Bay. I soon discovered the "magic" that Elsa had told me of all those years before.

Twin Islands/Grace Islands

Twin Islands/Grace Islands

Wendy Graham

During the 1920s, George Graham used as a shelter in the west island, a canvas tent which was also used to accommodate Y camp groups.

After the senior Killams arrived in 1928, George Graham assisted in many ways the people in the area, such as Magistrate and Mrs. Shaw with their cabin location where Peter Killam now has a summer place, Mr. McDonald, who built his house in Avalon Bay in 1933, which the Thrashers now own, and the Hebbs at Avalon Point. He notes going over to Bill Bailey's who lived on Vanguard Road opposite to Rita and Lex Hanson's home Bill was a good carpenter and helped build many homes in the area, including Mr. and Mrs. Henry Major's at a point between Avalon Bay and Burgess Bay next to Mr. and Mrs. Frank Fritsch waterfront home. George was a frequent visitor to both New Brighton and Grace Harbour where he visited the Stoddards, Tom Burns, Arthur Lett and the Larsens. Con Burns, son of Tom and Lillian, had a fish boat that came in handy for towing logs and transporting material.

Built in 1921 by George and Hugh Graham on Twin Island, it was left to Anne Northrup's dad, Arthur Graham and then to Anne and her family. Courtesy: Anne Northrup.

In February of 1933, George finished putting in the foundation for his house and building the chimney. He was not lacking for things to do. He notes that one day he had eight young ladies from the Killams visit him. Mr. and Mrs. Innes from New Brighton would come over for reading material. Often his neighbours from Gambier would visit. Killer whales would pass through the channel. Always something interesting happened. He was fond of flowers and mentioned the grouse hooting. This was a common occurrence in those days, and in the spring, they would have their young. Of late, the grouse have been conspicuous by their absence.

George would count the strokes of the oars of his rowboat when rowing to New Brighton and back from Twin, also to Hopkins and back. The number of strokes would depend on condition of the sea. It was not so much the time it took but the number of strokes, the calm sea would take far less, also there was the tide and wind to consider.

Among the friends he had in the area during the 1920s and early thirties to name a few there were: the Jewitts, Moxons, Killams, Hebbs, Tuohey, Morgan, A. Lett, Larsen, Burns, Ridley, Shaws, Harpers, McDonald, Bailey, Stoddards, etc.

1955 Anne Northrup's friend, Sharon Frances on Twin Island. A light house warns incoming ships of the rocky shores of Twin Islands. Courtesy: Anne Northrup.

In conclusion, for the last eighty-odd years, the southwest corner of Gambier Island— namely, Gambier Harbour, (originally named Grace Harbour), New Brighton, and West Bay, has progressed, thanks to the older property owners, at a slow and steady pace. Property assessments have not been quick to change, and that is why Gambier is the way it is today. Then came the "Island Trust" in the reign of David Barrett, and the NDP prior to this, subdivisions the size of city lots started to emerge, these islands, in the local area, commenced to be overtaken by building promoters with few restrictions, or regulations to control the venture in an orderly manner. At this point, the Island Trust was formed and all unauthorized building on the Gulf Islands and on the Howe Sound islands, which included Gambier, ceased.

A two hectare, minimum lot size was imposed on Gambier—this is approximately five acres per lot, thus slowing down the number of newcomers, due to the shortage of property in the future. The price of these lots, for those who can afford it, will be a good deal more than the smaller parcel of land. Do people really require and need a property larger than a half acre, with the increased taxes that are about to come? Eight odd years ago areas were divided into regular city lots of half an acre—but now all new subdivisions come under the requirements set by the Island Trust.

Nothing remains static—as the City of Vancouver grows, so will the demand in the surrounding areas grow. What is the future for Gambier?

Is it possible that these large two hectare parcels, at a future date, will be subdivided into smaller lots as the need for land increases, and as property taxes accelerate?

I will leave the answer to the reader!

In the 1920s, there was a certain amount of friendly rivalry between the three areas of West Bay, New Brighton and Grace/Gambier Harbour. Perhaps that rivalry still exists to a certain extent.

SS Capilano *traveling through the gap between Twin Islands and Gambier Island. The small island at the stern of the* Capilano *with the trees on it is Rose Island now belonging to the Ralph Killams. At the bow is the tip of Killams property. In the center back is Long Bay. George Graham's rowboat and float are in the foreground on Twin Island close to the house. Courtesy: Wendy Graham.*

George Graham's Log

George D. Graham was a bombardier in the Canadian Expeditionary Force in December, 1918. He was the first settler of Twin Island (which was later named Grace Islands during the second Great War). He moved permanently to the island in the early 1920s using his boat the *Ruby Marie* for transportation. George Graham was a great fisherman and if anyone could catch salmon, he could. His reputation was well known in the Sound. Being in an ideal location to watch the herring surface and the herring gulls dive into the water, George would know there were salmon feeding. In the *Ruby Marie,* he kept a log, and the following are some of the entries in that log.

A day's salmon catch at Twin Islands with friends. Second to left – Edmund Morgan, far right – George Graham. Courtesy: Wendy Graham.

March 25, 1932 until November 26, 1960

George Graham lived permanently on Twin Islands also known as Grace Islands from the early 1920s.

March
    25   found boathouse broken into and Turner 8 foot dinghy taken: also roll zinc, one gallon red paint and brushes and adze

           Fair Friday rain Saturday Sunday Graham Campbell Sloane via *Catala* and *Comox*

May
    21- 24 Graham Campbell

           Sloane windy, fixed wharf

    28-29 Graham two salmon and cod

June
    11-12 Graham, Wishart, Morgan, McCluny, F. Deeley Sr., F. Deeley Jr. No fish, launch taken up

September
    18   launch taken down

October
    1-2   Graham–cleaned well

    8- 10 one salmon Thanksgiving October 10

December
    2   sundown 4:15

    3   rain afternoon

    4   Over to Y camp

    5   over to store, fine and warm

    6   over to boat for papers. Change in weather, cold in afternoon.

    7   east wind-freezing.

    8   east wind until noon then westerly 4 inches of ice on barrels.

    9   back to town.

    16   cold spell broke on 15th so returned 16th.

    17   fine spring day.

    18   rain. *Invercraig* at mooring.

    19   very high tide, up to third slat on boathouse runway.

    20   still south east wind with showers. Down to New Brighton for papers.

    21   fair. One cod.

    22   heavy rain and winds. Tide up to 15.6.

    23   back to town. 1:30 to 9:00 on boat, *Britannia* call.

    30   brought radio up. Wharf loose.

    31   *Lilcris* up. Chained float.

1933
January

1	Stormy till 11:00 a.m. Fresh snow at seaside.
2	*Lilcris* down.
3	down to boat for papers. Killams up.
4	fine and warm. Doors and windows open all day. No fire on.
5	south west wind squalls all day. But warm.
6	rain going down to wharf.
13	fair-at night.
14	odd snowflakes in afternoon. Clear and bright at midnight.
15	find summer day. Frost at night. Down to Burgess with dogfish. Over to store – 45 minutes there and back. 550 strokes each way with ripple on water.
16	fine bright day but cool.
17	touch of snow through night. Down to boat for papers. 435 or strokes from New Brighton on smooth water. First 100 strokes to old camp, second 100 strokes to middle of Burgess Bay, third 100 strokes to north side Avalon Bay, fourth 100 strokes to middle of channel.
18	fair, sunny in afternoon.
19	fair, very mild-started to snow about 10:30 p.m.
20	2 inches of soft snow.

February

3	patches of snow in shade. Took up another radio, wire and spikes.
4	down to New Brighton.
5	Tim Hay up for a visit.
6	fine day, frost at night, birds singing.
7	down to boat for papers. Cutting wood and digging around a root.
8	freezing easterly wind all day and night. Sundown at 5:15 on south notch of Knob Hill.
9	Hay boys cut down the three fir trees at end of house. Coldest night according to radio for 20 years.
10	down to town.
17	snow all gone on the island.
18	cleaning up limbs of fir trees. Innes up for log.
19	cloudy with rain in afternoon. Put cover on Shaw's well.
20	south east winds. Rain.
21	down two vote for papers. Sunshine and clouds, mild. Rain at 10:00 p.m. *May Mac* up.
22	bright with south-west winds in morning, calming at noon and south east

breeze starting about 3:00 p.m. Very mild. Having supper with doors and windows open. The dark about 6:30 p.m.

23 spring day with gusts of wind and hail. Over to store and inspected the site for the community hall.

24 down to town. Slush on the hills overnight.

March

3 fine sunny day. Had battery changed by Burns.

4 mild cloudy day. Rain at night. Burning underbrush. *Lilcris* up. President Roosevelt's inauguration on radio.

5 Sunday-showery. Rain started at 4:30 p.m.

6 rains steady all night and today until 4:30 p.m. First day I've had to stay in the house.

7 sundown 5:45 p.m. 15 feet south of Mount Elphinstone Ridge. Down to boat for papers. Mended New Brighton wharf. First outboard of season.

8 Fine cloudless day. Burning brush. Police boat up.

9 summer day. Burning brush.

10 down to town. *Lilcris* down at 10:15 also first speedboat of season. Cloudy and cool.

1936 The Vancouver Police boat leaving New Brighton. Courtesy: Lynn Bell.

17 fine bright weather. First butterfly. Frogs croaking.

18 rain all night and morning. Cloudy all afternoon. First bumblebee. McCall moved to Gibsons. Dark at 7:25 p.m.

19 rain all day. Moved anchor block on float. Larsen's boat up for season.

20   bright but strong cold south westerly blowing all day. Sunset 6:00 p.m. over old Y camp. Water 2 feet from top of well.

21   south-westerly still blowing. Down to boat for papers via Shaw's and Grace Harbour. Back by Avalon Bay Trail.

22   sunny and breezy. Cleaned all badminton court. Trolling in the evening.

23   morning, cloudy, noon-sleet and rain, late afternoon fair. Towed in cedar log for float. Picked up 65 feet of rope attached to block of wood floating in. *May Mac* up in afternoon.

31   fair. Sunny and afternoon. Lumber for community hall at Hopkins up.

April

1   Cloudy but warm. The Arbutus is flowering and the currants are in bloom.

2   Sunday. Down to Cotton's Bay. Two cod. Fair and warm with a few drops of rain in afternoon and south-west wind at night.

3   Sunset 6:08 p.m. over Salvation Camp. Down at Camp Solitude cutting posts and planks for wooden shed. Fine day.

4   Down to the boat for papers via Avalon Bay. Putting up signs on way.

5   Put in six posts on woodshed. Beachcomber's boat in to dig clams between islands.

6   Getting dirt from Avalon Bay and sowing peas and carrots.

7   Down to town. *Comox* starts tomorrow.

13   up on *Capilano* and *Comox*. Cloudy

14   Good Friday. Fine but windy.

15   Sankey, *Martin* and *Smalley* up.

16   Sunday. Sankey down.

The Ruby Marie *at "Camp Solitude" Avalon Bay. Courtesy: Wendy Graham.*

17	Monday. Fine but breezy.

17   Monday. Fine but breezy.

20   *Martin* and *Smalley* down with McDonald on *May Mac.* Got radio back from Burns. Temperature 7 F°.

21   summer day. Peas above ground. Splitting wood. Lighted lamp at 7:50 p.m. not dark. School of black fish after dark.

May

11   dark about 8:40 p.m. All the pea vines pulled up by birds. Brought up 1000 feet of shiplap.

12   towed up lumber from New Brighton in four trips. 45 minutes to tow up 25 boards. Extra low tide so marked rocks for Captain Yates. West rock 2 feet 4 inches at low tide today and south rock 3 feet 2 inches.

13   took Mr. And Mrs. Harper off *Comox* and down to New Brighton. Repairing dinghy.

14   rain all day. Repairing dinghy. McDonald blasting at Avalon.

15   raining all morning. Finished roof on woodshed.

16   down to New Brighton to borrow plain and finished dinghy.

20   four Grahams and A. Mayse.

24   wet in morning and threatening. No one up.

27   cloudy but fine and warm. Took Killam's freight over from wharf. Bailey up to build house.

29   rain. Put back wall on woodshed between showers. Over to store in evening. Not dark until 9:20 p.m.

30   fine day. Down to New Brighton twice to tow up 300 feet of 2x4's.

June

1   finished boarding in wood shed. Had eight young ladies from Killam's visiting in evening.

2   Find summer day. Burnt paint off 10-foot boat. Picnic parties and launches around. King's birthday.

3   Fine hot weather. Painted boat.

4   Clouded up again with south-east breeze but warm.

10   fine and sunny. Weir, Sankey, Graham.

11   Conacher, Bowden from 11th to 24th

17   up with McDonald.

18   Sankey.

22   over to Y Camp for sand.

23   rain. Over to Y Camp for sand (two trips). Hebb's lumber up on gravel scows.

July

1   rain, and how. *Lady Evelyn.*

2	Fair. *Campbell* and Sankey up Friday night for a week.

October

31	up on *Capilano*. Fine and warm. *Cruiser* on opposite run.

November

1	rained all day. Made door for the woodshed. *Cruiser* down.
2	Election day. *Cruiser* up. *Comox* up.
3	Over to store. Unshackled float and towed around between the islands. *Cruiser* down and *Comox* up and down.
4	Fine, one arm and cloudless with frost at night. Over to Shaw's, Hebb's and McDonald's new house. Tearing old float apart.
5	Sunday. Got the cross pieces on new float. *Lilcris* and *Pladda* and *Cruiser* roundtrip and *Comox* down.
6	New float into position-2 x4's on. Fished for awhile in afternoon but only caught one dogfish. Summer day. Doors open.
7	Very mild. Down on *Capilano*.
23	on *Comox*. Little fog. Little rain. With sun in afternoon.
24	snakes out. Down to New Brighton for raspberry canes. Sundown at 4:10 p.m. over Gibsons.
25	planted blackberries. Went down to New Brighton from Gambier for float.
26	fished-no luck. *Makehew*, in and tied up a boom of logs. Over to Bailey's and Stoddard's. No low tides. Have seen the reef only at night by moonlight this month.
27	*Nova Arcadia* up. Planked the new float.
28	summer day with frost last night. Bright moonlight with hundreds of gulls flying around and raising a racket.
30	down to *Comox*.

December

5	up on *Capilano*. Stormy, could not land at Cowan's Point. Calmed down about 3:00 p.m., some stars at night. Exceptional tide.
6	Tried to get Killam's float off. Reckon the tide was 15 feet with the wind backing it up. *May Mac* up.
7	Down to New Brighton twice for 10 sacks of cement.
8	Dug excavation for fireplace and put in new foundation post.
9	Over to Hopkins to phone the shop. Digging gravel off beach in afternoon.
10	Over to Avalon with gramophone records. *Cruiser* down at 4:20 p.m. and *Comox* at 6:00 p.m. (Hopkins).
11	down on *Capilano* over to Britannia and Woodfibre and then direct to town as boat was unable to call their yesterday on account of Squamish wind. *Comox*

had to tie up at Gibsons 'til 10:00 a.m. today.

1934
January

5   Fine warm day like October. Logs steaming. No fire on in daytime. Down to New Brighton for cement.

6   *Cruiser* in New Brighton 4:05 p.m., *Comox* 5:30 p.m. Dark at 5:30 p.m. with the sunset over Gibsons. Arthur Lett over with apples.

7   fine and warm. No fire all day and no frost at night. Gramophone returned. Over to Shaw's, Killam's, Avalon, Bailey's and Stoddard's. Radio 3 batteries gone. *Comox* stopped in channel with my freight.

8   Mixed cement for fireplace 10:00 p.m. to 3:00 p.m. then collected more sand and gravel. Bailey over for short wave radio.

9   same work as yesterday. *Nova Arcadia* went to town. *Capilano* up and didn't return to Hopkins till 6:45 p.m.

10   concreted 'til all sun was gone. Then over to Avalon with mixing trough. Larsen over to borrow gramophone. (140 pails of sand and gravel, 30 pails of cement and 1000 pounds of rock to bring fire foundation level with ground).

11   down on *Comox*.

18   up on *Comox*.

20   rain and slush all day. Tide up Killam's float in pieces. *Cruiser* up in the afternoon. *Comox* up in the morning and afternoon. Both Grace Harbour and New Brighton both trips *Comox* at Hopkins when cruiser at New Brighton.

21   snow on mountains. Down to New Brighton and Grace Harbour. Killam's mooring disappeared. *Comox* through channel on extra trip at 10:30 p.m.

22   over to Avalon with records. T. Burns out to island in launches and towed back gangway.

23   cloudless with strong north wind from 10:00 a.m.to 11:00 a.m. and then change into southwest to sundown. *Capitol* scow now up and at Hopkins on return at 6:30 p.m. *Makaehewi* in with logs for the night.

24   *Makaehewi* still here ordered two float logs from across at the old mill to be delivered February 2.

25   down on *Comox*.

30   up on *Capilano*. Over to Avalon to get stuff shipped up on *Nova Arcadia*.

31   Pulling spikes out of part of old scow over at Shaw's. A. Lett cutting wood at Killam's. *Makaehewi* in and out to Roberts Creek. *Nova Arcadia* down. *Cruiser* called at New Brighton.

February

1   heavy Scotch mist 'til late afternoon. Townsend delivered float logs from

Avalon Bay, down to New Brighton for battery.

2   Over to Avalon to fix logs at high tide at 8:00 a.m. Strong south east through night changing into west at daybreak was squalls 'ill 10:00 a.m. and then bright and summer breeze. Collecting sand and carting away earth from fireplace excavation.

After 1935 the fish locker was on the porch of George Graham's house. If you put a fish in the locker in the evening it would still be alive for breakfast. Courtesy: Wendy Graham.

3   Fine summer's day. Tommy Burns out from New Brighton. We went over to Shaw's and found their outboard motor but could not find Killam's mooring. Over to store in afternoon.

4   Bought 10-pound spring salmon ($1.00) from fishermen. Over to Avalon and New Brighton, Sunday.

5   Finished foundation of fireplace. First bumblebee.

6   Finished dumping dirt from fireplace excavation, 208 pails down to Moxon's.

7   Alarm clock mainspring broke.

8   Down on *Comox*. Captain Muir on.

17   *Butler* up. Bumblebees out.

18   over to Bailey's and Stoddard. Down to New Brighton to catch boat. Mr. and Mrs. Innes over for reading material. Wilson Allen over.

19   over to Shaw's and finished pulling spikes out of old scow. Hutchinsons over from Keats and working at Killam's garden. City police boat up for Judge Harper.

20   over to store in morning. Started putting in cement foundation footings. Lots of butterflies out. New strawberries on Killam's plants.

21   down to see Bailey's stump puller.

22   summer day. Putting in foundation posts all day. Sunset on top of Knob Hill 5:15 p.m. Dark about 6:45 p.m.

23   over to see Hutchinson for about an hour in afternoon. Northern lights. School of black fish 6 to 15 passed through channel 11:15 p.m.

24   Killam's up. Working on wharf.

25   down to *Cruiser*, 4:30 p.m. to 7:00 p.m.

1949 George Graham's house fixed-up. Courtesy: Wendy Graham.

March

6   up on *Capilano* with five sacks of cement and seven 6x6's. Cool south-west breeze. *May Mac* up. *Cruiser* into Avalon with Larsen's.

7   Tommy burns out with the 6x6 timbers. Towed in two cedar logs for Filmers.

8   first hummingbirds. Finished putting in cement footings. Burns out with gas.

9   over to Killam's; dog-tooth violets in bud and flowering currant out. The store at New Brighton is open.

11	hottest day. William McRae up. Over to Avalon and New Brighton to store.
12	down on *Capilano*.
20	up on *Capilano* with Deeley. Walters, lumber for house.
21-23	working on house. Strike at Commercial Logging Company, fire broke out at 2:00 p.m.
24	working on house.
25	down to West Bay for rowboat.
26-27	working on house between showers.
28	over to Hopkins with Deeley and Walters to catch boat.
29	Killam's up. A. Lett over for board. Finished window cases with Battens. *Cynthia* at Grace Harbour 9:00 p.m. Heavy rain at night.

1930 Edmund Morgan at Twin Island's dock on ARIMIS. Courtesy: Anne Northrup.

30	Deeley up on *Aramis* with three boys and Harold.

April

1-2	Walters. Codfish.
10	up on *May Mac* with Walters and Deeley.
11	bricks up on scow on Monday. Getting brick and sand over from New Brighton with Burns' boat.

12 -14   on fireplace and new float. Deeley down Saturday on *May Mac*. Harold Walters up on *Comox*.

15   Walters and Postgate on *Comox*. Rain.

1956
March

1   Grouse hooting on island.

31   Northern lights.

April

2   Northern lights.

8   first bat.

13   hummingbirds and swallows.

26   Northern lights.

May

5   school of the minnows.

7   first sea bass.

8   first mosquito.

21   holiday.

June

1-4   rain.

5   Thunder. Grouse with eight young.

July

1   Dominion Day.

September

2   Labour Day.

October

8   Thanksgiving.

18   first snow at 2000 feet.

November

30   two rats.

December

1   four rats.

1957
February

26-28   cement base for water tanks.

Captain Larsen. Courtesy: Betty Larsen.

March

1   Northern lights.

17   Robins and sparrows singing. Grouse hooting. Moths on windows at night.

18   first frog.

22   hailstorm.

23   cold rain. Divers. Water tanks overflowing.

24   Northern lights.

25   first snake.

27   first butterfly. Northern lights.

30   first sea bass-Hopkins. First hummingbird and bat.

April

23   comet over Twin Creek-conspicuous 9:00 p.m. to 10:00 p.m.

28   three swallows back.

25-27   new roof-13 rolls.

30   thunderstorm.

May

21   *Gray Dawn* took old float away-Jewitt.

July

14   fresh deer tracks on beach at well.

15   *Bainbridge* through channel 9:00 p.m.

16   Gulls eggs hatched after three weeks and one day sitting.

23   *Smokwa* through channel four times.

28   rain all day, tanks full.

August

6   eleven lingcod, seven rock cod.

1958

January

12   no fish.

13   rain. Sea lions.

17   fine. No fish.

18   fine. Black fish.

20   sea lions.

22   record rainfall.

28   primroses at Moxons. Rosebuds.

29   two sea lions.

30   first salmon berry bloom. Manzanita bloom.

31   black fish.

February

4	cloudy and mild. Doors open.
9	2 inches over wall. Red Northern lights.

March

1	supper by daylight.
9	put up marker on reef.
11	Northern lights.
14	finished extension on wall.
17	first trip *Smokwa.*
18	steady rain.
19	first grouse hooting on the island.
25	Thrashers up.

April

14-18	steady rain.
19	deluge.
21	windy.

May

12-14	painted boats.

June

19-21	the mosquitoes are bad.
22	the mosquitoes are gone.
27	cloudy, cool and windy.

July

6	the swallows are gone.
25	the lighthouse battery is recharged.

September

Labour Day weekend stormy.

10	heavy wind storm 3:30 p.m. to 4:30 p.m. SW wind.

October

8	*Haulaway* took marker off reef. 4:30 p.m. *Lordell.* Shot full grown rat.

November

14	Bill Killam up.
23	*Surfrider II* at Mrs. Killam's.
29	Grey Cup day. Gale blowing all day. Reflection from Bill Killam's windows 8 minutes after ferry passes lighthouse going east.

December

25	Christmas morning. Cloudy. Sunshine in evening.

1959
January

8	water over garden.
13	high tide at 17 feet.
21	snow.
23	caught monster rat.
25	gangway broken. Moxons gone down. Purple flowers out. Also Manzanita.
26	eight whales off float.
28	water piping repaired.
30	marker replaced.

February

1	over to Jewitts. One rat.
3	one sea lion.
10	sunny and cold. Negroponte.
14	first spring evening.
18	over to Hopkins for capital *Naptha*.
20	black fish, sea lion and Northern lights.
26	water turned on.
28	tanks full. Doc Ridley fishing.

March

4	to Hopkins for laundry. Sunny.
6	grouse hooting. Rain.
14	one rat. Back from town. Cold rain at evening.
15	one rat and one bird. Rained all day.
17	to Hopkins. Fair.
20	snow on hills. Rain.
21	*Porpoise II* up. Gibsons. Hopkins. Langdale. Gambier.

August

4	sundown over Elphinstone 8:53 p.m.
14	no mosquitoes for a week.
15	*Hellowa* up.

September

4	up on *Sequin* with *Mahar II* and *Wilma K.* On Saturday. Rough trip. Boats down. Labour Day 2:30 p.m. to 3:00 p.m. heavy rain. Bill Killam closed camp Sept. 6. Fireplace on all weekend. Hopkins lights out.
12	caught four Grilse, lost five. Thunder in evening.
13	caught four Grilse, talking lure N.G.
22	caught five Grilse.

27 picked Damsons and Japanese lanterns. Thunder and rain in the evening. Daylight saving out. Sundown 5:40 p.m.

October

1 service X took the marker down 5:30 p.m.

8 high tide up to cross pieces on marker.

12 Thanksgiving. Mooring in boats up.

24 *La Rose* boom aground front of house, end of boom took marker.

November

3 moved to Camp Sunrise.

4 ice on water pails in morning.

7 fourth and seventh over to Twin Island. Moxon's up.

20 20th and 21st over to island.

24 Moxons down. Fixed gate post. Nailed dining hall.

December

3 to town 9:20 a.m. to 5:05 p.m. 17th and 21st.

1960

January

15 to town 9:20 a.m. to 8:10 p.m.

24 number seven broken into.

31 Moxon and Tuohey to February 2.

February

23 Moxon up.

24 returned to island.

25 to town.

26 keys, paper, address changed.

March

1 clear and cold. Squamish wind -28 Fahrenheit. To Gibsons.

8 water turned on.

9 to New Brighton, reef awash at 7 foot 3 inches.

12 to town 15th to 19th, 24th to 26th.

26 *Morgan* and Moxon up. First snake.

27 *Porpoise* and *Kat up*. Bill Killam's float's all awash on 12 foot 8 inch tide.

28 first hummingbird.

29 grouse hooting on island.

30 *Morgan* down.

April

3 first swallow.

28	29th to May 2 flock pigeons eating Arbutus flowers.

May

2	thousands of shiners under Gibson's wharf.
8	*Sea Fun* Men from Mars.
11	shiners arrived.
18	Simon Fraser charged lighthouse, seven men, two officers.

June

1	no mosquitoes so far-all drowned. Over to Hopkins. Fridge on.
15	water tanks overflowing.
16-18	Town.
26	*Sequin, Marlo, Comoro, Tecora, Ginger.*

August

14	rain, first since July 1.
22	marker gone.
24	temporary marker.
26	permanent 18 foot length, 1 foot rings, 11 foot to lowest crossbar.
30	tanks full up.

September

5	Labour Day. Fine and sunny in contrast to Sunday. Wet and breezy, water rough.
4	Lol Killam closed.
5	F.R. Killam closed.
7	down to New Brighton.
8	lighthouse boat around. P. Killam and Craig up. Water skiing.
10	Lee's house broken into.
12	Election Day.
15	15 pound Ling cod, five fish all different species.
18	*Sea Fun* with a crew of skin divers.
21	12 pound salmon. 12 pound dogfish on shiners.
22	11 inch Grilse.
25	daylight saving time off. Sundown 5:40 p.m. Killam's closed up.
27	one salmon, two Grilse.
28	three Grilse, lost two.
29	five Grilse, lost one salmon.

October

10	Thanksgiving-*Sequin, Glenean, Scamper.* Two Grilse.
23	no fish. F.R. Killam up.
24	five Grilse, lost two.

November

4	moved over to Langdale.
18	town, Major Knight up. Water off, telephone changed to automatic.
19	Embankment at S.A. Camp undermined.
25	Over to island and Moxons.
26	Grey Cup.

1961

January

11	to town and dentist.
17	three log float ordered Norm Jewitt approximately 8 feet by 38 feet.
21	over to Twin [Island] Red canoe with 4 persons around.
22	Y camp and Williamsons, out by Twin Creek Road.
28	Tuohey down, Moxon stay over to island.

February

10	10-12 to town.
13	Marker on reef gone *Stradi II* 4:00 p.m.
14	Moxon down . Anson away.
17	Paid N. Jewitt $80.00 on float.
21	S.A. officers up. North west gale 3:20 p.m. Power off 'til 4:00 p.m.
24	Moved back to island. Snowdrops and Manzanita out. Butterflies.
27	Cleaned water tanks.

March

13	Water turned on. To New Brighton to fix wharf.

End of log entries by George Graham. Courtesy: Wendy Graham.

George did Much Recording

Here are more entries from April 1934.

Bombardier - Canadian Expeditionary Force December 1918
Discharge papers - 1922

Taxation Act Amendment Act 1932
District Lot 838 Twin Island $3.00
1923 - $4.50
1924 - $6.00
Land registry act (description of real estate)
Bought Twin Islands in 1910 for $275 plus $5.00 tax = $280
1934 – Addition to house:

10 bags cement	$10.50
Windowsills	$1.15 per sill
Betsworth – windows and door	$11.25
Woodwards - roofing	$21.90
Tar paper - two rolls	$ 1.90
Nails	$ 2.50
6 x 6	$13.85
Lumber	$82.25
Freight	$15.50

May 12, 1933 marking rocks for Captain Yates at extra low tide marked rocks west rock 2 feet 4 inches at low tide and south rock at 3 foot 2 inches.

Smokwa and *Bainbridge*, were the first two small ferries to go through the channel between Twin Island and Gambier, July in 1957.

How can anyone ever say life on the islands was boring?

Late 20s to early 30s. George Graham's Twin Islands. Gambier Island in the background.
Courtesy: Anne Northrup.

1960s Jubilee Hall
Alexander and Isabell
Browning.
Courtesy: Diane Clark.

Errata

Miramar, A History of Gambier Island, is an account of the island and its inhabitants. Much information was gleaned from diaries, letters, and interviews with past and present, visiting and permanent persons of Gambier Island. Information from tax and death records, BC Archives, newspapers as well as the works of other authors on this subject provided the material that appeared in *Miramar.*

The best efforts were made to keep the information in *Miramar* as close to fact as possible. Unfortunately, some errors were recorded. Thank you to Art Harper, Gordie Mitchell, Dorothy Poore, and Jim R. Thomson for bringing these errors to our attention.

The following are the errors we are presently aware of:

From Art Harper—son of Judge Andrew Harper:

- Page 36   First paragraph should be Judge Andrew Harper and his wife, Ellen.
- Page 41   Bottom picture is of Judge and Mrs. Harper with Harry Burgess.
- Page 217   Second paragraph, second line, should be Judge Andrew and Ellen Harper. Third line should be art Harper was well known…
- My father was the judge, not me.

Early 20s Art, Andree and Judge Harper. Courtesy: Harper family.

From Gordie Mitchell:

- Page 155 Joe Mitchell did not have a limp, it was Kenneth Alexander.
- Ken's father was a judge in Vancouver.
- Gordie was born and lived in Long Bay for 6 years and went to school in West Van. He went back to Gambier at the age of fifteen and looked after the booming grounds in Long Bay for 5 years. At that time, it was Cliff Towing Steam Tugs.
- Mr. Lett would deliver groceries to the Mitchells. Often he would be rowing because his little motor would break down part way on his trip.
- Joe Mitchell bought the property in Long Bay in 1922.
- The steamship would come into a small float in front of Goodie's house once a

ERRATA

week with groceries.
- Less Farrow–one-armed man–had the place where John Cosulich is located.
- Linfoot Creek comes from the Linfoot/Gambier Lake. On the east side of the creek is one of the old shafts. It is just at the mouth of the creek; a thirty to forty feet high tide will enter it.
- In 1947-48, they walked Camp Artaban to Douglas Bay. The trek took about forty-five minutes, to do some logging. Gordie drove a cat then.
- The big tree picture in 1947-48 was hand cut and took two days to fall.
- Billy Fawcett would hand out mail on the dock at Daisy Bay. He is from Centre Bay.
- Gordie did a lot of machine repairs and caretaking.
- Mr. Breaker lived in Douglas Bay and had goats. The donkey engine cable would tighten up to a stiff log in the water and the goat would be dancing on the log.
- Camp Artaban was originally further out towards Point, a third way out. Joe Mitchell would take people out to the original camp.
- Joe Mitchell did a lot of shake cutting at Gambier.
- Major Picker would walk from the Army & Navy down to the wharf. He walked right off the end of the wharf with his beer cases and then hold them in the air and say, "Save the beer."
- Amy and Edna Laird owned Killams at first.
- Ridley made lunch for Owen when he went to visit. He would fish by Richardson's and catch nice flounders.
- Owen would take his dingy to Snug Cove and so some dancing with the girls. He would sleep under his dingy for the night then row the next morning. He rowed around the island in one day.
- There were big fires on the rock in Gambier Harbour. The store would donate a case of pop and there would be dancing on the wharf. Kids and parents would roast wieners and marshmallows.
- The steamship came Thursday and Friday.
- Many fathers would come to the island Friday nights by ship. Those ships were called the Daddy Boats.
- Boyds from Gambier Harbour had a place by Brads and sold eggs. It was called the Egg Farm.

From Dorothy Poore:

- Page 76   Footnote #47 "decadency" should be descendence.
- Page 79   Footnote # 93 "when he was lived" should be "where he had lived."
- Page 105   Line #1 "What or whom" should be "what or who."
- Page 114   Photo - on left: Grenville Allen (friend of Evan Boston), on right: California friend of Dorothy Poore. Picture taken by Dorothy Poore.
- Page 161   Dorothy Poore left the island in 2001, not 1997
- Page 164   Photo – Opposite page, lower photo: Charlie Poore, Cyril Hibberd, Hilda Smith, Gladys Hibberd, Dorothy Poore

From Jim Thomson:

Page 14   Middens – polite name for an old garbage dump.
- Page 88   Beachcombers – log salvager.
- Page 90   Loggers did not burn their abandoned camps at the end of the operation. The logged area was set alight in a controlled manner, usually the early fall, called a slash fire. This removed all the debris, cleared the ground and supplied fertilizer for the next crop. Fireweed always came up first. Some of our best stands of timber are now on burned-over land.
- Page 90   Except for use in local cabins (and outhouses) the cedar on the west side of Gambier, and elsewhere on the coast, was all cut into fifty-four inch shingle bolts, to be transported from stump to salt water over a skid road on horse drawn sled or stone boat, stacked in a 'crib' of cedar rolls and towed to a Vancouver shingle mill, there to be sawed into shingles of eighteen inch or twenty-three inch length. Shakes are split with a fro(e) and mallet.
- Page 92   It took 100 years to log Gambier not 10 years.
- Page 92   Loggers clear-cut all the trees at one time, only the swags were left. Trees were cut well above the ground to get clear of the swelling at the butt and in the case of most large cedars, the hollow section which extends up well into the tree. Further, the flare at the butt would have made the logs difficult to fit on the saw carriage at the mill. All trees

taper (therefore all logs) have a taper. Though the magnificent firs of Gambier showed very little in each length.

There were no flumes on Gambier; they require large volumes of water in their operation, of which Gambier Island has little. The closest ones ran from (now) Langdale to behind Gibsons on the ridge of Elphinstone. It used the flow of Langdale Creek, Gibsons Creek (twice) and Chaster Creek. Its length – three and a half to four miles.

- Page 93   The road to Gambier Lake started at Ekins Point with a hollowed log at the top of the switchback. Logs dropped by chute facing McNabb Creek.

- Page 92   Mike Fredea and wife Kitty were the first and only settlers in Andys Bay (1934 to 1950).

     Page 94   Bob Alsiger trucked timber to salt water at Andys Bay. Mannion Bay was never used as a dumping grounds. [This changed in the 1970s.]

- Page 107   Lapstrake (clinker built) rowboat and Caravel has smooth surface. Thanks to Turner Boat Works, the former outnumbered the latter by at least 10 to 1.

- Page 115   The Squamish Highway was completed to Squamish. I do not recall the Tymacs running to that port.

- Page 115   Easthope engines were used in smaller, 1.5 to about 6 h.p. and were the common inboard engines in the local small boats up to about 16 feet. Evinrude, Elto, and Johnsons were the common outboards, maximum horsepower was 35 in the Evinrudes.

- Page 119   Photo – Hull of the Sir Thomas Lipton – a sailing ship named after the famous tea merchant, Sir Thomas Lipton. It was never a scow.

- Page 232   Footnote #10 Frances Drage was Mrs. Drage's husband not son.

Bibliography

"Andys Bay." <u>Harbour and Shipping.</u> Oct 1952.

Armitage, Doreen. <u>Around the Sound: A History of Howe Sound—Whistler.</u> Madeira Park, Harbour Publishing, 1997.

"BCL goes visiting…a Boom Assembly-Line." British Columbia Lumberman, 1951.

Chaplan, Michael. <u>The Urban Treasure Hunter: A Practical Handbook for Beginners.</u> Garden City Park, NY, 2005.

Cooke, John S. and The Northern Miner. <u>Mining Explained: A Layman's Guide.</u> Don Mills, Ontario, 1998.

Cummings, J.M and J. W. McCammon. <u>Clay and Shale Deposits of British Columbia.</u> British Columbia Department of Mines. John F. Walker, Dep. Minister, 1952.

Dominion Department of Agriculture. <u>Soil Survey of the Lower Fraser Valley.</u> General References: Vancouver Area, Geol. Surv., Canada, Mem. 135,1923. Pub. 650, 1939.

Hudson, Rick. <u>A Field Guide to Gold, Gemstone and Mineral Sites of British Columbia Vol. 2.</u> Orca Book Publishers, Victoria, 1999.

Keller, Betty and Rosella Leslie. <u>Bright Seas, Pioneer Spirits.</u> Tanglewood Press, 2009.

McCulloch, Bruce, Randy Hughes and Burleith. "Andy's Bay – Past, Present and Future: Andy's Bay Log Sorts" Spring, <u>Western Matters,</u> 2004: 12

Miller, Brenda and Suzanne Paola. <u>Tell it Slant: Writing and Shaping Creative Non-Fiction.</u> McGill Hill, New York, 2005.

Pellant, Chris. <u>Rocks and Minerals.</u> Dorling Kindersley, Inc., New York, 1992, 2002.

Purvis, Ron. <u>Canadian Gem Stones.</u> Ron Purvis, Lillooet, 1962.

The Shorey Book Store. <u>Mining in Southern British Columbia</u>. ed L.K. Hodges. The Post-Intelligencer Seattle, Washington 1897. The Shorey Book Store, Seattle, 1967.

Sorensen, Jean. "A Perspective on FOREST POLICY." <u>ForesTalk Resource Magazine.</u> Spring 1978

Wrigley, Eva. <u>To Follow a Prospector: The Life Story of William H. Wrigley.</u> Hucul Printing Ltd., Salmon Arm, 2003.

Electronic Sources

www.for.gov.BC.ca/hfd/library/documents/glossary Ministry of Forests and Range Library.

http://encyclopedia@thefreedictionary.com/Teredo+worm The Free Online Encyclopaedia.

http://minfile.gov.BC.caMINFILE Record Summary MINFILE No 092GNW025. 24-Jul-85. BC Geological Survey (BCGS), 30-Jul-97 ed Keith J. Mountjoy (KJM) Name: Gambier Island, Gambier Island, Copper, MB, Daybreak, Copper Bay, Copper Cove, Gambier Creek, Gambier Lake.

http://empr.gov.BC.ca/mining/geoscience/pages/default.asx

www.leg.bc.ca Official Reports of Debates of the Legislative Assembly
Hansard – Legislative Session: 2nd Session, 32nd Parliament Monday, May 5, 1980 Afternoon Sitting Page 2273 and page 2274
Hansard –Legislative Session: 3rd Session, 32nd Parliament Friday, June 5, 1981 Morning Sitting
Page 6022 to pg 6024 discussion as to mining on Gambier Island and in Howe Sound

Jones, David Keith "British Columbia's Islands Trust on the Local Government Continuum: Administrative Agency or Local Self-Government." 1993.

www.bc.archives.gov.bc.ca/general/guides/preemptions-homesteads_research_guide.pdf

"British Columbia History." Journal of the BC Federation vol. 39 No 2

Fossil Article Windows Live® Microsoft Corporation. Search Results ©1993-2009

Maps Google imagery ©2009 TerraMetrics, Map data ©2009 Google, Tele Atla.